Mentoring
thru
Intentional Relationships

In Other Words . . .

This is a proven, cross-cultural model of leadership development that comes with lots of practical experience. It is not a book that increases the stress (ie. "I should be doing this!") but instead eliminates this pressure by creating a framework whereby the material can be worked through step by step with others. It is a guide for both mentors and those who want to be mentored. The scope of the material, with helpful graphics and a clear biblical foundation, has the goal to transform us into Jesus' image. It is definitely worth trying it out for yourself.

Axel Nehlsen
Director, Intercity Christian Network,
Together for Berlin

Relationships can't be built only at church meetings or home groups. We needed something else. Phil Jeske's course on mentoring is one of the best materials I have ever come across. It helps not only build strong relationships on the right biblical foundation, but enables future leaders to understand their character, to find their place in the Body of Christ, and to have a long range perspective. We as a group of churches, and I personally, have used it in mentoring groups of young leaders, both individually and as a group.

Pastor Valera Selezneva
Founder/Overseer
Family of Churches, Russia

Mentoring is a calling for each of us. It is something that I am very passionate about and feel very positive about participating in as I learn new things about myself. The self-reflection that can result from Mentoring thru Intentional Relationships *is a powerful growth experience and gives new insights about oneself. It provides an opportunity for renewal and regeneration – it a special transformation gift.*

Rt. Rev Deodatus Barwan Mwamba,
Bishop of *All Nation's Anglican Church*
Kinshasa II, Congo DRC, Africa

Mentoring Thru Intentional Relationships *has been the best resource for putting the concept of mentoring into action. We first heard about mentoring about twenty years ago, but only really began practicing when we found this tool. It has changed the way we relate to developing leaders and pastors. We highly recommend it as a practical guide for people who are serious about investing in the lives of others in a meaningful* way.

Doug Friesen, Academic Dean, Pacific Life Bible College
Leadership and Church Developer, *Foursquare Gospel Church of Canada*
Rebecca Friesen, Director of Operations, *Foursquare Gospel Church of Canada*

Having travelled in over forty countries of the world in order to present the Good News of Jesus Christ, I have seen something of the enormous lack in the area of discipling and equipping not only new believers, but also Christians in leadership. It takes strong, mature leaders to produce healthy, strong churches . At our Church in Berlin, through the Mentoring thru Intentional Relationships *model, I have observed firsthand the amazing results of changed lives for service.*

Volkhard Spitzer, Pastor
Berlin

For many years Phil has had a consistent passion to help men and women become more useful and fulfilled in the service of Christ. He instinctively knows the need for experienced servants of Christ to get personally involved in the lives of those who desire to serve, but don't know how. He also knows how vital it is for a person to both build and learn effective ministry on a strong foundation of Godly character and healthy personal relationships with God and man. His focus is on helping others succeed and in pleasing Christ. For Phil, a fulfilled life is a life of service in Christ. His deep conviction of both the need and possibilities released through intentional mentoring is contagious, and I pray it will ignite a fire in every leader and student that studies this material.

Walter Rusnell, Bible Teacher/Author
Spiritual Growth Seminars
British Columbia, Canada

Congratulations Phil on completing this Mentoring thru Intentional Relationships *study manual. I am confident it will make a significant contribution in equipping leaders. Our Lord modelled Kingdom Life and mentored His disciples to impact their world. His final admonition to "make disciples of all nations," if obeyed, results in Christians with a firm foundation, disciplined lives and Christ-like maturity. I have field tested this training methodology over decades and have watched the Holy Spirit raise up an army of world changers.*

Jim Argue, Founder & President
Genesis Discipleship Training Center
California, USA

I commend you for your dedication to the task of not only equipping and mentoring others, but in providing the resources for others to do the same. From your early days at Genesis in California to the present in Europe, with so many experiences in-between, you have stayed true to the principles of discipleship in life and in deed. Working with you in a church setting, having served on your Board of Directors and enjoying the friendship of you and your family, all confirm in my mind that you are fulfilling the call of God to "go and make disciples," equipping them so that they "are fruitful and that the fruit remains."

Pastor Roy Holmquist
North West Family Church
Calgary, Alberta, Canada

This Mentoring Program has helped me to look at myself and others in the church and in Christian ministry with new eyes. One of the major lessons this program taught me is to value differences in Bible-believing Christians and churches and to acknowledge the need for these differences to complete the Body of Christ with "arms AND legs." I also now have a better understanding of the particular gifts God has given me and my limitations. I believe this will help me form more balanced teams to advance God's kingdom and help God's people grow....taking many of the things I learned in the Mentoring Program to new groups and mentor others.

Matthias Lohmann
Participant, Europe

Mentoring

thru

Intentional Relationships

A Model for Growth & Development
Through Mentoring Relationships

Phillip T. Jeske

Zinzendorf Publishing
Canada

About the Author

Phil Jeske is the founder and president of International Christian Ministries in Canada. As a missionary in Africa, he helped develop ICM's in-service training programs, as well he has lived in Europe, equipping and training emerging leaders there. He has a BTh., MA, and is finishing a PhD. He has co-authored the book, This Pile of Stones, 2002 with Nancy, his wife since 1982. It is a moving narrative of their experiences and God's faithfulness in fulfilling his purposes in our lives, even in the midst of confusion, disillusionment, and heartache. They have an adult daughter who is also running her race with excellence and purpose.

ICM and Leadership Development

International Christian Ministries, ICM (www.icmcanada.org),   is an interdenominational, international mission organization that seeks to serve the Church around the world through training, mentoring, and coaching Christian leaders. This includes various leadership conferences as well as mentoring and coaching ministry teams using this Mentoring Manual and the materials from our Ministry Coaching Network . For more information regarding this material, or this ministry, go to our website. You may also contact us there regarding having one of our ministry coaching teams come to your country.

To my father,
Rudolf K. Jeske

Thank you for showing me the heavenly Father;
Thank you for being a godly example and faithfully running the race.

I am proud and blessed to have you as my father.

With Gratitude. . .

I am well aware that I am who I am today due to the grace of God (the grace of my wife being a close second!) and the blessing of being able to build upon the foundation of others.

Thank you to those who have personally influenced me (and if you are willing to admit it, you know who you are!), from family and friends, to my early days of formation at "Genesis," to other professors during further studies, and ministry colleagues. That which is good in my life is due to your efforts, and the areas still needing growth confirms my continual need of your friendship. Thank you for your input in my life and being models and mentors for me to follow.

I am also indebted to the many spiritual leaders, past and present, who I have profited from and have been influenced by, if from only a distance. The writings of some of these have been listed in the Reference Section, but of course there are many others who have not been included here. Where specific thoughts can be traced to one definable source I have attempted to give specific credit. I am grateful for the input of those whose thoughts and ideas I have directly or indirectly been influenced by over the years. Hopefully I am as faithful as they in passing on the baton and leaving a legacy.

Table of Contents

Preface

Before you is a journey!

What you have before you is not so much a set of notes, but an opportunity to take practical, intentional steps to discover WHO God made you, WHAT gifts He has given you and then HOW you can best serve the Body of Christ in the 21st Century. This is the goal of our mentoring journey.

This journey is not always an easy one, but can provide those that embark on it lasting results. This journey of personal discovery and life change will shape who you are and your ability to reach your potential in Christ.

If you are taking part in this journey with others (in a small group) you will not only have the opportunity to develop a personal relationship with your mentor, but will be able to walk this road with fellow sojourners. With all of our obligations and responsibilities we often do not take the time for this type of intentional relationship – either to give to someone else of what we have learned, or receive from someone who has walked a few steps ahead of us.

You are most likely part of the majority who have never had or taken this opportunity. Yet to have someone intentionally walk along side of us can be a profoundly positive experience in helping us become all that God intends us to be. Unfortunately, this has become a lost art, which can explain why so few have taken advantage of such an experience, and fewer still never initiate such a relationship. *Mentoring thru Intentional Relationships* as a mentoring model is only meant to be a tool or compass to assist you in intentionally mentoring others or to help you become mentored by someone else.

The classic biblical example of this is the Apostle Paul with Timothy. We see that the ultimate goal of this relationship was not just for Timothy's personal benefit, but that Timothy would find his place in the Body of Christ – equipped to serve others. It was Paul's intention that, "...the things you have heard me say in the presence of many reliable witnesses entrust to reliable men who will also be qualified to teach others."

I first developed this resource as I was looking for a tool to assist me as I was mentoring others. At the time I could not find a resource that had what I was looking for in one place. Then after publishing this mentoring manual in 2003, I discovered that many others – from a variety of countries and backgrounds – were also looking for just such a tool to help them mentor others and be mentored.

It was been rewarding to hear how this manual has been helpful as others have used it to invest in others. Since then it has been translated into German, Russian, Spanish and French and is being used in a variety of settings in many countries around the world.

Be encouraged, You are not alone! Many others are on this journey of mentoring others. So it is a privilege to offer you the 2005 edition of this resource for your use along the journey. Together let us continue running the race.... and finish well!

Phillip T. Jeske
August 2005

Beginning the Journey

Foreword

I deeply appreciate the growing awareness developing in the Body of Christ for the need of mentoring. After serving as a pastor in the United States and now more than twelve years as a missionary in Bulgaria and Germany, it is clear that this need is universal. Wherever we want to raise-up properly prepared Christian leaders, mentoring is needed.

I have experienced first-hand the awesome results that come from having a caring and committed mentor in my adult life. I have also experienced the tremendous joy and fulfilment that comes from mentoring others, helping them discover their individual path and destiny in God.

While the Body of Christ is beginning to recognize the tremendous benefits resulting from mentoring, many people feel lost, not knowing how or where to begin this process. You hold in your hands a wonderful tool intended to help move you along that path. In this manual, Phil has masterfully written and assembled materials that will enable you to begin and continue mentoring relationships that promise to profoundly affect the lives of those involved.

We have now been ministering for several years in Berlin and it has been a privilege to partner together with Phil in implementing this model here. We have seen wonderful fruit in the lives of others and it has been a time of great discovery for us. One of our main discoveries was that this journey will be different for each mentor and mentoree. It also has become clear that this manual is extremely valuable as a general guide for both mentors and mentorees as they journey down this sometimes obscure road of mentoring.

This manual is a specialized tool in the Kingdom of God that will enable mentors to fulfill the very special honor they have of helping others discover and fulfill their destiny in God. At the same time this manual can provide mentorees the invaluable knowledge as to who they should seek to influence their lives as a mentor.

As each Christian leader seriously embraces the responsibility to mentor others and the heart to mentor others is passed on with the help of this manual, I am confident that the Kingdom of God will expand beyond even our wildest expectations. Not only will we experience immediate benefits, but future generations will have the potential to reap from our simple efforts.

Let us arise and courageously choose to pour ourselves into others by
Mentoring thru Intentional Relationships.

Jim Johnson, Director
Impact International
Europe

In Your Hands ...

Mentoring Model: An Introduction

Mentoring
thru
Intentional Relationships

An Introduction

AN INTRODUCTION TO MENTORING

A Personal Journey

This manual and model grew out of the need to have something to assist us in our ministry in Europe. For years we had been working with an organization whose purpose it was to serve the Church by equipping Christian leaders. This work had began in Africa in the late eighties and all of the programs we developed were designed and implemented as in-service and on-the-job, so that leaders could stay in the ministry while they were receiving further training.

As we were in transition to Europe, I was personally entering that mid-life phase when one traditionally begins to reconsider priorities and even realign personal and ministry purposes. Coupled together with the reality of the needs of the Church in Central/East Europe, was a personal re-evaluation of how I could be most effective in equipping another generation of leaders. There was a great hunger in our current setting for a model whose emphasis had a much more direct relational emphasis and focus.

In my personal re-evaluation I realized that in all my training and education, I had never strayed far from my discipleship roots. I had began my adult life journey and ministry at a discipleship school over twenty years previous and then during this mid-life period realized afresh that this value was the thread which had remained constant throughout my ministry over the years.

So out of the desire to leave a legacy and the needs of emerging leaders in Europe, this model began to take shape. Combining my own personal values, varied ministry experiences and life journey, I began to develop *Mentoring thru Intentional Relationships* with the following question in mind, *"What would I have wanted to know or what concepts would have been helpful to be exposed to early in my ministry that may have saved me some heartache and fruitless effort?"* Then the second question, which is just as important as the first, *"How could these truths about life and ministry be best discovered and learned?"*

Mentoring – *thru Intentional Relationships*

The answer to these two questions resulted in this *Mentoring thru Intentional Relationships* Model. Of these two, the *How* (intentional relationships) is more important than the *What* (the material used). The material and topics chosen for this manual addressed the first question, while the focus on mentoring as a basic structure addressed the second question.

A group began to form of those who desired to participate in this developing network. They met together to discuss the material, while at the same time being paired with a mentor – someone who had walked a few steps further in life and ministry. The purpose was to join the informal nature of a mentoring relationship within the context of a flexible structure (a *model*) with the goal of facilitating the development and growth of another generation of Christian leaders.

The following notes are an overview of the mentoring process, as well as some practical steps gleaned from my personal experience. My prayer is that it will serve

Two Key Questions

you well in your own mentoring journey – both being a *mentor* as well as being *mentored*.

Mentoring as Lifestyle

Mentoring has become somewhat trendy, both in and out of the church. While mentoring is not identical to discipleship – the differences of which we shall discuss – it does incorporate some of the same values, particularly its relational emphasis. The term, *mentoring*, has many different meanings and implications, however this is not intended to be a book *about* mentoring, rather a tool to help you participate in the mentoring process.

The obvious must first be stated. The term, *Mentoring Model*, or even, *Mentoring Manual*, is really a contradiction in terms. *Mentoring* by its very nature has a relational focus, but for it to effective in the routine of every day life there does need to be some structure, albeit a flexible one. While no model or structure can make mentoring happen, without some sort of flexible structure it often does not just occur on its own. An external motivation can be helpful in assisting us become more intentional in our mentoring relationships; for without a focus or plan, the best of intentions often only remain great ideas.

At the root of mentoring is relationship and walking together with someone down the road of life. Having a flexible structure can help us turn our good intentions of raising up leaders into reality. So while mentoring cannot be reduced to a model, it is helpful to have some sort of structure to help us accomplish what we all need and want. That is the purpose of this mentoring model. It is a basic framework for you to use as you intentionally are mentored or become a mentor.

Positive habits can be powerful tools for good in our lives. They can help us fulfill our intentions, even when we don't feel like it. This model is like the wood forms which hold the liquid concrete of a foundation in place until the concrete has hardened. Of course, once the concrete is solid the wooden form is no longer required. Likewise, *Mentoring thru Intentional Relationships* as a model is to help you give some form to your intentions of developing others through relationship. The goal is to help you establish a lifestyle of mentoring others through intentional relationships. At that point the form itself will no longer be necessary.

Character, Skills, and Knowledge

While mentoring by its very definition is relational, it does require a tangible focus. While different authors define mentoring somewhat differently, the primary focus is to come along side of someone else and help them reach their goals; helping them become all that God intends them to be. It is not just personal spiritual discipleship, the impartation of knowledge, or ministry skills, it is a combination of all three.

Ideally it balances all three: *Character*, *Knowledge*, and *Skills*. Relational mentoring should encompass the Heart, Head, and Hands, each being defined as follows:

- Heart: character development – instilling the love, values, and passion of Christ in the leader.

- Head: knowledge acquisition – development the understanding, knowledge and wisdom in the leader.

- Hands: skill development – developing the ministry and life skills of Christ in the mentoree so that they may more effectively fulfill the Great Commission.

A Process not a Destination

Heart...
Head...
Hands...

The most effective way to bring these all together in the Christian leader is through the mentoring process, for without the mentoring process we do not really have the right structure necessary that will practically assist us grow in all three – character, knowledge, and skills. While we may desire and strive for this goal, without the intentionality of a mentoring relationship this goal is seldom achieved.

Biblical Examples

We need those around us who have learned to be godly people of influence and can model that for us. We all need these mentors – those who have gone on before and can help us with input and perspective. Those that can help us establish healthy habits and foundations, particularly during the early stages of our adult lives and ministry. Then as we enter mid-life we need someone who challenges us not to plateau and become complacent in our lives and ministry, but can motivate us towards continual development. Finally as we approach the latter period of our lives peer mentors can then help us to finish well – fulfilling the purpose that God has for our life; even as David served God and *"fulfilled God's purposes in his generation"* (Acts 13:36).

We see a mentoring example in Paul and Barnabas. Barnabas took Paul under his wing during the early period of their relationship, but it was Paul's ministry who exceeded Barnabas (Acts 4, 9, 13, 15). But where would we be today if it had not been for a Barnabas who selflessly mentored Paul? Barnabas' Kingdom influence was realized through his mentoree, Paul. Perhaps Paul was thinking of Barnabas when he penned 2 Tim 2:2, *"Entrust to reliable men who will then be able to teach others what I have taught you."* This is the multiplication factor. We have the opportunity to multiply our ministries as we mentor others.

Other biblical examples from both the Old and New Testament include Eli and Samuel, Elijah and Elisha, Moses and Joshua, Jesus with Peter, James and John, Paul and Timothy, to mention just a few. This biblical pattern, as well as our own experience, should be enough to dispel the myth of the image of the "self-made" person. No such person exists in the real world – we are all beneficiaries of the input of others. This emphasizes the priority that this should have in our lives. As the Body of Christ we are to be *interdependent* on each other, not *independent* of each other. This principle is particularly valid for Christian leaders within the Body of Christ, for it is we who are to lead by example.

More than a Program

The purpose of *Mentoring thru Intentional Relationships* is to be a tangible way in which the relational mentoring process can be focussed. Its intention is to help you recognize the need for mentoring and then give you a vehicle with which to mentor others and be mentored by others. This is not a typical manual in that the material is NOT the most important component. Its purpose is to help provide focus for a mentor/mentoree relationship. While it can be used to assist you in your personal growth and effectiveness, it is intended to be used in the context of a mentoring relationship.

You may have picked up this manual because you desire such a relationship in order to grow and reach your potential, or you may realize that you have something to offer someone else as their mentor. The following introductory pages will give you some insights into the mentoring process as well as provide some practical ideas as to how this material can be used. Regardless if you know much about the mentoring process or if the idea is relatively new to you, the following will assist you to become more intentional in your own growth and your development of others.

> "Entrust to reliable men who will also be qualified to teach others"
> 2 Tim 2:2

A Focus for Mentoring

The
Necessity
of
Mentoring

WHY MENTOR?

Globalization and Cultural Context

■ <u>Shifting Values</u>

While the need of mentoring is particularly evident in societies in which people are disconnected from each other, globalization is beginning to produce these same negative factors in what were once relational societies. With the growth of urbanization and the increased reliance on technology, this is becoming a global phenomena.

At its root is the lack of value placed on maintaining the basic family structure. Increased individualism has also negatively affected the long-term committed relationships in a society, where learning through relationship has traditionally occurred. What has taken generations to decline in western culture is happening at an accelerated pace in other societies around the world. This typically occurs initially in urban centers, but then affects the complete infrastructure of the society. This phenomena is particularly evident in both the post-communist lands, as well as in the urban centers of African societies. But of course it is not limited to these regions, as this is becoming a world-wide pattern. It is further compounded where there is a general breakdown in the value of the family unit as succeeding generations are not nurtured as they should be.

■ <u>High Tech - High Touch</u>

Simultaneous to the breakdown of the relational ties in society is the greater emphasis on technology and the subtle inference that it can solve these systemic problems. Of course technological solutions are not bad in and of themselves, for they can actually be very helpful in many fields including the educational process.

But these technological tools will not be able to solve the leadership crisis. *High tech* solutions are only effective as they can supplement the relational component of leadership training. The greater the reliant a society is on *high tech*, the greater the need for solutions that are *high touch*. Distance education, internet courses and a host of other innovations can help in the development of Christian leadership, but they cannot replace the need for personal relationships – personal mentoring remains essential.

Growing
through
Relationship

The tendency for training and teaching to become merely an academic or theoretical exercise is a constant challenge. We have also noticed this tendency as a ministry. For while the purpose of our training programs in Africa are more than merely imparting biblical knowledge or theoretical theology, we must always guard that they do not gravitate to become only this.

As we then expanded the ministry into Europe, we saw again this need for practical training, but due to the dynamics of the society (as outlined above), there was also a greater felt need for the relational component in the implementation of the "how" of any training. *Mentoring thru Intentional Relationships* began to take shape as a response to this need. For many emerging (and current) leaders, this component of learning ministry and leadership from others within a relational context was something they had never experienced.

Re-evaluation Necessary

These factors affect the Church and how we develop Christian leadership. Within many cultures, as well as within the church, we see the erosion of generational and societal connections which at one time were common. Consequently, in much of Christendom, we have lost this emphasis of training Christian leadership through the context of relational mentoring. Many preparing for ministry, or already in places of leadership, have no one along side of them to encourage and *bless* them. The sad reality is that many currently in leadership have experienced this disconnect from previous generations, which makes it very difficult for them to model for someone else something that has never been modelled for them.

Specialists in the field of leadership training tell us that the majority of today's leaders have had no leadership training or courses, but have rather learned it after being in a position of leadership or after having been given leadership responsibilities. Most leaders have just learned leadership by doing it, not through special classes or training.

These factors have combined to produce the current state of Christian leadership and explain why we need to re-evaluate how we equip the next generation of leaders. At a time when mentoring has become a way of training within many secular fields, Christians need to rediscover its biblical roots and benefits.

It is within the context of mentoring relationships that another generation of spiritual leaders is best developed. Other structures, such as educational institutions or church programs, are not best suited to accomplish this goal which by very definition is relational. *So how can another generation of Christian leaders find their place and be equipped to be effective for the Kingdom?*

New Paradigms Required

■ Relationship versus Position

As those in leadership know, leadership is much more than a title or a position. True leadership could perhaps be better described as someone who has influence. John Maxwell in his writings on leadership emphasizes this aspect of leadership and how each person can be used of God to positively influence others for good, regardless of their official title or position. As we develop others and help them be used of God in more effective ways, our sphere of leadership increases in proportion to our level of influence. True leadership is more dependent on our willingness to apply ourselves in order to be used in greater measure by God for his purposes, than it is on what title or office we have. It is not a career choice as much as it is a life choice. We all have the opportunity to be partners with God in accomplishing this – to be persons of influence; leaders within the sphere of influence he has given us.

■ Releasing versus Controlling

Current leaders must resist the fear of having those closest to them surpass them in ministry and influence if they invest in developing them. So instead of helping, those leaders closest to the next generation of emerging leaders often hinder their development. So often the current leaders are the very ones *closing the doors*, instead of *opening doors* for the next generation and releasing them into their calling. Yet it is very difficult to pass on something we have never received or never received in the right way. So while it may be best to learn leadership and ministry through a mentoring relationship, few have had this experience, and so do not naturally pass it on.

■ Accountability versus Independence

Most often leaders fail due to inner issues, not outer issues. This is the reason why accountability and a circle of relationships is so important. Both young growing leaders as well as mature leaders need accountable mentoring relationships that

A Paradigm for Developing Others

Key ?

Becoming a Person of Influence

provide them with perspective. Having an open relationship with someone who has been through some of the very same waters, and has safely navigated through them, can be a lifeline for a floundering minister. Leaders do not need to fail before seeking out such relationships and the wise leader does not wait until the waters of crisis are upon them before developing such relationships. By then it is often too late. Having such relationships are preventative safety measures for our ministries and lives.

Over the years we have had many such peer relationships. While in Berlin we were blessed to be part of an intentional group of four missionary couples who met once a month. These peer relationships helped to keep us honest and real with ourselves and others, as well as keep a proper perspective on ourselves and our ministries. Solomon understood this as he wrote in Proverbs 27:17, *"As iron sharpens iron so one man sharpens another. He who tends a fig tree will eat its fruit..."* Though it is not always easy, those who make the effort to tend the tree of relationships will enjoy the fruit it produces.

Open and Vulnerable Relationships

We all have the need for peer mentoring relationships. Ironically, the further ones moves in leadership the greater the need for these types of relationships and yet the more difficult they are to find and develop. *Is there someone who knows how you are doing personally? Is there someone you can share openly with?* If this is not the case, you are in a very precarious place in your life and the potential for damage to you, your family and your ministry is immense. These various levels of relationships are safeguards for leaders and need to be pursued with the same zeal as our other ministry goals. Failure to do so has the potential to jeopardize all that we have worked for in our lives and ministry – often even without us being aware until it is too late.

■ <u>Vulnerability versus Pride</u>

It is a sad commentary that so often we as Christians in the church remain disconnected from each other. This often occurs, for we feel threatened by others and fear they will surpass us should we invest in them. Pride and fear often keeps us from these relationships. The truth is that it is a risk to be a vulnerable leader, particularly if we believe the lie that the leader must always be perfect. Yet for those that are willing to take the risk and sacrifice their own pride, will reap the benefits in their lives as well as in the lives of those around them.

As Ecclesiastes 4:9-11 reminds us,
"Two are better than one, because they have a good return for their work, If one falls down his friend can help him up. But pity the man who falls and has no one to help him up! Also if two lie down together they will keep warm. But how can one keep warm alone? Though one may be overpowered, two can defend themselves. A cord of three strands is not quickly broken."

In the book of Hebrews (10:24-25) we read that we are to *"...encourage one another, particularly in light of the days we are living in."*

Pouring our Lives into Others

■ <u>God's Kingdom versus Our Kingdom</u>

Our goal in leadership should not just be to gather followers, but to develop leaders. The more leaders we grow and develop around us the greater our influence will be. Leadership is key. As someone has said, leadership is relatively simple: knowing what God wants to do and then knowing how to do it. Christian leadership is more than just pulpit or "visible" ministries, but mature Christian men and women in all arenas of life.

So while we all need the input of mentors in our lives, we also need to be mentoring others – pouring our lives into others. Others need your input and what you have to offer and as you invest in others you will be challenged and grow in your own life and ministry. Helping others grow motivates us to keep current in your spiritual, personal, and ministry life. But this does not just happen automatically – we must take the initiative and become intentional in our relationships.

Inherent in the mentoring process is the fact that mentoring is not an event that occurs among the masses. Yet if every leader consistently mentors one, two or three leaders at a time, imagine the impact for the Kingdom over the course of a lifetime. As a leader or pastor you cannot mentor large numbers at a time, but you can leave a legacy as you influence others through mentoring.

Mentoring Options and Possibilities

There are many possibilities to practically mentor others. Perhaps you can think of several young leaders in your life who you could give some of your time to and help guide them as they develop in ministry and life. You may only consider yourself a young leader and yet there are those around you who would appreciate any time you gave them to motivate and help them grow.

Many years ago as a youth pastor, my wife and I spent extra time every week with five teenagers in the youth group. We ate meals together in our little apartment, went on walks together, had ice cream together – all with the goal of modelling (with our imperfections) what it meant to be a disciple of Jesus. To this day we have remained in contact with some of these youth, most of which are now married with families of their own. It is impossible to overstate the long term impact that simple, intentional relationships can have.

Besides working with youth, there are all sorts of other possibilities. Women are encouraged in Titus 2:3-5 to be mentoring the younger women. Christian businessman or other Christian leaders can mentor someone in whom they see potential. Imagine the impact and legacy that would last decades after your life through those who you mentor during your lifetime.

At a missions conference several years ago I was reminded again of the power of such relationships. A young man approached me and introduced himself by name and explained how he had attended a youth group that I had led as a young pastor. I immediately remembered him as a somewhat troubled youth who never seemed to show much interest in spiritual issues. He continued to tell me what an impact my life had on him...with the result that he was now a youth pastor. Luckily I was near a chair and able to sit down! What would have happened had I been even more intentional about my interaction with this young man? This is the challenge to all of us.

Mentoring is the Key

So then how can we train another generation of Christian leaders? How can this be accomplished? First, it does not just happen by itself. We must be intentional. Current Christian leaders have the privilege and responsibility to develop, equip and bless the next generation of leaders so that they will fulfill God's purposes in their lives. This material is to help you give some structure and motivation to be successful in accomplishing this goal. Its purpose is to provide some practical steps for your good intentions. Either as a mentor or as a mentoree, you can have a key part to play in how effective future generations of Christian leaders will be for the Kingdom.

Unfortunately, seeing this need, or even having good intentions, does not go far enough. While as an individual leader you many not have it within your power to

A Model:
Options and
Possibilities

Intentional
Relationships
Develop
Equip
Bless

Leadership
through
Relationships

change the whole of society, we all have it within our power to mentor others within the sphere of our own ministries and influence. We can make the effort and take the time to develop emerging leaders. Even if you may never have had this opportunity yourself, you can offer this gift to someone else.

A Flexible Tool

This is at the heart of why it is important to become intentional in developing mentoring relationships. The purpose of *Mentoring thru Intentional Relationships* is to provide you with a flexible structure that will help you become intentional in developing others through relationship. As we are all too well aware, it is often our personal concerns, challenges and leadership responsibilities that hinder us from doing this very thing, yet we each have something to offer and can be an integral part of the solution to this problem.

Leadership, and particularly Christian leadership, is best learned through relationships. Relationships that are *Intentional*. Perhaps this is exactly what you have been looking for. Perhaps this is how you can lay the foundation for renewal, revival, or even a church planting movement – by *Mentoring Others thru Intentional Relationships*. You *are* part of the solution.

WHAT IS MENTORING?

Types or Styles of Mentoring

But what actually is mentoring? In many ways mentoring is easier to describe than it is to define. It is more of an art than a science. At its very core, mentoring is a relationship in which the mentor seeks to assist the mentoree reach their full potential. The mentor's task is to help the mentoree achieve their life priorities and goals. The mentor is one who has walked a few steps ahead (in some area) of the mentoree and with their experience is willing to help the mentoree become the best they can be.

Helping
Others
Reach Their
Full Potential

While in its purest form mentoring may describe a life-long relationship, this is not always the case and does not need to be the case in order for it to be effective. There are a variety of mentoring intensities and commitment levels ranging from being a model for someone (which may even be from a distance); to more occasional mentoring, such as in a counselling or teaching situation; to more intentional and higher level of commitment, such as a coach, spiritual guide, or discipler. Of course, no one person can be all that another person needs and we all need more input than just one or two mentors during the course of our lifetime.

Mentoring thru Intentional Relationships is intended to facilitate a mentor/ mentoree relationship that is focussed and intentional, as opposed to haphazard and superficial. At the end of the structured period of this model, the relationship between the mentor and mentoree may transition to become a more occasional one, though this need not be the case.

Mentoring and Discipleship

Mentoring, and this mentoring model, does not have the same focus as spiritual discipleship – discipleship being defined as having to do with teaching a new believer basic spiritual truths and how to follow Christ. While *Mentoring thru Intentional Relationships* does address issues such as spiritual disciplines, its focus is on the "discipling" of a leader. In this way it is more than just a narrow definition of spiritual discipleship. It seeks to help the mentoree discover where they are at in their development in key areas of their life, and then how to take practical steps to establish new life/ministry patterns and disciplines. The mentor is the mentoree's partner in this journey.

Mentoring is the process of practicing how to live a life of integrity and how to implement these spiritual disciplines – within the context of our humanity. Knowing the right answer is usually not the problem, the issue is more of the need to learn through observation how to live these "right" answers in everyday life. This often needs to include accountability in order to consistently make the right choices. This is what is meant when we say that the "material" is important, but not *the* most important component. The interplay between receiving the right resources and implementing them into our lives is both the purpose, as well as the challenge, of the mentoring relationship.

It is assumed that participants in this model have reached a certain level of personal and spiritual maturity. Of course, this does not mean that participants are *perfect* or that they do not have areas of struggle in their lives. It only means that they already have a biblical foundation in their lives and are beginning to display the fruit of being a disciple of Jesus. At any given point in the process, the needs of the mentoree determine the issues which need to be dealt with and the necessary pace of the change. The material is important to introduce the basic areas all leaders have to deal with in their lives and ministry, but the mentor functions as an accountability guide to help the mentoree determine the priorities and steps of that growth.

The Mentor is Not:

■ A Parent

In this role as guide, the mentor should not become the mentoree's parent. The relationship should be more of a peer relationship, based upon mutual respect. Though the mentor may have more experience in certain areas in which the mentoree desires to grow in, the relationship is not a parent/child one – this style of relationship will actually hinder the growth of the mentoree. The mentor is certainly not in a role which entitles them to determine, or interfere, in every decision the mentoree must make. In this way it is also not a type of unhealthy *shepherding* or even an unhealthy discipling relationship.

The mentor is someone who has gone a few steps ahead and is willing to turn around to help someone along the same path. The focus is helping someone mature. Fortunately, the mentor does not have to have all the answers. They are more of a resource person, directing the mentoree to where they may find the right contacts, ideas, books, tapes etc. The mentor is not the resident expert, or parent. It is the mentoree who must take final responsibility for their growth.

■ A Model of Perfection

Fortunately, the mentor does not need to be a perfect model either. No mentor is perfect, merely someone who has gone a few steps ahead and is willing to share that with someone else. But while the mentor is a model for the mentoree he is more than this. We all have models for our lives, those we know personally and those we have only read or heard about. Yet, by definition, a mentor is someone that the mentoree knows personally (or will get to know personally). It is in this *walking together* that the real learning takes place. Not merely classroom learning (though knowledge may be imparted), but a practical, *This is how I have handled this type of situation.* or *This is what I did when...*

This does not require perfection on the part of the mentor (perfection being an assumption that keeps many from becoming a mentor of others), but does require

The Mentor as Guide

Mentoring is Not...

a certain vulnerability. Openness, not perfection, is required, for this type of relationship can only be effective as the mentor is open and honest in his relationship with the mentoree. Of course for many this can be threatening, especially if the mentor assumes that perfection is a requirement for respect. But it is openness and vulnerability that produces respect. The greater the respect the greater the commitment; the greater the commitment the greater the mutual accountability; and the greater the accountability, the greater the growth.

■ A Resident Counsellor

The role of the mentor is also not that of a teacher or counsellor. While the mentoring process includes aspects of these roles, neither of these are the primary task of the mentor. He does not have to be an expert teacher, outstanding counsellor and gifted discipler, all rolled into one. Rather, the mentor is a resource person who walks alongside of the mentoree in order to help them achieve personal and/or ministry goals.

Some of these other roles, such as the teacher or counsellor, may be needed for short periods of time, or perhaps in a specific area of career or skill development, but are not central to the mentoring relationship. Mentoring within this model is a relationship that is intended for a longer period of time than a one time seminar or counselling session. The mentor will be teaching the mentoree from their life, even though they may not consider themselves a teacher in the formal sense of the word.

■ An Elder Patriarch

Another misconception is that the mentor must be much older than the mentoree, or that a mentor must be a certain age in order to mentor someone else. Yet a mature young adult could mentor someone who is not as mature or developed in certain areas. The mentor is someone that the mentoree respects and wants to learn from, regardless of age. The key is that the mentor must have a certain level of maturity and experience in an area of life and ministry that the mentoree wants to grow in – something which can occur long before the retirement years! On the other hand there is no upper age limit beyond which we cannot mentor. As we continue to grow and develop throughout our lives, mentoring is something we can do throughout our whole lives.

Whatever age the mentor is, the mentoree must have a respect for them and their values. The mentor must want to see the mentoree succeed in life and it is also critical that there be a certain amount of chemistry between the mentor/mentoree displayed by their enjoyment of each other's company, or the relationship will be more of a frustration than a benefit. While there can be short term times of tension in the relationship, frustrations over the long term need to be resolved or the relationship needs to be ended. For the purposes of this model there may be some arbitrary matching necessary, which will function for the short term of perhaps a year or so (maximum), but for the relationship to be mutually beneficial longer term, there must a be mutual respect, similar values and somewhat parallel life direction.

THE WHO OF MENTORING

For the Mentoree

Chances are if you have read this far, you have a hunger to grow and be mentored. The reality is that in the majority of cases it is the person desiring to be mentored who must approach a potential mentor. This is the first potential hurdle: *Are you willing to take this initiative?* I'd encourage you to do so, as the implications for your life could be incalculable.

Perfection
not Required

Mutual
Respect

■ Finding a Potential Mentor

Yet finding a mentor is not such an easy matter. Many current leaders are very busy and have their own set of challenges. Even if they desire to see you grow, these factors may very well obscure their well-intentioned desire to raise up another generation of leaders.

But let me offer a few thoughts to help you in your search. First, make a list of those closest to you and ask yourself: Who do I already know who shows an interest in me? Who seems interested in my growth? Can I imagine this person committing themselves to me? Are they someone that I see as a model? What do I admire about them? Do I want to develop these same qualities in my life and ministry? Are they someone who will be humble and willing to be transparent with me? Having thought these through, approach a potential mentor.

■ Approaching a Potential Mentor

Perhaps the hardest task is determining how to approach a potential mentor. It is important to realize that many potentially good mentors do not feel like they are competent or up for the task of mentoring someone else. It is helpful to put them at ease by letting them know that they are not the *ONLY* person in your life and that you are not asking them solve all your problems ("Would you like to be *ONE* of my mentors."). Instead it is helpful to let them know that you see qualities in them that you would like to emulate and that you would like them to consider being a special influence (one of several) in your life.

■ Expectation and Commitment

Your mentor is not the person who will make your choices for you and is not your professional counsellor that is on call for you day and night. Also, your mentor is not your best friend or *buddy*. While a friendship should develop, and for the relationship to be mutually beneficial you will have to enjoy each other's company, do not expect this relationship to have the familiarity of a *buddy*. The mentor is to help challenge and assist you to grow in areas of your life, which at times may not be all that comfortable. This is why you must admire certain qualities they have and want to emulate that in your own life. You must respect and trust that they can help you do this.

It is also important to put your mentor at ease regarding the weekly time commitment, as well as the duration of the *Mentoring thru Intentional Relationships* model. For this, it may be helpful to provide them with a copy of this manual as an introduction to the mentoring process and the details and requirements of this model. From the outset it is important to discuss the expectation you have for the relationship; what you are looking for and what you feel they have to offer. If there seems to be an agreement in values and direction, the next step would be to go over the Commitment Form together in order to discuss the direction of the relationship, level of accountability, frequency of meeting, confidentiality etc. If you do not know this person very well, realize that it will take time for this relationship to develop. Start slow.

It is important to not miss scheduled meetings and to be prepared to discuss issues. Remember, your time with your mentor is for you, not them. You need to understand your priorities and the areas in your life that you want to grow, this is not primarily your mentor's responsibility. When you meet together have questions ready or issues that you are prepared and wanting to discuss. They are there to help you, you are not doing them a favour by showing up. It is also important not to monopolize your mentor's time. While it should never be a problem for you to contact your mentor, as this is the purpose of this type of relationship, you need to be respectful of the mentor's time.

...For the Mentoree

Finding a Mentor

Having Realistic Expectations

For the Mentor...

Who to Mentor

■ Your Motivation

The greatest motivation for your mentor will be when they see you change and grow. It is important for you to regularly and frequently let your mentor know that you appreciate them and their time. While they may want to do this, it does take effort on their part and does mean certain sacrifices. To the degree that you are motivated and follow through is proportional to the degree that you will benefit from this model and the mentoring relationship. You may not always agree with your mentor's point of view, but always show respect and be prepared to see things from another perspective. You can be respectful even if you disagree; you are not in competition with your mentor.

■ Your Influence

New-found knowledge is powerful, in and of itself. This new knowledge will increase your influence, however there is a danger that this can be used inappropriately. As you grow in knowledge and influence there is the very real temptation to use this influence wrongly or prematurely. There may be the tendency to try to increase your own influence or ministry through the very assistance or contacts you have received from your mentor. However, it is *never* appropriate to build your ministry or sphere of influence at the expense of your mentor (and anybody else for that matter) and his ministry!

Develop in your own sphere of ministry and influence; do not be in competition with your mentor and his ministry. Never by your actions or attitudes cause your mentor to be able to question your loyalty and trust. If differences or tensions arise it is best that the mentoring relationship ends before irreparable damage occurs to each other or your ministries.

Thoughts for the Mentor

■ Choosing a mentoree

You may be a pastor, church leader, or Christian in another vocation and see mentoring as a practical way in which you can be intentional in your relationship with someone who you may want to help develop. If you have this desire, you can learn to be a mentor. Yet though this may be your desire you may have wondered how to choose who to mentor.

Ideally the mentoree will be someone you already know or from within your circle of contacts. In any case, they should be someone in whom you see potential and are willing to commit yourself to in order to see them grow and develop. They do not necessarily have to be someone who is a close associate or co-worker, though this could be the case.

It is important that your mentoree respects and admires you (though it is not necessary that they worship the ground you walk on!). On the other hand, it is important that the mentoree is not intimidated by you. Usually the relationship will not work if they feel intimidated by you, for they will not feel free to share their weaknesses or failures and, consequently, will not grow. If you feel this is the case, you should maybe rethink mentoring this person, or at the very least discuss this issue with the potential mentoree.

Other helpful questions to ask are: *Are they self-motivated? Do you see God's hand in this person's life? Are they teachable, willing to learn? Do you see indications that they are motivated to make changes in their life? Can you imagine spending time with them and enjoying their company?* Your potential mentoree may be from your ministry or circle of contacts and so the answers to these questions may be self-evident, however if they are not it is often best to enter the relationship for a specific period of time to determine if it will work.

■ Inferiority Complex

While you may be the one taking the initiative, you may also be reading this having been approached by someone wanting to take part in this *Mentoring thru Intentional Relationships Model*. To this point, mentoring may not have been that high on your priority list and you may not even necessarily feel capable of being a mentor, but do not let doubt and fear stand in the way of you sharing your life with someone else. As you reflect on what God has done in your life you will realize that you have a lot to offer. The potential to positively impact a life should far outweigh your own sense of inadequacy.

To reiterate, mentoring does not mean that you become a person's parent, resident expert, full-time counsellor or model of perfection. Perfection is not required, but rather a commitment of time and energy in order to positively influence someone else. It is important to remember that you can be a mentor even if you have not been mentored yourself.

Imagine the opportunity to help someone so that they do not have to make some of the same time-consuming mistakes that you may have made along your journey. Imagine being able to help someone achieve their full potential and perhaps have a greater sphere of influence beyond even your own. Instead of this causing us to feel threatened, we can share in their joy as they stand on our shoulders and see horizons we may never reach. As you develop other leaders around you through mentoring, your ultimate sphere of influence will grow.

■ Taking Initiative

Instead of waiting for someone to approach you, why not consider taking the initiative and approaching someone within whom you see potential? It is important for you (and them) to realize that you are *not* offering to be *the* most important person in their life. So that there is no misunderstanding, it is best to phrase the question in terms of, "I would like to be *one* of your mentors." as opposed to "I would like to be *your* mentor." This can help to establish the parameters of the relationship and eliminate some of the false expectations that can occur in the initial stages of the mentoring relationship. There is a great hunger and yearning for mentors and if you make yourself available God will bring people your way whom you can offer this gift. A certain level of *chemistry* must develop in order for the relationship to function long-term. However, at the outset, this is not always evident, which is why it is wise to initially commit for a limited time. Perhaps make an initial commitment for a certain period of time such as the first six chapters, or perhaps you could commit to them for the length of time it takes to go through all twelve chapters of the manual (one to two years). This gives the relationship a time limit, but leaves the door open if your hearts are knit together and you would both like to continue the relationship beyond this model.

You would be agreeing to mentor them in their personal life, as well as in your particular area of expertise. If you are in full-time ministry, then you would probably choose someone who has the same calling, though they may have a differing gift combination. Though they most likely will have less experience, it is important that you believe in them as a person and see their potential.

■ Personal Honesty

It is also important to honestly evaluate what you feel you can offer the mentoree, taking into consideration your personality, giftings, experience and stage of life. Fortunately we do not need to be an expert in every area of this manual. Some

Influencing
Others

Taking
Initiative

areas will be more familiar to you than others and some you will want to place greater emphasis on than others. What is important is that you consider what is the best contribution that you can make in their lives.

■ <u>Meeting Regularly</u>

Being intentional in our relationships does not mean that our meetings together with our mentoree have to be formal – the discussion and interaction should be as informal as possible. You are seeking to develop a relationship and this takes time. Growth occurs out of mutual respect and trust, as these are the foundation of the mentoring relationship.

It is not helpful just to meet to talk, but also plan other activities together. If you are in ministry and can include your mentoree in these activities this is also very helpful, as we learn by both observing and by doing. If you are mentoring a protege in ministry the more you are able include them the greater the level of their growth and skill acquisition. As you do this you will also be multiplying your own ministry influence – attracting and developing leaders, not just followers.

You may want to begin your actual time together by discussing any issues arising from the manual, focussing on the application of the principles in the mentoree's life. *What has the mentor discovered about themselves, life, ministry and how can you as the mentor help them apply this knowledge in their own lives and ministries?*

It is also important to keep track of the issues that your mentoree is dealing with and follow up on these in subsequent meetings. This may take the form of encouraging them in certain areas or holding them accountable in those areas in which they have indicated they would like to be held accountable (ie. spiritual disciplines, personal life etc).

The longer the relationship the greater the tendency for the relationship to plateau or slump. As mentor you need to be aware of this and continue taking initiative in order to keep the relationship positively moving forward.

Mentoring Limitations

■ <u>Direct Advice</u>

There are times that the mentoree may desire direct advice, but it may not be helpful for the mentoree's growth for you to give direct answers or solve their problems. While there may be times for direct advice when asked, it is important to remember that it is the mentor's responsibility to direct the mentoree to Christ, not to themselves. As mentor you must resist the temptation to abuse or overstep the permission that the mentoree has granted you in their life.

In healthy adult mentoring relationships the agenda should be determined by the mentoree. This does not mean that the mentor does not speak into the mentoree's life, for this is one of their key roles, but it should never be done in an overbearing, condescending, or controlling manner. If this occurs regularly it would most likely be in the best interest of the mentoree to find another mentor.

■ <u>Expectations</u>

It is also very important to discuss ahead of time the expectations that each have of the relationship. *How often will you meet? How will you handle confidential matters? How often will you evaluate the relationship? What particular areas are you wanting to grow in (as mentoree)?* or *What do you particularly feel you have to offer (as mentor)?* The degree of accountability desired by the mentoree and the

"Being" and "Doing" Together

What to Avoid...

degree of accountability expected by the mentor should also be discussed. In discussing these issues, it is important that the mentor does not dominate, but instead allows the mentoree input in helping to establish the parameters.

■ Leaving Well

If at some point in the relationship you may feel that you need to stop or make changes in the mentoring relationship, it is important to be honest and loving in doing so. It is not so much a matter of confronting, but rather of clarifying the issues. It may have to do with expectations not being met, which is why it is so important to have discussed and filled out a *Commitment Sheet,* ahead of time.

Often these necessary changes in the relationships can be seen as merely a new phase in the relationship, not necessarily anyone's failure. Even if change is necessary, with the right attitude the emphasis can be on the positives of the relationship. On other occasions the relationship may outgrow a mentor/ mentoree and become more of a peer relationship. This can be very positive and may signal more of a longer term relationship, though the level of contact may change.

■ Who Should Not Mentor

While everybody *can* mentor, there are some people for whom it may be best to postpone developing a mentoring relationship. These would include those who find themselves in the following situations:

• Any personality type or gift mix can mentor, but it does require a certain selflessness and a person who always desires to be at the center of attention will find it difficult to mentor. Some of this may be due to personality and some of it may be due to ministry style, both of which can be adapted if mentoring is seen as a high enough value and priority.

• Also if someone is just surviving in their life and ministry, it may be best to postpone mentoring someone else. If someone is suffering from burnout and is disillusioned in their life and ministry, mentoring will be very difficult, as they really have nothing left to give. Yet as we go through these valleys, we often have even more on the other side to share with others, if we are open to God using even our pain as a positive gift to show the character of Christ.

• For what would seem obvious reasons, it is also not wise to mentor someone of the opposite gender or have a non-Christian Mentor in spiritual matters.

THE HOW OF MENTORING – *Mentoring thru Intentional Relationships*

The Mentor as Guide

Mentoring thru Intentional Relationships is designed to be used by a mentor or mentoree who wants to become intentional about their growth and increased effectiveness for the Kingdom. Depending upon the strengths of the mentor, as well as the needs of the mentoree, some attributes of each of these roles (discipling, spiritual guide, teacher, counsellor, model, coach) may be expressed at times.

It is clear that one person cannot provide all of these to a mentoree, nor should they be expected to, however, the mentor is key as a guide to the mentoree in their growth and in assisting them in achieving their God-given goals and ministry objectives. Much has been said regarding this and more will follow, but at this point let us focus for a few moments on how this manual itself fits into this intentional relationship.

Clarification Required

Pathways to Mentoring

The Mentor and the Manual

The Manual as Guide

▪ Its Purpose

The material in the manual is not intended to be teaching notes as such, but rather reading material for the mentoree and mentor. However, "covering" this material is not the ultimate goal of the model. It is merely a vehicle to "prime the pump," as it were, to help the mentoree and mentor discuss some of the key issues which affect the Christian leader – from his personal life, to his ministry in the Body of Christ. Some chapters will be more applicable than others and some you will want to spend more time on than others. The material is only a starting point, it is the impartation by the mentor of his own personal life and experiences that will be the key to the growth of the mentoree.

▪ Parts of the Whole

It could seem to be a rather clinical approach to have each chapter refer to only one area of life and analyze it. But while each area is looked at separately, it must be remembered that they are all part of the whole. The purpose of introspection in each of these twelve areas is for the whole to be healthier and more effective.

For example, though the pieces of a car are taken apart in order to be repaired, the real purpose is for the car to be put back together and function for its intended purpose. Likewise this material may appear to be separating elements that actually belong together, but as with the car, the purpose of looking at each individually is only with the intention of putting it all back together. This is important to keep as a focus throughout the process.

The material is in outline form for it is not intended to be exhaustive or all inclusive. It points the participant in a direction. The degree of emphasis on each area should be according to the agenda of the mentoree. If there are several mentorees/mentors in a local region who meet regularly to discuss the material (recommended), the facilitator will have to take the needs of those in the group into account and direct the discussion accordingly.

The material could also be described as a building where each chapter is a door to a room. While there may not be time during the formal period of the program to fully *furnish* every room, the doorway of each chapter points to a very important *room* that the mentoree must deal with if they are going to be effective in their lives and ministry. To the degree that each room is *furnished* during the program will be determined by time factors, the needs of the mentoree, as well as the dynamics of the group (if you are also meeting with a discussion group).

A Beginning Point

▪ Only a Tool

The material is to be a helpful tool in giving direction to what the mentor and mentoree need to discuss together. It is not intended to be the *only* resource that the mentor/mentoree use as input on the particular subject, it is merely a beginning point. Additional reading resources and materials have been included for further study.

A discussion group may also decide to read at least one additional book per chapter and then discuss this. If these are not available in the local language perhaps there are locally written books which can be substituted that deal with similar topics. [To determine if this manual, *Mentoring thru Intentional Relationships,* is already in a particular language or to receive permission to translate it, please contact the author or ministry by mail or internet.]

■ The Contents

The Mentoring manual itself is divided into four sections or quarters, each of which has three chapters:

PERSON
- Your Personality: Who You Are
- Your Gifts: What You Have
- Your Calling: What You Do

DISCIPLE
- Your Foundation: The Personal Disciplines
- Your Challenges: The Big Three
- Your Direction: Being Led of God

LEADER
- Your Foundation: Servant Leadership
- Your Development: Growing as a Leader
- Your Legacy: Developing Others

MINISTER
- Your Motivation: Being God's Person
- Your Mission: Having God's Heart
- Your Ministry: Following God's Strategy

1.0 PERSON

The first three chapters focus on who we are as a person. Each chapter is designed to help the mentoree discover who they are – from their basic personality style, to their spiritual gifts, to their life calling. Before we can influence others we need to know who we are; who God made us and what he has given in our hand to bless others with. We must also understand his dealings in our lives in the past and how this can indicate his specific future purposes in our lives. These first three chapters help the mentoree begin to discover and reflect on these issues. Those who have done some of these types of exercises will be enriched as they will be able to reflect on these at a deeper level with a mentor. Those who have never been exposed to these will have the opportunity to do so within the context of a personal relationship for the first time.

2.0 DISCIPLE

Just as the elements in the First Section address who we are at the core of our person, this section addresses the core of who we are as a disciple of Jesus. Before we can influence others we must have a solid spiritual foundation. These three chapters are somewhat of a spiritual checkup. Even those who have been in ministry for some time will appreciate this opportunity. The mentoree will be able to reflect upon the spiritual disciplines in their life and take an inventory of where they are at. Since hearing from God and learning to do so is so key in the disciple's life and ministry a chapter in this section will deal with this. Finally, issues which have derailed many a life and ministry, even causing some to not finish the race, will also be addressed. Specifically, mentorees will be encouraged to deal with issues regarding their attitude towards money, dealing with their sexuality, as well as the temptation to lead based upon manipulation and power.

...Person
...Disciple
...Leader
...Minister

An
Overview
of the
Journey

Some Possible Formats

3.0 LEADER

This section focuses specifically on issues of leadership. We begin with the foundation of all spiritual leadership: that of being a servant leader. *Is this is contradiction of terms? How is it possible to lead without being overbearing or domineering? How did Jesus lead?* These are some of the issues dealt with in the first chapter of this section. The final two chapters in this section deal with how we can personally grow in our effectiveness as leaders and then the principles necessary if we are going to be effective in developing others. Practical matters such as the role vision, priorities and values play in determining the leader's success are discussed, as well as the attributes a leader must develop in order to be effective in mentoring others. The mentor will find these chapters particularly helpful.

4.0 MINISTER

But why do we want to discover and learn who God made us and what gifts he has given us (Section One)? Why is it so important to develop spiritual disciplines, avoiding pitfalls (Section Two) and then learning to lead from the perspective of a servant (Section Three)? Understanding and applying these previous sections are foundational in order to deal with the matter contained in the last three chapters of Section Four. God has an ultimate plan for the ages and specific purposes for each of our lives. *Yet since not every believer is called to a career in full-time ministry, how does the believer fit into God's purposes?* Issues arising from the Great Commission and principles of church planting will be discussed with the intention to help the mentoree formulate and evaluate their particular Kingdom contribution.

Potential Two-Stage Model

For those wanting to use the material over a two year period (one chapter every six-eight weeks), there is a natural break between the Second and Third Sections, which would allow for a two year format. The first two sections (one year) can be used separately from the last two sections (the second year). This may be helpful for those who only want to focus on only the first two sections of personal growth (1.0 and 2.0). Perhaps if being taken as a group, some may even want to continue with Section 3.0 and 4.0 and others may not. This provides a natural break for a reevaluation by each participant.

For those who want to allow two years to go through the material, Sections One and Two could be taken in the first year and Section Three and Four during the second year. This latter approach provides more time for discussion, as well as the opportunity for the mentoring relationship to deepen.

The Text

Notes Column

The wider column on every page includes key principles, thoughts, and challenging input for the participant to think about and interact with. These notes are intended as an overview and starting point on the subject.

Application Column

The main focus of the text is personal application. The narrow column along the outside of the page has various icons and questions to help direct the mentoree and mentor to the key issues of the chapter and then guiding in the application of the principles into practical life.

■ <u>Insight</u>: These are questions which seek to probe for a deeper meaning. Some of these may be discussed in class, but to gain maximum benefit the mentoree should take time to answer these on their own.

 ■ <u>Discussion</u>: These are specific questions and comments that seek to provide a context for the group discussion. Discussion should actually make up the majority of the small group time. These questions are also helpful in providing discussion between the mentor and mentoree.

 ■ <u>Application</u>: These questions are designed to lead to personal life change and/or specific tasks or actions that the mentoree needs to consider doing. They are at the heart of the material and should be the main emphasis of the mentoring relationship.

 ■ <u>Mentor Matters</u>: Specific questions to discuss with mentor or insight to be gleaned from your mentor, as well as specific actions to which you can be accountable with your mentor are signified by:

A Journal

It is recommended that participants keep a personal journal to write down what God is doing in their lives throughout the model (and beyond). Those who regularly practice this discipline have gleaned much in their lives. Each entry need not be lengthy, perhaps only a few key thoughts that will be important to remember. This will be a valuable tool for the mentoree as they develop a written record of God's dealings in their life.

HOW TO USE THIS MODEL AND MANUAL

While there are many options and variation, there are essentially two components of the *Mentoring thru Intentional Relationships* Model.

   1. One-on-one Mentoring Relationships
   2. Synergistic Discussion Groups

The Mentoring Relationship

■ <u>The Focal Point – A Relationship</u>

As mentioned above, this is NOT just another manual of notes to go through or a seminar to be taught. The emphasis of *Mentoring thru Intentional Relationships* is the *One-on-One* relationship between the mentor and mentoree. Without the development of such a relationship, the ultimate goal of this model will not be achieved. We believe that emerging Christian leaders can best learn leadership and Christian service through intentional relationships. This takes both a willingness on part of current leaders as well as a humility on part of the up and coming leader who most likely will already have responsibility in positions of ministry.

The focal point, or pivot, on which the whole model turns is the mentor/mentoree relationship. Without this component of a one-on-one relationship with a mentor, this is nothing more than just another manual with some interesting, informative

A Mentoring Model

Mentoring Dynamics

material. While going through the material on one's own would be helpful, the reader is encouraged to seriously consider finding a mentor/mentoree with whom to go through this together.

The material can become the reason to initiate and give context for a potential mentor/mentoree relationship. Having such a manual means that the mentor does not have to develop their own subject matter or questions, and the mentoree has a tangible reason to approach someone to be their mentor for a specific time period. For instance, you could approach someone to enter into such an intentional relationship with you and offer this as the core of material that you would like to discuss on a weekly basis.

Since a certain chemistry is needed in the relationship between the mentor and mentoree, it is usually best for them to find each other and begin to use this model within natural existing relationships. However, the model has also been effective when mentorees are paired up with willing mentors for short periods of time, that include regular times of reevaluation.

As the relationship flourishes and both want to continue it beyond the duration of these twelve sessions (a calender year or two), this is also an option. In other cases it may be better to end the formal part of the relationship. Yet even if the relationship is only for a certain time frame, it can be very helpful for the mentoree's personal growth and development.

■ Frequency and Duration of Mentoring Time

It is helpful to coordinate the mentor/mentoree time with the discussion groups. For instance, if the discussion group meets every two weeks, on the alternate week the mentor could meet with the mentoree to follow up on the material covered. Two times a month is considered a minimum amount of time for the mentor to meet with the mentoree, though this may vary.

To begin with it is often helpful to begin by meeting once a week. However, it is better to be realistic in terms of how often one can meet and keep to this than create false expectations that cannot be fulfilled. The key is to be intentional by scheduling this as a regular meeting, so that the busyness of our lives does not crowd out this time. This requires discipline and commitment on behalf of both the mentor and the mentoree.

The duration of each meeting together is also something which needs to be discussed between the mentor and mentoree. Usually two to three hours is desirable. Again, the mentor should not feel the pressure to have to be the resident expert. Their responsibility is to discover where the mentoree is at and determine what aspects of the chapter relates most to the mentoree, so that they can help the mentoree achieve their goals and encourage them in that direction.

Not every aspect or point from each chapter will be applicable to the mentoree at any given time; the effective mentor will listen to the mentoree to discover what they need to focus upon. The material is designed so that the mentor can quickly see some of the key points and, utilizing the questions along the margin, guide the mentoree towards personal life and ministry application.

If, however, the mentoree is quite young or has not had much exposure to the themes of the chapters, it may be necessary for the mentor to be a bit more directive. This however must be done with care so that it corresponds with the agenda and needs of the mentoree. This emphasizes why it is so important that the mentoree share the same life and ministry values as the mentor.

At those times when the mentor may have a perspective that differs from the way the subject matter is handled in the manual, they have the opportunity through the personal relationship to discuss these matters with the mentoree from their perspective. An attempt has been made to discuss these themes in general terms, intentionally allowing for the mentor and mentoree to fill in the specifics depending upon their cultural and/or church setting.

Synergistic Discussion Group

■ <u>Frequency of Meetings</u>

Ideally, this manual was developed with the intention that it could be discussed regularly in a small group setting together with other mentorees. In this group setting key issues can be highlighted and discussed, with specific applications being discussed later in the personal mentoring setting. This discussion group could meet every week, twice a month, or some other variation depending upon what is convenient for the participants.

At the very minimum, each chapter usually requires at least two sessions together. If participants meet twice a month then a chapter could be completed in one calender month, and the program could be completed in one calender year. However, this would mean meeting together for twelve consecutive months, which is not always that realistic. Consequently, the manual usually takes longer than one calender year to complete.

It has also been the experience of some groups that meeting together for only two times per chapter is not enough time to discuss each chapter. Various other options could include meeting each consecutive week (four times in a month), which would mean more discussion time and still completing one chapter per month. Another variation would be to only meet once every two weeks, but take six to eight calender weeks to complete a chapter. In this case it would take longer than one calender year to complete all twelve chapters.

If the group decides to divide the material into two parts (Chapters 1-6 and Chapters 7-12), then each chapter could be easily covered every two months and each half of the model would fit conveniently into one calender year. The entire model would then be completed in two years. However, how it is organized is not as critical as ensuring regularity and consistency. The specifics will be dependent upon each group and their particular needs and setting.

■ <u>The Discussion Group</u>

Regionally
The small group usually consists of fellow mentorees in the program. Several mentorees within a city or region can meet together, each also meeting personally with a mentor from either their own church or circle of contacts. Then while each mentoree has one-on-one time, each also has the opportunity to interact with others, who may be from the same (or different) churches/groups in their area.

Local Church
Another option is for a local church to have several of their key leaders go through all or some of this material and facilitate discussion for all those participating in the program. While this would then be more of a program of the local church, it is crucial to remember that the mentoring relationship is really the key to the whole model. To this end it is important that everyone be partnered with a mentor who will accompany them through the program. This is sometimes more difficult logistically as they are not always enough willing mentors within the setting of a smaller church.

Synergistic Discussion Groups

Small Group Options

Facilitating the Small Group

Focus: Discussion and Application

Missions or Educational Setting

Perhaps you are a missionary and would want to use this to mentor some national leaders or perhaps as an educator you want to utilize it to facilitate the mentoring of students in your program. Another option might be to organize a discussion/accountability group of peer leaders who would like to discuss this material and share with one another from their own life. Again it is rather easy to adapt the material to fit within any of these settings and even others not mentioned here.

The advantage of a combination of both the small group and personal mentoring components is that the participant receives the best of both. The small group provides motivation to continue through the model as well as the opportunity to learn from others and build friendships. Yet not everybody in the small group is at the same stage or needs the same emphasis, which is why the one-on-one time with the mentor is so important. While the discussion group helps keep forward momentum and provide motivation, it is important to realize that the mentoring relationship is crucial to the effectiveness of the model.

■ The Group Facilitator

While it is not required, it is often helpful to have, or appoint, someone that can facilitate the small group discussion meetings. Ideally, this is a person who has some experience in leading small groups, but again this is not necessarily required. The important factor in facilitating synergistic learning at a small group level, is to ensure that the time together does not deteriorate into a lecture or seminar-style session. While this is affected by the participants and their level of maturity, this should be the key goal of the facilitator.

The purpose behind the material in the manual is not to have someone "teach" the material in the traditional sense of teaching. It is designed that participants read the material ahead of time, if possible doing some additional reading and then meeting together to discuss how to apply it in their lives and ministries. The manual is to facilitate discussion and practical application, not be taught line by line. Therefore, the facilitator does not need to be the resident expert with all the answers. It is a group that is walking down the path together offering insights, personal illustrations, and life application with each other.

There are various possibilities as to who can be the facilitator. A local church leader could serve as the facilitator for the discussion group, or perhaps a mature mentoree from within the group. Alternatively it could be a mentor of someone in the group. If this model is being sponsored by a third party (such as a mission agency), then they may provide a facilitator. Another option would be to rotate the facilitator week to week so that a variety of input is provided and more participants are involved (particularly if mentorees are serving as facilitators).

Lesson plans have been included as a help for the person facilitating the small group meeting. These of course will have to be adapted depending upon how often the group meets and how many times they wish to meet together per chapter. In any case, these are merely guidelines from which to develop one's own plan. It is very helpful for the facilitator to do extra reading on the topics in order to be able to offer other perspectives. At the very least the facilitator should be willing to read the one key book per chapter.

Again, the purpose is not to teach another class or seminar, but to lead a synergistic discussion focussed on certain aspects of the material. The benefit of the small group time for the participants will be directly proportional to the degree to which the facilitator creates a non-threatening atmosphere where participants feel free to share and learn from one another.

Regular & Periodic Reevaluation

As trust develops and the mentoring relationship grows, the commitment to the mentoring relationship needs to be evaluated. This is important for over time situations change affecting the dynamics of the mentoring relationship, requiring a re-clarification of expectations. A natural built in point to do this is after completing Sections 1.0 & 2.0 (the first six chapters). While the first six chapters are applicable for every believer, Sections 3.0 & 4.0 (the last six chapters) have more of a leadership/ministry focus.

This point is a natural transition enabling mentor/mentoree to evaluate if it would be valuable for them to continue. This not only gives the mentoree the opportunity to consider if they would like to continue, but also the mentor. If from the very outset of the program participants understand this, then it can be a positive way to end the relationship in its current form or confirm that they would like to continue, but perhaps with some adaptations (of course this should be occurring throughout, not just after Section 2.0).

The last six chapters (Sections 3.0 & 4.0) are not just for those in positions of leadership, but for all those who want to increase their effectiveness as *those who have influence*. However, depending upon where the mentoree is at personally, it may not be the right time for them to go through this material. This is something that the mentor/mentoree can determine at this point. To receive the most from these chapters the mentoree should already have a certain level of understanding and acceptance regarding their giftings and calling. Though not required, the mentoree will receive more from latter chapters if this is the case.

It may also be helpful to reevaluate after every section. However, minor or momentary frustrations should not be used as an excuse for a mentoree to leave the program prematurely. Often being committed through these times can prove to be very helpful. This is particularly the case with someone who has never developed much discipline and may have trouble following through with basic commitments.

This is why a certain level of maturity and discipline is required by those participating in the program, so that as issues need to be dealt that are not that easy, they will have the maturity and commitment to persevere so that they will see greater growth in their life.

Mentoring thru Intentional Relationships may also be used by leaders as an ongoing process to discover and develop other leaders around them. Having these natural points of reevaluation can assist the mentor to find the key people and determine their leadership qualities, without having to commit long term with those who may not be ready.

A word of caution however is in order. As mentors we must be careful to not judge too quickly or allow momentary disappointments determine our decision to not continue. This must be a matter of prayer and we need wisdom to see the potential in others that may not be initially evident.

It is healthy to regularly evaluate the mentoring relationship and process. It is best to avoid open-ended relationships, for if things are not going well this type of mentoring relationships rarely end positively. It is better to reevaluate where the relationship is and where it is going, than just letting the relationship end slowly. If changes need to be made then the natural transition points mentioned above can help facilitate the change, rather then merely spontaneous decisions motivated by temporary relational or emotional difficulties that may occur periodically.

The
Evaluation
Process

Running the Race...

...Leaving a Legacy

FINAL THOUGHTS

- Run the Race

You and I are part of that *cloud of witnesses* that the writer speaks of in the twelfth chapter of Hebrews. This cloud of witnesses is leaning over the balcony of heaven, cheering us on, motivating us to *"throw off everything that hinders and the sin that so easily entangles,"* and to *"run with perseverance the race marked out for us."* In our generation we are part of that continuum which includes all those who have gone on before us and all those who will follow us. To successful complete our lap around the track, we need each other.

- Leaving a Legacy

As members of the Body of Christ we all have the same goal and purpose, yet none of us can fulfill God's purposes for our lives on our own. We need each other. Not just those who are with us as peers now, but those who have gone on before and those coming behind us.

We have received the baton from those who have walked this path ahead of us and our mentorees are those whom we will pass our baton to. We need to build upon the lives of those before us and then, as our race comes to an end, we can know that we have faithfully passed on the baton to others.

Mentoring thru Intentional Relationships is intended to help each of us in this process – those who are prepared to share their lives with others as mentors and those who desire to be mentored. In reality, we are actually both of these at the same time – needing to be mentored by others as well as being a mentor for others.

May you run the race in such a way that those following you will also be equipped to pass on the baton to yet another generation.

SELECTED READING

Two other important additional resources:

Chapter 1.1 deals with our personality and so the *Personality Style Survey* by Walk thru the Bible Ministries (located at the end of the manual in Resource Material), would be very helpful, however, any DISC personality test can be used (www.walkthru.org or Inscape Publishing, Minneapolis).

Chapter 1.2 deals with our spiritual giftings and so it would be helpful to do a Gifts Survey also. An excellent resource is the book, *The 3 Colors of Ministry*, by Christian Schwarz (this is available in many languages). Again, other gift surveys can be used such as the one by Peter Wagner (*Your Spiritual Gifts Can Help Your Church Grow*) or by LEAD Consulting (Raleigh, NC).

Additional reading will be an invaluable addition to this manual for both the mentoree and the mentor. As mentioned, the manual is not intended to be the final word on each of these subjects, but rather a beginning point for the journey.

There are many good resources on each of the topics we cover, however at the very least the following will give a starting point for additional reading for every chapter (others are included in the *Resource Material*):

Chapter 1.1 - *Solving the People Puzzle*, Walk thru the Bible Ministries
Chapter 1.2 - *The 3 Colors of Ministry*, Christian Schwarz
Chapter 1.3 - *The Power of the Call,* Henry Blackaby and H. Brandt
Chapter 2.1 - *Celebration of Discipline*, Richard Foster
Chapter 2.2 - *The Challenge of the Disciplined Life,* Richard Foster
Chapter 2.3 - *Experiencing God*, Henry Blackaby
Chapter 3.1 - *Upside Down*, Stacey Rinehart
Chapter 3.2 - *Developing the Leader Within You*, John C. Maxwell
Chapter 3.3 - *Becoming a Person of Influence,* John C. Maxwell
Chapter 4.1 - *Spiritual Leadership,* Henry Blackaby
Chapter 4.2 - *The Church is Bigger than You Think*, Patrick Johnstone
Chapter 4.3 - *The Purpose Driven Church*, Rick Warren

....One Additional Resource per chapter

Person

Chapter

Mentoring
thru
Intentional Relationships

1.1

Your Personality: Who You Are

INTRODUCTION

- As we begin this mentoring journey we will begin with several aspects of who we are as a *Person*.

- While the four divisions are rather arbitrary, for we cannot really separate one of these aspects from the other, we will attempt to do so, so that we can look at each individually.

- Before we are a *Disciple*, a *Leader* or even a *Minister*, we are a *Person* and so that is where our journey will begin.

- It is a journey that begins with self-discovery, as we look at our *personality*, our *gifts* and our *calling*.

Why Begin with Personality?

- Those knowledgeable in the field have observed that our basic personality is largely determined by the time we are five or six years of age. If this is the case then it would be helpful to discover how important our personality is in affecting our attitudes, values and actions.

- Having predated our adulthood, our personality is fundamental to who we are. This also means that who we are, our personality, has predated most relationships that we have and even our spiritual conversion.

- So in this program, whose emphasis is *Mentoring thru Intentional Relationships*, understanding our basic personality and how this affects how we respond to others is foundational. It is also helpful to understand so that we may get the most from the mentoring relationship.

- To begin with we need to discover who we are and accept ourselves, so that we are not always trying to change the very way God made us. This is not always a matter of determining between just "right" or "wrong," but rather seeing the variety and value in the basic personality types.

- As we better understand both ourselves and others we can become more appropriate in our actions and more effective in positively affecting others for the Kingdom.

The Good News

- This is not a fatalistic look at temperaments – which has the view that we are prisoners of our own personality – but rather an approach which gives hope for potential change. Not necessarily trying to change who we are, but learning how to *adapt* our basic personality style to better deal with others and situations.

- Much of our natural response has to do with our values and motivations which are grounded in our basic personality style. Yet at the very core of being successful in life is being able to adapt and change how we respond to situations and others in order to act appropriately.

Do you think your personality is something you are born with or develops in our early years?

How important are our experiences in forming our personality?

What about your personality would you like to change? What characteristics have caused you problems which you have not been able to change, though you have tried?

- So first understanding who we are (in terms of our personality) is essential if we are going to be able to adapt and change some of the potential weaknesses of our natural personality style.

Do you think it "unbiblical" to study personalities? Why or why not?

Is This Biblical?

- Often many of the interpersonal conflicts and issues we deal with throughout our lives have to do with not understanding the basic characteristics of our personality style.

- Many times interpersonal conflicts are not clear-cut issues of right or wrong, good or bad, but rather have to do with something as simple (and complex) as who we are at the core of our beings – our personality.

- Understanding our personality, or temperament, is not so that we have an excuse for wrong or sinful behaviour – nor is it a fateful, *"God just made me this way and everyone has to deal with it...."* Rather our goal is to be conformed to Christ's image and live a life which positively influences others.

How have you seen others abuse this teaching? Discuss your biases with your mentor, then make a choice to look afresh at this topic from a balanced perspective.

A Balanced Perspective

- This chapter is a tool to help you discover your natural personality style. This will help you understand your behaviour tendencies in various situations and then learn how to adapt your instinctive reactions to more productive ones.

- We will discover that each of the four personality types have both strengths and weaknesses. There can be a tendency to use this material to put ourselves or others in a box (ie. "You are a ...." or "That is why you always...." or "I can never do that because...."). But a healthier attitude is to use it to discover our natural "starting point" in terms of personality and then learn how to adapt our response with others to a more healthier one.

- Learning our personality mix can help us determine these strengths and weaknesses.

- We need to first see that everyone has strengths and then learn to appreciate the strengths in us and others – thankful for the way God made us (Psa. 139:13-14). Only with this understanding can we maximize our particular strengths.

- While we all have strengths, we also all have weaknesses. We must also recognize this and allow God to help us with those weaknesses (2 Cor. 12:9-10). Understanding this can help us to minimize the impact of these weaknesses.

- Being a better Christian does not mean trying to change the way he has designed us – God's desire is to make us the best that we can be, which includes understanding the particular strengths and weaknesses of our personality type.

- So to begin this journey of self-discovery we will begin with a look at our personality – a look at who God made us. While there will be many other discoveries in the coming chapters, this first section will deal with the core of who we are as a *Person*.

Some Cautions:

- While this can be very helpful, if not fully understood, the knowledge we acquire can be misused and abused and so a few cautions are in order.

- First, it is important to not categorize or label people. While our personality style is a large part of who we are, it is not the *only* factor. We cannot assume that we know or understand the complexities of every person – their attitudes, values, background, as well as the many other factors which affect who they are – just by understanding something about their personality style.

- Knowing our personality style is also not a tool to use to excuse sin or to justify destructive behaviour. The negative or weak aspects of our personality type can and need to be changed by God's grace and our effort.

- This leads to the next caution: We all have the potential to change. With God's help, and a fresh understanding of who we are, there is hope for all of us to improve in this area.

PERSONALITY BASICS

Four Basic Types

- Regardless of our culture, age, or background, there seem to be four basic personality types or temperaments, though no person is only one of these types. Each person is a combination of these four basic personality temperaments.

- Further, research seems to indicate that the majority of people have two personality temperaments that predominant and two which are less dominant.

- As far back as 400 B.C. Hippocrates observed and tried to quantify these four personality types. He used body fluids to describe four personality types: Choleric - the active type (*D*); Sanguine - the lively type (*I*); Phlegmatic - the slow type (*S*); Melancholy - the dark type (*C*).

- There have been many models since to describe these four basic personality types, but perhaps the easiest to remember and identify with, is the widely used *D-I-S-C* model.

D-I-S-C Survey

- To help determine a person's basic personality type, various forms of the *DISC* test has been developed.

- You may be doing a shortened version of this which has proven to be very accurate (provided in *Reference Material*), or you may have acquired the full-length version which is more thorough.

- It is important to recognize that this is an indicator, there are no right or wrong answers and this is not the final word on your personality type.

- For best results you should answer the questions as you really are or feel, not the way you think you should, or how you think a "Christian" should answer these questions. Again, this is not an indicator of character qualities or flaws, but personality tendencies.

- Before proceeding in the notes, do a DISC survey test now if you have access to one.

Determine not to "label" others or use your personality to excuse destructive behaviour.

Spend some to think about what your main motivation is. Reflect on how this affects your relationships and ministry.

Quadrant Personality Graph

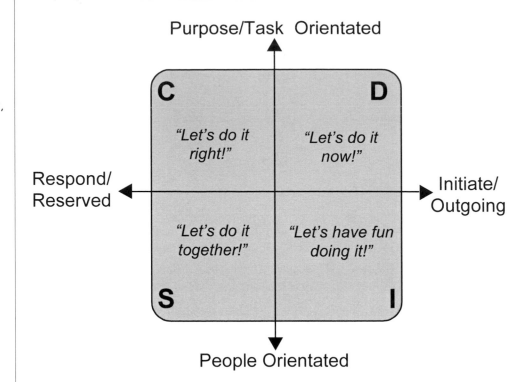

Before doing the DISC Survey, in which two quadrants do you think most of your positive personality traits will be?

After doing the DISC survey and reading through these qualities, what have you discovered about yourself? Were there any surprises in your discoveries?
Discuss these with your mentor.

- Each quadrant represents a personality type and can be described by the preceding graph.

  - The upper half indicates people that are naturally orientated towards *Purpose* or *Tasks* while the bottom half represents those whose have a *People* focus.

  - The left half of the graph represents those who *Respond* or are more *Reserved* and slower-paced while the right half of the graph represents those who take *Initiative* or are *Outgoing* and have a faster-pace.

  - It is important to remember that everyone is a combination of these four, with two styles (represented by quadrants) most likely being the most prominent (though this is not always the case):

    D - type personality takes initiative and has a purpose/task orientation.

    I - type personality takes initiative and has a people-orientation.

    S - type personality is more responsive/reserved and has a people-orientation.

    C - type personality is more responsive/reserved and has a purpose/task orientation.

PERSONALITY CHARACTERISTICS

- Each personality type is motivated by different factors; they see the world with a different set of values.

- No one person has all the positive characteristics listed, nor all of the weaknesses. To the degree that someone has matured is the degree to which they will have balanced their personality and display more of the strengths and fewer of the weaknesses.

- This is why two individuals of the same personality type may be quite different – one may have worked on increasing their strengths and decreasing their negative tendencies, while the other may be an example of most of the negative attributes and a few of the positive ones.

- The following lists represent both the *best case* (the positive list) and *worst case* (the negative list) potential.

The *High "D"* Personality Type – Dominance/Decisive

■ Basic Need and Motivation

- The *High D* personality is motivated by a challenge.

- Those strong in this quadrant have a high need to have control of the situation in order to be motivated to take charge.

What positive High D characteristics could help bring more balance in your life?

■ Positive Character Tendencies

- They are usually dominant and have a dynamic type of personality.

- Their focus is to get something done and they are often very practical.

- They are also problem-solvers and the decision-makers of this world.

- They love to accept a challenge and are persistent enough to see it through to completion.

■ Potential Character Weaknesses

- However, they can also be very dogmatic and defiant.

- This can lead to insensitivity to others and being too demanding of others.

- Their persistence can also lead to inflexibility and impatience.

- Their overconfidence can lead to overlooking risks and cautions.

- When pressured or under tension, there can a be a tendency to be overbearing and dictatorial.

Begin to look at your potential weaknesses and identify what specific areas have caused you problems in your interpersonal relationships.

■ Biblical Character

- Apostle Paul could be an example of a person with strong tendencies as a *High D* personality style.

- He went from *passionately* killing Christians (Acts 22:4) to *passionately* following Christ (Acts 20:24).We see his determination in expanding the Gospel and his direct manner with the churches he planted.

- However, he needed to be controlled by the Holy Spirit (Gal. 5:16-22), so as to mitigate his character weaknesses.

The *High "I"* Style – Influence/Inspirational

■ Basic Need and Motivation

- *High I's* personality types are motivated by a need for recognition.

- They need to feel the approval of others.

What positive High I characteristics could help bring more balance in your life?

■ Positive Character Tendencies

- *High I's* are inspirational people who can naturally influence others.

- They tend to be optimistic and personable; they are warm and everyone likes them.

- They are verbally articulate, persuasive, outgoing and friendly, as well as compassionate.

- Their people-orientated personality means that they usually know many people and are networkers.

■ Potential Character Weaknesses

- While they are influential, they can also be easily influenced, which can lead to inconsistency.

- They can also be impulsive and lack follow-through.

- Their verbal ability can lead them to talk too much, which can manifest itself in their being verbally manipulative.

- Being generally optimistic can lead them to misjudge their capability and over commit themselves.

- When under pressure there can be a tendency to use superior verbal ability to strike out and attack.

■ Biblical Character

- The Apostle Peter is an example of an example of a *High I* personality type.

- He often spoke first and thought later, which was positive when in control (Matt 16:13-17), but negative when out of control (Matt. 16: 21-23).

- We see him as the one who speaks to the gathered crowd on the Day of Pentecost and though he was optimistic and could take great risks, his tendency for impulsiveness led to problems for him at times (John 21:4-7).

The *High "S"* Style – Steadiness/Supportive

■ Basic Need and Motivation

- Those strong in the *High S* quadrant are motivated by close interpersonal relationships.

- They usually have a need to sense the appreciation of others.

■ Positive Character Tendencies

- *High S's* are supportive people who are loyal and agreeable, without even trying!

- They are reliable, stable, and steady and usually liked by everyone for their sweetness.

- They like being with people, but like to choose who they are with, as opposed to just being with a crowd.

- They are easy-going and desire to maintain the status quo; they don't like changes.

■ Potential Character Weaknesses

- They can be indecisive and in wanting to please everyone be indirect with others.

- They avoid conflict and are overly tolerant, even when a direct approach is required.

Take some time in your personal devotions to focus on your positive traits and thank God for who he made you.

Begin to look at your potential weaknesses and identify what specific areas have caused you problems in your interpersonal relationships.

What positive High S characteristic would help bring more balance in your life?

- They also can have a tendency to procrastinate and can have difficulty with deadlines.
- Due to their agreeable nature they can easily be taken advantage of, after which they can pull within themselves in efforts to try and protect themselves.
- When they are under pressure or stress they have a tendency to just give up and give in.

■ Biblical Character

- The Apostle John is an example of someone with *High S* tendencies.
- He was in the inner circle with Jesus and was quietly loyal to the Master.
- Though he wrote some of the New Testament, he was in the background. He never mentions his own name, always referring to himself as "the other disciple."

What positive High C characteristics could help bring more balance in your life?

The *High "C"* Style – Conscientiousness/Competent

■ Basic Need and Motivation

- *High C's* are personality types who are motivated by excellence.
- They have a high need for right answers and doing things with quality.

■ Positive Character Tendencies

- *High C* type personalities are generally self-disciplined, orderly and very thorough and analytical.
- They are competent individuals who are cautious, calculating and precise.
- They are often compliant and conformists, unless they can see how to do it better (which they usually can!), which is where they can take charge.
- They are also consistent and conscientious to see a project through.

■ Potential Character Weaknesses

- Those with this personality style predominant, can tend to be too cautious and rigid and their attention to detail can mean they lose sight of the big picture.
- They can tend to be moody, pessimistic, or even critical, as they usually can see what is wrong and not what is right.
- They can also have a tendency to be unsociable, working on projects opposed to being with people.
- Not wanting to make mistakes they fail to take risks and opt to stay "safe."
- When under pressure or stress they will avoid and become even more introvert, having the potential to harbor ill-feelings for long periods.

Which biblical Character do you particularly identify with?
Do a character study of this person from the perspective of their personality and how God dealt specifically with them.

■ Biblical Character

- Moses is a biblical example of this *High C* personality type.
- He was careful, cautious when facing a challenge (Ex. 3:10-11). His competence made it difficult for him to share responsibility with others (Ex. 18:13-18).
- We see him receiving God's law and then expected complete compliance to it (Deut. 4:1-2).

Different Yet Valuable

- Comparing your survey results and the above descriptions, you can probably identify most of your own characteristics in one or two of the four personality styles.

- Everyone is a combination of these and everyone has positive qualities which can be associated with these personality styles. Each person is valuable and brings to every situation the potential of their positive qualities.

- Yet, each of these various styles are separated in what motivates them and in what situations they operate at their best. For example, the use of time and resources, as well as how we make decisions is affected by our personality mix.

- Most people cannot point to a time when they learned many of these qualities, rather they have always seemed to be a part of them, to a greater or lesser degree.

How does your specific personality combination enhance your strengths and limit your weaknesses?

The Mix

- It is important to look at our top two personality styles as opposed to just the top one, since the vast majority of people have a combination of two main personality types. Seeing how these balance each other is important for it is this mix that explains the complexity of our feelings and actions.

- Note that "*D*" and "*S*" are opposite, as are "*I*" and "*C*". All other combination have some common traits, either in their *priority* or *pace*.

- From the graph, note the similarities that some of the temperament styles have (*People/Task* Orientation or *Initiators/Responders*). Each quadrant has at least one of these in common with another style. It is our top two styles and the similarities and differences of these top two which determine many of our personality traits.

- Often in relationships very opposites may attract (D-S or C-I) as we try to meet the need in others, but these two combinations are unusual as the top two in any one individual. *It is more common to have a mix with an adjacent quadrant on the graph, as opposed to across the diagonal.*

How do you cause stress in other personality types just by being you?
Consider how this affects your leadership style; your influence on others; your ministry.
What steps can you take to be more effective?

We Create Tension

- In situations every day we can cause stress in those with other personality types, just by being who we are, with our natural personality style.

- We must recognize this and not judge others (or ourselves) for this reality – it is the way of human personalities. It is often not even a matter of *right* and *wrong* or sinful behaviour.

- The fact is that others can help to balance our own weaknesses, but if we only focus on the weakness of others and not their strengths, relational problems are magnified.

- To the degree that we can learn to accept others and adapt ourselves appropriately to meet differing situations/people, is the degree to which we will be effectiveness in our positive influence for the Kingdom (we will discuss this further in Section 3.0)

- This does not mean that we must "change" our very personality and be something that we are not, for in many ways this is not really possible.

- However, it does mean that we can recognize how our personality style affects others and how we can best interact with others according to their particular personality motivations and needs.

- Paul's concept of the Body of Christ, with all its diversity and unity, addresses the idea of differing personalities all joined together in common purpose in the Church.

- God wants to use others to complement us and use us to complement others.

ADAPTING OUR STYLE

- To be successful in our personal lives/ministry we need to learn how to adapt our personal style to meet the needs of others.

- This begins as we understand our *personality mix* – who we are. For example, a strong D/C needs to recognize that they must increase the weaker I/S qualities (focus on people not just the task) and so on. It is not so much a matter of *changing* who we are, for we will probably always have a natural tendency in the direction of the particular personalty style strengths. But it is more of a matter of adapting our behaviour to be more appropriate or effective, given the understanding of our natural personality tendencies.

- This is usually a challenge for we come to relationships with biases that arise from our personality style and this causes others to react to us and vice-versa.

- However, the ultimate purpose of learning to adapt, is not so that we can be self-serving or manipulative, but rather that we can learn to genuinely help others be all that they can be.

Discuss with your mentor steps you can practically work on in adapting your particular personality mix with relationships that you have.

Steps in Understanding Others

- The first step in this process is coming to an understanding of who you are and accepting that.

- Then, by using the DISC graph as a tool, we can begin to observe others with the intention of identifying their basic personality style.

  - Ask yourself, *Are they in the upper half (Task or Purpose Motivated) or are they more focussed on People (S or I)?*

  - *Are they faster paced (D or I) or are they responders (S or C)?* Or in other words, *Do they tend to 'Tell Others' or do they 'Ask Others'?*

  - Again, the purpose is not to put people in a box, but to understand their needs and how to best motivate and communicate with them.

- We must then make a commitment to focus on the positive attributes of every personality style and recognizing the needs of each.

- Having understood others, as well as our own particular personality style, we can take the following steps to adapt to meet each others' needs.

Practical Steps for Each Personality

- In order to minimize the negative impacts of each personality style, there are practical steps that each of us can take (according to our natural personality style), in order to be more effective in our lives.

Using your two highest personality styles as a guide, read the suggested steps you can take to improve yourself and ministry.

- ■ The *High "D"*

- Those strong in the *D quadrant* would benefit from slowing down and listening more.

- Their efforts would also be helped by being more focussed on the people-component of any endeavour.

- They also need to be warmer and more open and more willing to submit.

- As a leader, *High D's* need to be willing to play a secondary role at times and not dominate.

- It is important for them to be supportive, explaining the why's of the decision and better evaluate the risks, particularly for those who are following their leadership.

- An effective *High D* leader is one who has allowed God to "break" them and one who learns to lead from a foundation of servant leadership – open and vulnerable with others (see Chapter 3.1)

- Biblical truths that can be developed: James 1:19, Matt 20:26, 28; Prov. 1:5; Luke 14:28-30; Is. 40:31.

Discuss with your mentor specific steps you can take according to your starting personality style.

■ The *High "I"*

- *High I's* would benefit from pausing and focussing on results.

- While *I's* tend to be people orientated, they must discipline themselves to focus on the details and facts and be more realistic.

- They need to evaluate their activities and be less impulsive in their actions and manage their time.

- This also means learning to control their emotions and not relying completely on their charisma to influence others.

- They must be careful not to manipulate others with their superior verbal and persuasive skills and learn to listen more and talk less.

- To be an effective leader, an *High I* also need to learn personal discipline and limit their natural tendency to socialize.

- Various biblical truths that they can develop:1 Cor. 14:40; Prov. 14:29; 2 Cor. 8:11; Prov. 10:19; 2 Pet. 1:5-7.

Be accountable to your mentor to change in areas that you may have struggled with most of your life.

■ The *High "S"*

- *High S's* would benefit from taking more initiative and being more decisive.

- They will be more effective as they learn to be more direct and be less sensitive in their dealings with others.

- As leaders this also means learning to confront when appropriate and not be motivated in their actions just so that others will like and accept them.

- They will also have to work at increasing their pace and be open to change – stability at all costs is not always beneficial for them or those they lead. Change can actually provide new opportunities!

- *High S's* need to learn to say "No" and though they naturally are servants, they will need to know the line between being a servant and not being taken advantage of and abused – listening to God's direction and not others is key for them.

- Biblical Truths to develop: James 1:5; 2 Cor. 3:12; Prov. 27:5; Eph. 5:15-16; Phil. 4:13.

■ The *High "C"*

- *High C's* will be more effective as they develop their people skills.

- They need to realize that all the facts cannot be known and sometimes decisions have to be made on less tangible issues than just facts and figures.

- This may mean taking more risks, which they usually find very uncomfortable.

- As leaders they will have to learn to react more quickly and not get consumed by details and losing sight of the big picture. They must see the need and begin to meet deadlines.

- In dealing with others, *High C's* need to focus on being more optimistic and focus on the positive, not just see the negatives which arise from the decisions of others.

- They also will be more balanced as they make the effort to develop relationships and become more spontaneous and flexible.

- Learning to deal with the inconsistencies and variables of leadership is crucial, as they need to see the art and not just the science of leadership.

- Biblical Truths which they can develop include: 2 Tim. 1:7; 2 Cor. 3:5; Prov. 18:24; Phil. 4:19; Heb. 11:6.

Reflect on your top two personality styles and which is stronger and which is weaker.
How does this combination affect your actions and relationships?

Relational Needs

- Each Personality Style comes to relationships from a different vantage point and has different needs and values.

- Since we assume that all people are like us, it takes great effort to deal with others the way they need to be communicated and dealt with, not just the way someone of our particular personality type finds most understandable.

Consider your family members, those you work/minister with: What personality mix are they and how has this affected your relationship with them?

- It takes effort for each person to deal with other personality styles the way they need to be related to. Yet doing this not only helps us in our relationships, but ultimately helps us to be more effective in our tasks – both the mundane and the sublime.

- Depending on the person we are dealing with, it is helpful to relate to them in a way that they can best accept according to their personality style. Specifically this affects the differing ways that we try to communicate, convince, motivate and even disagree with the various personality styles.

■ Communicating with:

High D - Be direct and challenge them.

High I - Be positive and enthusiastic.

High S - Be patient and easy-going.

High C - Be specific and thorough.

■ Convincing a:

High D - Be results orientated: focus on the bottom line.

High I - Be enthusiastic and focus on proven results in others.

High S - Be warm and friendly and take time.

High C - Be methodical in what needs to be done and its importance.

■ Motivating a:

High D - Let them take charge and determine how to do it.

High I - Allow them ample input and recognize their efforts.

High S - Do things together and minimize conflict.

High C - Work closely together and give them time to do it right.

■ Disagreeing with a:

High D - Give them a way out without direct battle; offer various option for them to decide.

High I - Have patience, often in time their enthusiasm will fade without confrontation.

High S - Focus on relational issues and affirm the stability of the relationship.

High C - Have facts in place and present them clearly; giving time for it to sink in.

What personality was Jesus? Discuss your views and opinions regarding this.

What Personality Type was Jesus?

• Jesus was divine, but at the same time completely human – yet without sin. Yet how did this issue of personality affect him in his humanity?

• Jesus was completely human and perfectly balanced in his personality – the perfect balance of all four types, appropriately responding in every situation.

• For example perhaps Jesus was a *High D* when he cleared the temple, yet not out of control (John 2:14-17) or a *High I* in front of the crowds inspiring and motivating, yet under control (Matt. 15: 29-39)?

• We could also view him as a strong *High S* as he attracted the most vulnerable to him, yet serving others without being manipulated (Matt. 9:18-21). We also could see him as a *High C* answering questions of the religious leaders with competence, and yet without arrogant (Luke 20:1-40).

• While this is speculation, it is interesting to see how Jesus dealt with others and realize that he did adapt to various people and situations.

• We see Jesus motivating, communicating, confronting, and explaining truth to others in ways that they could best comprehend and accept. We as leaders can learn from him and follow in his footsteps.

• The Kingdom is built on relationships and so our success in dealing with ourselves and others is essential if we are going to effective in positively influencing others towards God's purposes.

Commit to your mentor which top three steps of action you want to take and give your mentor permission in the coming months to ask you how it is going in these areas of change you have determined as your priorities.

SUMMARY

• In this first chapter we have seen that the first step in understanding ourselves and others is to discover more about the issue of personality and how fundamental it is to our attitudes and actions.

• We have discovered that not only do we have a natural personality style, but it is possible to adapt it in order to be more effective in our relationships with others.

• In this first section, in addition to our understanding of our personality style, we will look at the gifts that God has given us and the calling that he has on our lives. This will be our focus in the next two chapters.

Mentoring
thru
Intentional Relationships

Your Gifts: What You Have

1.2

INTRODUCTION

- In addition to a basic personality style, we are also given gifts as Christians to help us in our service of others.

- They are interrelated in that our personality style does affect the expression of our gifts. To this end, it is helpful to consider how they affect who we are, as well as our particular ministry.

- Our personality style, the gifts that God has given us, and our particular calling, all combine to form the three aspects of who we are as a person, which we will discuss in the first section of this material.

- This is not an in-depth look at the subject of spiritual gifts, as there are many good teaching books which have been written on this subject. These notes are merely to direct the reader to the appropriate issues and motivate the mentoree to work through some of these issues in their own life and ministry, particularly if they have not already done so.

- To have a greater grasp of the topic, as well as being able to do a gift survey, Christian A. Schwarz's book *"The 3 Colors of Ministry"* is highly recommended reading for this chapter. It contains one of the most thorough gift surveys, as well as an interesting approach to being a balanced Christian/Church (ministering from the perspective of God's revelation as Father, Son and Holy Spirit). This book can be ordered on-line (www.NCD-international.org) in various languages, or by writing one of the *Natural Church Development* offices.

- The purpose of this chapter is not to change someone's particular theological position regarding the topic of spiritual gifts. As a mentoree you need to be aware of the teaching in your particular setting and be in unity with that understanding. If you are mentoring someone from your own denomination or group this chapter will give you the opportunity to explain your position and why, however, if your mentoree is from another particular church tradition you will need to discuss these matters with sensitivity.

- The variety that God has designed within the Body of Christ seems to indicate flexibility in the interpretation of the biblical texts regarding this subject. So our approach is intended to be a practical one in order to discover our gifts and how we can better use them to serve others.

> Discuss with other mentorees or mentor who has influenced your understanding and usage of the Gifts. In what areas are you open for change, in what areas are you not?

> Have you had any misconception regarding what gifts are and what their purpose is?

A BIBLICAL OVERVIEW

Definition and Overview

- Schwarz defines Spiritual Gifts as *"a special ability that God gives, according to his grace, to each member of the body of Christ to be used of the development of the church."*

- According to the Scriptures, every believer has received at least one gift (1 Pet. 4:10; 1 Cor 12:7-11), however, most believers have never taken the time to discover what spiritual gifts God has given them.

- This chapter is intended to help us appreciate the need for spiritual gifts and then take the steps necessary to encourage their expression in our life and ministry.

- Each gift is for the benefit of the whole Body (1 Cor. 12:17-20) and is not just to be expressed or used in isolation – their very purpose is to serve others.

- They are not given as rewards according to our righteousness (Rom. 12:6), nor are they the same as the *fruit of the Spirit*, which has to do with character. Rather they are distributed according to God's will.

- Consequently, it is possible for the spiritual gifts to be expressed in an immature, or even harmful manner, by those who are not spiritually mature.

- Though most Christians acknowledges the existence and value of the gifts, there is much variety as to the particular emphasis and expression of the various gifts. Some see them as life-long, others only as given when needed, some as official offices, and others only as ministry gifts of service. All these variations, however, need not cause division, but actually indicate the flexibility that there seems to be in the Scripture as to the expression of the gifts.

Biblical Passages

- While there is no shortage of gifts mentioned in the Bible, it does not seem that any one particular order or system is of greater importance than another.

- Of the three main passages where gifts are listed, the gifts are listed in different orders, with no apparent hierarchy.

- In Romans 12:6-8 we see, Prophecy, Service, Teaching, Exhortation/Encourage, Giving, Leadership, Mercy.

- In 1 Corinthians 12:8-11 we read of, Wisdom, Knowledge, Faith, Healing, Miracles, Prophecy, Discerning of spirits, Tongues, Interpretation of tongues, and then verse 28, Apostle, Prophets, Teachers, Miracles, Healing, Administration, Tongues.

- The third main passage is Ephesians 4:11 where we see, Apostles, Prophets, Evangelists, Pastors & Teachers.

Some Observations:

- Though each list has the same author, there is no clear list or order of hierarchy. We know from Paul's writings that he is capable of making a hierarchal list when he intends to do so, but does not seem to do so with the gifts.

- These lists seem to be reflections of what was actually happening in the early church, not necessarily intended to be exhaustive or exclusive.

- This lack of definitiveness has led to many different types of organizational systems for the gifts. These range from the idea that some (or many) of the gifts ended with the passing of the first century Church, to a variety of charts intended to organize the gifts.

- Some within the Body teach that the nine gifts of 1 Corinthians 12:8-11are the main spiritual gifts and all the others as more natural abilities (or natural motivations). Others believe that all the gifts are "spiritual gifts," and yet others see a difference between the *gifts* and the *offices* (which we may call roles). Further multiple combinations of each of these teachings can also be found in the Body.

- Our approach here is that each of these views have merit (except the concept that the gifts ended in the first century!) and that it is more important to encourage and exercise the various gifts for the good of others, than arguing over their terminology or definition.

Has your exposure to the gifts through your church life been a generally positive or negative one?

Do you think these are all the gifts there are, or are they only illustrative?
Do you think that would be possible for there to be divinely inspired spiritual gifts today not listed in the Bible?

From your study of scripture discuss your views regarding the differences between natural abilities, spiritual gifts and offices or roles.

- In order to provide some consistency for those doing the Gift Test in the book, *The 3 Colors of Ministry*, Schwarz's perspective that each of these gifts is a spiritual gift will be adhered to. As a more general approach, it will serve as a good beginning point in our discussion on the gifts, allowing those who have specific emphases to expand upon this general foundation.

The Equipping Gifts (Ephesians 4)

- The Gifts in Ephesians 4:11 has been described as the *Equipping Gifts.* These four or five gifts have been seen by many in the Body as gifts primarily used to *equip the saints to do the work of the ministry* (4:12).

- Over the course of church history some of these gifts have evolved into more of an office or an officially recognized position and, depending upon the particular church group or church era, each gift has received varied emphasis.

- In many church circles, the pastors is the most identifiable position, while among other groups the apostle is preeminent, or the prophet, evangelist, or even teacher. Other churches have added other offices such as elders, deacons, bishops, superintendents etc., usually based upon Paul's writings in the Pastoral Letters.

- The purpose here is not to make a biblical case for any particular position or view, but rather to focus our attention on a few obvious observations.

- First, in terms of equality, is the fact that there is no separation in the Scripture between the clergy/laity, while it is clear that our gifts do create opportunities for us of varied service and function.

- Unfortunately, it is possible to have an officially-recognized *office* and not have the necessary *gifts* to fulfill the task of that office. The challenge and opportunity for all of us is to align our service to others with our God-given gifts.

- Though perhaps obvious, it needs to be stated that, if a position is attained due to personality, prestige, reputation etc and not according to gifts, the Body of Christ will ultimately suffer.

- So regardless if these four or five gifts are seen as "offices," gifts, or combination of both, it is crucial that they are used in the Body so that all believers will be built up.

- Leaders (see Chapter 3.1 on servant leadership) need to particularly ensure that they are operating within a sphere of ministry and influence that fits their *Gifts*, *Personality* (Chapter 1.1) and *Calling* (Chapter 1.3).

Do you believe that the equipping gifts of Ephesians 4 are roles or offices only, or can a believer have one of these gifts without the role? In your view, what determines an "equipping" gift?

Are you ministering within a role for which you have corresponding gifts?

What Gifts are Not

- To help us better describe what is meant by the term "gifts," it may be helpful to discuss what a biblical definition does not include.

- Gifts in the biblical context are not just *Natural Abilities*, the *Fruit of the Spirit*, or *Christian Attributes*.

■ Natural Abilities

- God-given gifts are more than natural ability or talents, though we often use the general word "gifts" to also describe these (ie. "She is really gifted.")

- Obviously God is also the source of these natural abilities, since he has created us, but these abilities, natural and developed, are expressed in both Christians and non-Christians alike.

Distinguish between your natural abilities and spiritual gifts?
Are there similarities? Differences?

- In contrast, these gifts mentioned in the Bible have been called by some as "spiritual gifts" to distinguish them from just natural abilities.

- Unfortunately the term, "spiritual gifts" can lead some to wrongly conclude that they operate in only mystical settings, as opposed to very human, natural, and practical contexts.

- Therefore, it is important to realize that there is a difference between just a natural ability (which we recognize as, ultimately, God-given) and spiritual gifts which are given to believers to be used to serve others. Yet it is not a biblical perspective to view these "spiritual gifts" (listed above) as only operating in church-type services, for they are to be practical expressions to serve others in everyday human life.

■ Fruit of the Spirit

- The *Fruit of the Spirit* relates to the character and *maturity* of a believer, while Gifts relate to the *service* of the believer with others.

- The evidence of the "Fruit" in a believer's life is Christian growth, maturity and holiness. This can lead to confusion in the Body of Christ for not all those who exercise their spiritual gifts are mature, living holy lives, or particularly "spiritual."

- While the gifts can be expressed in less than effective ways by immature believers, they will be more effectively used by those who are mature, holy and of sound character. But the manifestation of the gifts can never be taken as a confirmation of a person's spiritual growth or maturity.

Do you agree that the fruit of the Spirit is more important in the believer's life than the gifts? Why or why not?

- While we can discover our Gifts, the *Fruit* in our life is not discovered, but developed.

- As Paul taught in the Corinthian letters, the Gifts are temporal for they are task-orientated to meet needs, but the Fruit will last for eternity. This is why the chapters in the second section of the manual will deal extensively with the spiritual disciplines necessary in order to foster the growth of the Spirit's fruit in our lives. Grasping this truth will help in the effective application of our gifts.

■ Christian Attributes

- As with our *fruit* as Christians, each believer needs to be growing in the Christian attributes that should characterize every believer.

- For example, all believers need to be growing in faith (Eph. 2:8,9; Gal. 5:22; Heb. 11:6), serving others, being a witness, and being hospitable. Yet this may not mean that every believer has the spiritual gift of *Faith, Service, Evangelism,* or *Hospitality*.

- Regardless of our particular gifts, as Christians we all need to be growing in our capacity to express Christian attributes.

■ Counterfeit Gifts

- Satan can and does counterfeit every gift on the list (Matt: 24:24; 7:22,23), but as see when Moses was before Pharaoh, his power is limited (Exod. 7, 8).

- Many of Satan's techniques are nothing more than mere copies of these gifts that God gives. The key difference is in the result of the exercise of the gift: *Does it draw people closer to Christ and love him more? Do they have positive, practical result?* This is the critical issue in the proper use of the Gifts.

Are Gifts Discoverable?

- There are varied views regarding the issue of if we should actively try to discover our gifts.

- Some take the position that it is not healthy to try to discover our gifts, as this can lead some to rationalize not fulfilling basic Christian duties, or even a self-deception, as they may think they have gifts which they do not have. While this is a valid position, it is not the one we will take in this chapter.

- While these concerns are valid, they can be mitigated with good teaching and accountable relationships. In Romans 12, Paul encourages believers to think soberly of themselves; not thinking more highly than they should, but nevertheless having an accurate estimation of themselves and their place in the Body. Many have found such a self-discovery helpful, as well as have many churches.

- As members of the Body recognize and learn to appreciate what gifts God has given them, they are better prepared to serve each other. This leads to personal growth, as well as Kingdom growth, as every member of the Body becomes more effective in meeting the needs of others with the gift that God has given them.

Do you think it is important to discover your gifts? Why or why not?

Availability of the Gifts

- As alluded to previously, there are basically two schools of thought regarding the availability of the gifts for the believer.

- Some hold to the view that the gifts are given by God at specific times to the believer to meet specific needs. Others hold to the view that the believer *has* their particular gifts for the duration of their lives (or for regular, long periods of time).

- While it is not possible, from Scripture, to definitively determine which view is more accurate (there are Bible scholars on both sides), the practical application of these views is what is important.

What school of thought (or combination) do you hold to with regards to the availability of the gifts (ie. lifelong or as needed)? How does your view affect your ministry?

- Those who see the *gifts* as tools which are at the disposal of all believers – to be used as required and needed – see them as a divine empowering to meet particular needs, not special attributes. Yet it is obvious from the praxis, that some believers operate more frequently (and even regularly) in the realm of certain gifts. Some would then label this as someone's "ministry," or a "sphere of service" within which they more regularly function.

- Those who hold to the view that believer's have certain gifts for the duration of their lives, still believe that all believers should be open to see God work through them in new ways, depending on the specific need. However they would assume that a person would have greater success operating with those gifts which they have particularly been given as "their" gift.

- So regardless of the starting point, both views are very similar when it comes to the practical expression of the gifts.

- Consequently, it is not so important which view one holds (or combination thereof), but to see that the gifts are there to meet a need and that we will most likely have some gifts which are more regularly manifested through us. These regular occurrences, may then develop into a particular *ministry, sphere, role,* or *calling* that God has for us in the Body of Christ.

If you have access to Schwarz's book, The 3 Colors of Ministry, take the test on page 35.
Discuss your results with your mentor (particularly looking at pages 38-40 in Scharz's book)

Talk to your mentor regarding where you are at and steps you can take to become more balanced.

What do you think of Schwarz's three-color model? Do you see this in your own life? In your ministry? Which area and with what gifts do you feel most comfortable?

A BALANCED APPROACH

Lack of Unity

- Historically, the subject of Spiritual Gifts has unfortunately been more divisive than unifying. Often different segments of the Church have put greater emphasis on differing gifts.

- Though "balance" has been a word that has been somewhat *overused*, it has unfortunately not been *overpracticed* in the Body of Christ.

- As with our study of Personality types (Chapter 1.1), it would seem that many of these divisions could be eliminated with a greater appreciation that many of our differences originate from merely not really understanding each other – our values and motivation.

- For example, some in the Body of Christ emphasize those gifts that focus on a *power* experience, while others place greater value on the gifts whose focus is *commitment*, and still others the gifts that have a *wisdom* emphasis.

Three Dimensions of Life

- In his book, *The 3 Colors of Ministry*, Schwarz refers to these three general areas (power, commitment, wisdom) as three dimensions of life, patterned after the revelation of God to man as Father, Son and Holy Spirit. He uses three colors to illustrate each of these dimensions as Christ-centred (Red), Holy Spirit centered (Blue) or Creator centered (Green).

- The Red color represents *Commitment* and Obedience, the Blue color represents *Power* and the Green color God's *Wisdom*. He then organizes each gift into one of these three areas according to their emphasis.

- While one could dispute the exact placement of each gift, the reality is that, due to a variety of reasons, we all have a tendency to value some gifts more than others.

- Others have used various other models to describe this reality, yet this has been an observable phenomena throughout church history, as well as in local churches in every culture. Have you ever wondered why some churches (mostly unintentional) seem to focus on teaching, while others on community service, and yet others on a manifestation of the Holy Spirit's power?

- None of these is more important than the other, yet one emphasized to the detriment of the others causes an imbalance to occur in the Body. Often it occurs as leadership emphasize some gifts over others; being more comfortable with the outworking of some gifts, often due to their own gifting.

Some Applications

- These various emphasis, both in our personal life and in the life of the church, can be due to natural tendencies, particular gifts, what is valued within a particular church setting, a person's needs, or even personality style. All these factors (and others) determine the value structure and what becomes one's focus. Often our focus tends to originate from our perception of God or which area has been a greater revelation for us.

- Yet this varied emphasis is not the real problem, as this is a common human tendency. The problem occurs when we lose sight of the fact that other's gifts and focus are just as valid and valuable as ours and that we actually need each other.

- Our perspective needs to shift to one of seeking balance in our lives, so that we can appreciate all the gifts and their place in the Body (ie. Paul's discussion regarding the various members of the Body, 1 Cor. 12:12).

- Just as individuals can lose this balance, so can churches emphasize one area to the detriment of the others and no longer have a balanced ministry. Since they then communicate (usually non-verbally) that they value only certain gifts, those with other gifts leave, compounding the lack of balance in the local church.

- The good news is that once we realize this (as individuals and as a local churches), we can take intentional steps to foster balance in our lives. Greater fruitfulness can occur as we have a greater integration in our lives of each of these three areas. We can adapt and become more accommodating with each other in the expression of our gifts (having a balance of all three).

Some Practical Steps

- If you have not already done so (and have access to Schwarz's book) take the time to do his *Diagnostic Indicator* (page 35). It is important to note that this is not a personality indicator, it merely reflects our current feelings and where we currently happen to be. It can help you to see in which of these three regions you find yourself right now.

- As we saw in our study of personality, each of us is very complex and we do not just fit neatly into one of Schwarz's "colors." However, people do tend to discover themselves in either one area or a combination of two of these areas, though the variety and intensity may vary, just as we saw with our personality styles.

- Usually it is easy to see which of these areas is our emphasis or which we most value or gravitate towards. Schwarz arranges the gifts according to each of these three areas. Though somewhat subjective, it does help us see how most gifts have certain emphasis and hence why balance is so important.

Are you strong in two of these but weak in one or focus on one and not the other two?

- Schwarz further describes the ramifications of imbalance for each of various areas.

  - Those who emphasize *Wisdom* but not *Power* and *Commitment* focus on knowledge, but can miss the powerful demonstration of God's power.

  - Those who emphasize *Commitment*, but not *Power* and *Wisdom* focus on the commitment to the task, but can miss spiritual anointing necessary for ministry.

  - Those who emphasize *Power*, but not *Commitment* and *Wisdom* focus on spiritual experiences, but this can lead to a lack of emphasis on practical planning in ministry.

  - Those who emphasize *Wisdom* and *Commitment*, but not *Power* can have a tendency to burn out.

  - Those who emphasize *Power* and *Commitment*, but not *Wisdom* can have a powerful ministry, but can also cause harm if not tempered by wisdom.

What action steps can I take in order to develop balance?

  - Those who emphasize *Power* and *Wisdom*, but not *Commitment* can have a powerful ministry, but can lack the commitment to follow through.

Gifts and Our Calling

- Our gifts are also directly related to what we do; our ministry or role in the Body.

- In Chapter 1.3 we will be looking more closely at our role and how the idea of "calling" is related to our particular place in the Body. But the gifts that God has given us often determine our particular function in the Body (using the Apostle Paul's metaphor of the value of each member of our physical body). This is why

How do you see your gifts relating to your calling? Discuss with your mentor your understanding of your calling, role or purpose.

understanding the gifts and how to best use them is very practical as we grow in our service of others.

- A believer's task (*ministry* or *sphere of influence*) should correspond to our giftedness or stated another way, *our gifts will make room for us*.

- Therefore it is important to use your gifts, for by doing so you can best fulfill the call that God has on your life. Further, knowing our spiritual gift can actually help us determine our "call."

- While each believer has a *general call* to do God's will, there is also a *specific call* or purpose that God has for each of his children. Our gifts are an integral part

  of this and can even help us determine what that purpose is. This will be discussed further in the next chapter.

Some Cautions

■ <u>Avoidance</u>

- Often excesses in teaching or practice by others can cause us to avoid certain biblical topics. Yet the improper handling of the topic of Gifts, which can lead to extremes and immaturity, is no excuse to avoid this topic in the Body.

- The even greater tragedy is when *abuses* and *misuse* to lead to *no-use* at all. Instead of forbidding the use of gifts, or allowing fear to limit their expression, we need to learn how use them so that the Body is built up and edified.

Have you discovered ways in which you project your gift on others, or communicate that your gift is most important?

Have you used your gift or lack of gifting as an excuse for areas of disobedience in your life?

■ <u>Assuming Everyone has our Gift</u>

- As we discovered when looking at the topic of our Personality, we can also have a tendency to assume that everyone is like us, or at least *should* be like us. This is manifested in that we think that just because we enjoy doing something, or find it easy, everyone else will find it easy also.

- The fact is that, having a particular gift often does make tasks and service easier for us than for someone who does not have that particular gift. This is important to acknowledge, so that we assume all are like us and should be able to function as we function.

- Carried to its logical conclusion, this would mean that the whole Body of Christ would be made up of members with the same gifts, equipped to serve in exactly the same way. The reality is that the Body is made up of a variety of members with various personalities, gifts and callings, but unified in purpose.

- Instead of laying guilt on others, we must acknowledge that it is the Head of the Church who gives the gifts as He wills (1 Cor 12:11) and we can learn to trust in his wisdom.

Discuss with your mentor steps can you take to improve in these areas.

■ <u>Assuming our Gift is the *Most* Important</u>

- Another tendency is to exalt one gift over another; seeing certain ones as more important than others. Yet each of the gifts are intended to serve others, they are not "rewards" or badges of honour.

- The need and the situation often determines the relative value of the gift at any given moment. They are not ends in themselves, but means to an end (1 Cor 12:28). If someone needs wisdom, the gift of hospitality, at that moment, may not seem as valuable as a word of wisdom.

- As discussed previously, Paul's lists of gifts are usually not arranged in any definite order or hierarchy. Whenever there is an order, it seems to be related to the particular needs of the reader, which determines which gift is most appropriate for them at that particular time.

■ Using Gift as an Excuse for Disobedience

- It can also be a temptation to excuse or justify one's own lack of commitment, or even disobedience, due to not having one gift or another. For example, someone may say, "I am not an evangelist or do not have the gift of evangelism and therefore I do not need to share my faith."

- Gifts are related to needs and so if we are in a situation that requires the use of a gift, our first response should be, "Lord do you want me to meet this need (his will), and if so give me your power to do so (his way)".

Gift Combinations

■ Individually

- As we are a combination of personality types, so each of us have a combination of gifts.

- The initial process in discovering our own gift combination is to evaluate which gifts it is likely that we do not have (since most believers have only several gifts, those that we do not have is usually a majority of those listed in the Bible).

- 1 Corinthians 12:4-6 speaks of gifts (*charismaton*), ministries (*diakonion*) and activities (*energematon*). This has led to various explanations regarding these differences. Some see *ministries* as the *sphere* of area that a gift is used and others make the distinction between the *degree* to which the ministry is manifested.

- Each person in the Body has gifts that are for the benefit of others in the Body. This increases our dependance on others, as we all then need each other.

- Even those who have the same gift often express it differently from those with the same gift. Instead of comparing ourselves and our gifts with others, we need to be open to how God wants us to implement and use the gifts within the sphere of ministry that he has given to us, for there is not just one context in which to use even the same gift.

- Also, individuals have been given gifts in varying degrees. For example while two individuals may have the gift of teaching, one may most effectively exercise it within the sphere of smaller groups and the other to larger groups. It is important to not only understand what our gift is, but also the sphere and scope to which God has particularly intended that we serve others with that gift.

- With our unique personality and calling, the expression of our gift may be quite different from someone else with the same gift. In addition, we seem to have both primary and secondary gifts. An individual usually has one or two main gifts that are strongest and secondary ones that are perhaps not as strong or evident.

- Schwarz (as well as others) in his *Gift Test* uses the terms, "manifest" and "latent" to describe those gifts which are evident already, and those which we have potential to develop.

- God has given to every believer at least one gift with which to serve others. The gifts are not for the individual themselves, though there is joy in expressing them. Their main intent is for the service of others, so that the Body is built up and the Kingdom expanded.

■ As a Body

- As we have seen, the purpose of the gift is not for the person with the gift. It is

Evaluate one of your primary gifts as to its particular intensity in your life. Spend time in prayer and contemplation in order to discover what sphere or scope you feel God has for your gifts expressed in your particular ministry. Ask others that have been influenced by your ministry/gift their opinion.

Can you think of other settings or varied ways of applying your gift(s)?

What steps can you take so that your gifts function better within a body of believers?

for others in the Body, as they are functioning appropriately with the other gifts in the Body.

- When all the gifts are functioning within Body, there is greater balance and a more accurate revelation of who God is. This is why a gift that is expressed outside of the accountability of the Body of Christ loses its true power.

- However, by the very nature of the gifts, there is diversity in the Body, as to the emphasis of the gifts and how they are manifested. Respected Christian leaders can, and do, differ on how the gifts should be used and yet this does not need to cause disunity in the Body. Ministries with quite varied perspectives regarding the gifts have built successful ministries, so we must be careful to avoid labelling one another in the Body as *right* or *wrong* and instead choose to be unified in the midst of our diversity.

- The key is to accept the variety and see it as God's different mix within his Body, without trying to impose our views on others as the only or *right* way.

- As individual believers we need to evaluate our particular gifting and find a local body within which we can exercise our gift with freedom.

- As we discovered with personalities, often (though clearly not always) the differences in the gift-mix between local churches has more to do with church culture as opposed to *right* and *wrong*. Differing church cultures often determine which gifts are emphasized and encouraged and even this varied expression of the gifts among churches is part of God's design.

If you are in leadership in a local church, evaluate how your particular church culture emphasizes and values certain gifts over others.

- We need to have the maturity to allow for these differences and not try to fit others into our mold, or impose our manifestation of the gifts on others as the only biblical way (this of course does not mean that obvious unbiblical expressions, which are not glorifying Christ and building up the Body, should be condoned).

- Only with this attitude of unity will the Body be built up and unbelievers convinced of the reality of the Good News.

EXPRESSING YOUR GIFTS

Discovering your Gifts

- As previously mentioned, the gifts referred to are given to believers, they are not just natural abilities or talents.

- Yet just being a Christian does not automatically mean that you know what your gifts are or how to use them. It is important to both seek the gifts and then learn how to use them.

- The initial starting point for both of these is the Bible. Then after knowing what the Bible says, it is also helpful to read other good books to gain insights and discover truth through others.

If you have not done so already, and have access to Schwarz's book, do the gifts inventory beginning on page 65 (or a gift test from another source).

- If you have not done so already, do a diagnostic gift inventory test to help you have an indication as to the gifts God may have given you (this is only one of the steps).

- It is also helpful to spend time with those who already function effectively in the gifting you feel God has also given you. Look for someone to help mentor you in their proper use.

Discerning the Body of Christ

- Members of churches typically discover gifts in areas in which their particular local church is strong. This underlines the importance of being in relationship with those whose values you share.

- Asking ourselves several questions can help us in the process: *What kind of gifts are predominant in your church? Is your gift recognized and valued? What is the mission purpose of your church and its core values – are these compatible with yours?*

- If we cannot be loyal and respectful in our church, due to a difference in our perspective, instead of staying and causing disunity, it is better to find a local church that shares our same values and then be committed and loyal there.

- Instead of reacting negatively to other church "styles," we need to be open to experience God in new ways, leaving aside our labels of others and focussing on the nature of God the giver of all the gifts. The goal is not to imitate one type of church or another, but rather to reflect the multi-faceted character of God.

- No church or leader can *produce* spiritual gifts, but they can create an atmosphere in which they can grow and mature.

What steps have you taken to discover your gifts? What gifts bring you joy as you serve with them?

Applying Your Gift

- In order for effective ministry to take place, the gifts must correspond and fit the need.

- As we see needs around us we should be available to meet them through the gifts that God has given us. In James 1:5 we read that God desires to show us as we ask him to do so.

- Effectiveness begins by taking into account our spiritual giftedness before engaging in any type of ministry.

- Knowing our gifts, however, is not always easy, for they are not always so self-evident. This means that we must be open to serving others with our gift even before we have learned to perfectly express or use that gift. A greater anointing, or usefulness, comes only as we begin to use the gift at our current level of understanding and ability.

- Caution must be exercised, however, for the consequences of the improper or immature expression of some gifts can be negative.

- Though the gifts are supernatural, through proper training we can become more effective in our use of them. Seminars, reading, further experience, constructive criticism, can all assist in our greater effectiveness. Merely having a gift is not a guarantee of its proper use.

As a member of a church are your gifts valued in your particular church and made room for? If not what steps do you need to take to use your gifts, while still maintaining the unity of the believers.

Defining Your Ministry

- With this in mind, it is important to reevaluate the ministry we are involved in order to determine our current or potential effectiveness.

- *What tasks or ministries are we currently involved in?* We must first evaluate what must be accomplished, what problems solved, or what needs met.

- From what we have learned through experience, as well as the gift test, we can begin to determine what gifts we have that uniquely prepare us to accomplish a task or meet a need? We can also determine what other abilities or talents we may have which can assist us in our sphere of ministry, in addition to evaluating our personality style and how we may have to adapt it in order to be more effective in our ministry.

- After reflecting on this, we must then consider if we are the ones that should be meeting a particular need or engaging in a particular ministry.

Is it possible for a local church to be balanced in most of the main gifts or is it inevitable that certain gifts will have greater prominence?

- Other questions to help us in this process of defining our particular ministry are, *Is there other training or equipping that may be helpful at this time for you to increase your effectiveness?* and *What other resources are necessary, both tangible and personnel, to meet this need?*

- A final consideration is to establish criteria to help in determining if our ministry actually met the need or accomplished the task.

Evaluating Your Gift

■ Internally

- God made us and is the one who has given us gifts – he knows what gifts fit with our personality and calling and has designed us to uniquely fulfill his purpose through our life.

- If we are fulfilling God's purpose in our lives then the implementation of our gift should bring joy in our own lives; it should be more than just duty. However, ministering to others takes effort and at times our own fatigue may make it hard to distinguish between this and the joy we feel in serving others with our gift.

■ Externally

- In determining our particular gifting and place in the Body, it is important to observe the results of the use of our gifts. Gifted people produce results through the exercise of their gifts in their ministry.

- If we consistently do not get results when *expressing* a certain gift, there is a high probability that it is not one of our gifts. However, these results (or lack thereof) need to be evaluated for this could also just be due to the immaturity in exercising our gift. Wise counsel and practical help from a mentor or other leader can help in this regard.

- The confirmation by others is also a helpful tool in determining effectiveness. If we are trying to exercise a gift and nobody else in the Body thinks we have this gift, we indeed may not have that gift (though this is not always the case). This is important to evaluate, for the gifts are *for the Body*, not *for the person* who has the gift. They are for the edification of Body.

- As we more regularly express our gift in the Body, others begin to expect us to exercise our gift, which means that we become more accountable within the Body for the use of our gift.

Appreciation of all Gifts

- While we may know what our primary gift is and even some of our secondary gifts, we must remain open to God using us to serve others through other gifts. At times he may even serve outside of our "comfort zone" in order to stretch us and teach us that he is the one that really meets the needs, not us, or the gift. As we are open to God, he will enlarge our capacity to be used of him with others and this often requires functioning with gifts we may not quite feel "ready" or "comfortable." But service to God and others has to do more with *availability* than *ability*.

- At our conversion we did not receive all gifts that we ever will have. They are not static; discovering them is not just a one-time event, but a dynamic experience. Paul writes in 1 Corinthians 12:31; 14:1 that believers are to eagerly desire the gifts.

- In Matthew 25:21 Jesus teaches us that if we are faithful with little we will be given more and this is certainly true of the gifts. As we are faithful with what God

---

What gifts do you feel you have, but as of yet have not used?
Is there somewhere where you can begin to do this?

Discuss the statement, "If you consistently do not get results when trying a certain gift, it probably is not your gift."

has given us, God will give us more gifts in order to bless others.

- Churches and Christian leaders need to also pray and expect God to lead the right people at the right time to the local body with the gifts that are needed.

- These gifts that God gives are beyond the natural; they are "supernatural." However this does not mean that we cannot be relevant and real in their expression. Jesus during his ministry had *supernatural* power, but operated so *naturally* with others that they were surprised at the humanity with which he expressed the gifts. This should also be our pattern.

SUMMARY

- In this first section we have begun to discover not only our personality style, but also the gifts that God has given us in order to serve within the Body of Christ.

- This process is not a one-time event, but areas of constant growth and development.

- In our last chapter in this section, on who we are as a *Person*, we will be discussing the issue of our *call* and how this coincides with the discussion of our personality and gifts.

- We will begin to grow in our understanding of the most effective context within which we can then express our personality and gifting-combination.

Discuss with your mentor ways that your gifts can be expressed in very "natural" ways in your ministry – ways that other can relate to and receive from.

Person

Chapter

1.3

Mentoring
thru
Intentional Relationships

Your Calling: What You Do

INTRODUCTION

- In the first two chapters, we have looked at both our personality style, or basic temperament, and our gift combination.

- We have discovered that each believer has been given at least one gift and that this gift(s) is to be used for the edification of all believers. Our function or place in the Body can be described as a *ministry* or *sphere of influence.*

- But to understand our *sphere of influence* or the purpose God has for us, we need to also look at the issue of "calling." For this, together with our gifts, affects both our role in the Body of Christ and the degree to which we will be an effective influence in the community.

- Some of the issues to be discussed in this chapter are, *What does it mean to be called? Does everyone have a calling?* and *How do we discover our calling?*

What is your understanding of your concept of a "calling?"

THE CHRISTIAN CALLING

Set Apart for a Purpose

- God created us and desires to work in partnership with us in order to accomplish his purposes.

- However, even before service and activities, God wants to have a relationship with us. This is actually our highest calling and that for which we have been set apart. Our highest purpose is to love him and worship him forever.

- Yet having experienced this oneness of a relationship with God, it is inevitable that we begin to share God's heart for all people (see Chapter 4.2) – a heart that seeks partners in a desire to reconcile all lost sons and daughters to himself.

- All believers are called to be these *ministers of reconciliation* in a fallen world (2 Cor. 5:18). This calling is not just limited to a few believers, but is for all, we are all a *chosen people* and a *royal priesthood* (1 Peter 2:5, 9-10).

- Throughout church history there has developed in every era (to a greater or lesser degree) the false concept that some Christians have this priestly calling and others do not, perhaps originating in an Old Testament view of the priesthood.

- Yet it is clear from biblical teaching that all believers have this calling and privilege to stand in the gap – to be those *priests*, showing others to the heavenly Father. This is not a calling for just an elite few.

Discuss the statement, "Every believer is called."

Discuss the biblical concept of the priesthood of all believers. How does truth apply to you in your ministry?

Responding to the Call

- Though God initiates the *call*, it is we who must recognize and respond out of a free will to that call.

- God called Jeremiah while he was still in the womb and, though at first he thought his youthfulness was an excuse, he eventually responded to the call (Jer 1:4-12).

- In Ezekiel 22:30-31, we read that God was looking for someone who would stand in the gap on behalf of the land, which was reminiscent of Abraham interceding for Sodom and Gomorrah in Genesis.

- Again in Isaiah 6:8 God asks, "Whom will go for us" and Isaiah responds with, "Here am I!"

- Responding to the call is also a matter of timing as we see with Queen Esther who came to the Kingdom, "for such a time as this." (Esther 4:13-14)

- Further in the New Testament we see Jesus calling each of the disciples while he walked the earth and then in a vision calling Paul, as well as the next generation of disciples (Paul's mentoree, Timothy in 2 Tim. 1:3-7).

- In each of these cases, and others not mentioned, God makes the initiative to call a person to a task. The person must then respond to this call, often overcoming personal challenges in the process.

Requirements in Fulfilling the Call

- The first step in effectively fulfilling our call is to develop inner maturity and character – allowing the character of Christ to be developed in us. This begins with us being conformed to the image of Christ (Rom. 8:28-30).

- We see in Jesus' life, characteristics such as, brokenness (John 11:33-35), compassion (Matt. 9:35-36), concern (Matt. 9:12-14), willingness (Matt: 8:1-3), forgiveness (Lk 23:34), humility (Phil. 2:5-7), self-sacrifice (Jn 10:14), servanthood (Jn 13:14-17), obedience (Jn 15:10), and unconditional love (Jn. 15:12-17).

- Living as those *called and set apart* means making efforts to maintain a pure heart. Even as we follow after God we must "work out our salvation" as the Word says. This is not just another set of requirements in order to receive God's free gift of salvation, for this is by faith alone. It is also not an effort to live the life of the Spirit through self-strength, for only by his Spirit can we live the spirit-life.

- God's grace does not excuse us from our personal responsibilities, such as confessing our sins and faults to God and even with others when appropriate and being open to his correction and discipline.

- This growth in inner maturity, which is reflected in character growth (2 Peter 1:3-11), can only be sustained through a life of walking in the Spirit and is only accomplished through our response to the Holy Spirit as he faithfully deals with us.

- Our *call,* or sense of calling, can never be a substitute for the process of inner maturity in our life. Only as we are committed to spiritual growth will we be able to adequately fulfill God's purposes in our lives.

OUR CALLING AND OUR VOCATION

Calling and Career

- But how does our calling as Christians, to be those reconcilers in a lost world, relate to our career or vocational choices? How does where we spend most of our waking moments relate to our spiritual calling as believers?

- As a Christian wanting to do God's will, our understanding of how we can best fulfill this *calling* within our daily lives should greatly affect our choice of career and vocation.

- This does not mean that the only place to fulfill this *calling* is in *full time* or *vocational* ministry. Clearly not everyone can (or should) work full time within the church, yet we all can take steps to fulfill God's purpose in our lives (Chapter 4.2).

- God has a purpose for every believer, within the varied expressions of their job and career. Regardless if that career has been by choice or by chance, God desires to work through the believer to touch others that they are best suited to influence.

- This, of course, emphasizes the obvious: Service for God is not limited to *volunteer* or *paid ministry*. As we shall see later (Chapter 3.2 and 3.3), leadership is a *sphere of influence* and we can be of positive influence for the Kingdom right where we are.

- To limit *calling* and *ministry* to either the church or vocational ministry (sometimes called "full time" ministry), is to limit what God wants to do through his people worldwide.

- For the believer there is no such thing as *secular* work. Every believer is a servant of God and can be an ambassador and a *minister* reconciling God with man, regardless of our profession. The believer has been set apart for a purpose, which God desires to express through the daily activities of our lives.

- The Christian in his home, on the job and every other arena of life has a purpose and calling that spans time and eternity. In the *here and now*, it means that it cannot be just *business as usual* as with those who only have a temporal view. This broad understanding of calling will inevitably affect the believer's very motivation, priorities and decisions (Chapter 4.2).

Some Misconceptions

- This idea of *calling* has led some to various misconceptions regarding ministry and service.

- One such misconception is that the most effective way to serve God and show commitment to him, is through full-time vocational service, either in a church or an organization, etc. However, the fact is that all believers, regardless of career, are called to be a *minister of reconciliation*.

- Another misconception is that vocational ministry is defined by where we earn our income. However, the reality is that at times God uses other means to provide, be it side jobs, tentmaking situations, whether in our home country or abroad.

- A third misconception (perhaps not as prevalent as it once was) is that full-time ministry is primarily for those who have one or more of the five-fold ministry gifts of Ephesians 4:11. However, though these are ministries given to *equip the saints for works of service*, they are not limited to only those in vocational ministry. Perhaps as never before in church history, there is an understanding that there are a variety of gifts and abilities which can be expressed through the vehicle of vocational ministry.

- A further misconception is that being called as a vocational minister must always be a life-long calling. While it seems that this may often be the case, the reality is that there are different seasons in our life. At various times, God may lead someone into vocational ministry for a time and out of vocational ministry at other times. We must be careful not to judge others or assume that we know God's plan for everyone's life.

A Proper Perspective

- Though not for the majority of believers, there is a calling for some to vocational ministry. While this is usually considered *full-time,* as discussed, this may not always be the case.

Discuss with your mentor how you can fulfill your call within your particular job or vocation?

If you have not seen your job as a means by which to fulfill God's purposes for you in this life, what steps can you take to realign your perspective?

Consider your current sphere of influence. Who do you influence? What kind of influence are you?

Which of these misconceptions have you had, or do you have? Do you agree with these? Discuss this with your mentor.

Is your ministry focussed on activity, or on equipping others? What changes do you need to make to be an equipper? What are the advantages of being an equipper?

- Though this vocational calling is not limited to just those with the equipping gifts (Eph. 4), it seems that those who are called to "full-time ministry" (understandably, a term difficult to define) do have a greater responsibility to equip the *saints for the work of the ministry* – the ministry of reconciling God with man.

- However, this does not place greater value on some believers over others, as the classic artificial split between clergy and laity does. Instead, it refers only to the varied functions in the Body. Those with these gifts are not the ones to "do" all the ministry, rather they are to "equip" others to do the ministry.

- This type of call is more than a career move or vocational choice. While every believer needs to have a sense that they are where God wants them to be, the call to vocational service has unique personal challenges and direct implications for the rest of the Body, necessitating divine confirmation.

- Even after sensing a divine motivation to enter vocational ministry, and having this confirmed in various ways, a person should evaluate their motivation for vocational ministry (not guilt, obligation or even desire to serve God). Some have advised that if a person can imagine being content in any other career, then perhaps they should reevaluate their *call* to vocational ministry.

Wrong Motivations

Spend some time with the Lord to consider your motivations for entering ministry. Allow him to show you your heart and deal with any false motivations that may be there.

- In our desire to follow God, some often feel that the only way they can really serve God is through full-time service or vocational ministry. Yet as we have seen, God's purposes in our lives can include a range of vocations with which to serve him and others.

- Though seemingly plausible, there are several clearly wrong motivations for becoming a vocational minister (as well as wrong motivations for engaging in ministry of any type).

- While a desire to help others is admirable, this, or being motivated by other's needs, is not a good reason to enter full-time service.

- Also a desire to spend more time studying scripture and receiving enjoyment by teaching others is also not a reason that will sustain someone in vocational ministry.

- A positive experience that one had with a minister in which one was helped is good, but not reason enough for full-time service, nor is the desire to thank God for his deliverance from a dramatic experience (or for the gift of salvation) a good reason to enter vocational ministry. Deathbed-type promises rarely lead to long-term success in vocational ministry.

- Finally, feeling pressure after having received training or ordination by a church denomination or organization is perhaps one of the weakest reasons for entering full-time service.

- Additional motives which are even more negative include entering vocational ministry out of a need and desire to receive the affirmation of others, the desire to follow in the footsteps of a relative or a friend that is greatly admired, or the desire to want to gain instant success, for seemingly little work (ie. only preaching once a week on Sunday!)

- Full-time vocational ministry should only be pursued as a response to a divine call. While it is a noble calling, it is not more valuable or important than the purposes that God has for every believer. *Calling* is not a matter of worth or value, but a difference of function (sphere of ministry) according to our gifts.

Characteristics of the Call

- The call to vocational ministry usually begins with a growing awareness that God has a specific *sphere of ministry* or purpose for us to fulfill. It is more usual for this to be in the form of a growing impression and understanding that God is moving us in a particular direction, than a dramatic and instantaneous revelation (though, of course, this also can happen).

- Together with this growing awareness, there is usually a growing conviction that nothing in this life will give us as much satisfaction as serving God through a full-time commitment to vocational ministry.

- If this occurs while someone is already in another career, the transition is usually gradual. Over time, the desire for the present career usually begins to wane and the passion for vocational ministry grows.

- As stated, this call originates with God, but needs to be confirmed by others. This is a pattern we see throughout the Scriptures. While the specific role or sphere of ministry is not always evident, initially, this becomes clearer as steps are taken to fulfill the call.

- There should also always be clear confirmations, such as a growing peace and faith to walk the path ahead, as well as continued spiritual growth, confirmation from the Word and others (who are spiritual and have proven to be trustworthy).

- So the *call* itself is often a growing awareness which is accompanied by various confirmations. This gradual and steady process ensures against hasty *vows to God* that he has never intended we take. Having the patience to go through this process is particularly helpful during later times of discouragement and struggles, when the reality of our call will be inevitably, and often severely, tested.

> Retrace God's calling in your life to ministry. What confirmations did you have?
> How did God reveal his will to you?

Challenges with the Call

- In the initial stages of responding to what we sense is God's call, doubt is often the key obstacle to responding to that call, *Did he really say what I thought he did?* or *Surely he could not mean me?*

- From Scripture we can see that initially many of God's people had excuses. For Jeremiah it was his age; he thought he was too young to respond to God's call (Jer. 1:7-8), Moses tried to volunteer Aaron for the task as he thought he was a poor communicator (Ex. 4:10), and Gideon was insecure regarding his family standing and background (Judges 6:15).

- Isaiah, on the other hand, recognized his unworthiness and thought this disqualified him (Is. 6:5), Amos saw himself as only a shepherd and therefore not someone God could use (Amos 7:14), while Paul, had to live with the memory that he had martyred many Christians.

- Throughout history those who God has called have had inadequacies, weaknesses and even failures. But God's call is not according to our greatness or ability, but according to his intention to partner with imperfect men and women so that he might be glorified in the earth. This is why fulfilling a call is more than just gaining education, experience, or skills – it must begin with a divine call.

- Throughout our ministries, these inadequacies or weaknesses can haunt us and even attempt to thwart what God wants to do. This is why it is so important that we can point back to a divine call and a confirmation of that call.

> Were there particular challenges that you have faced in fulfilling your call?
> How have you gained victory over these?
> What areas do you still need God's grace to overcome?

The Right Motivation

- *Ministry* (vocational and other) is not a position or even just accomplishing a task, it is sharing *life message* from a position of brokenness (2 Cor. 3:1-3).

Have you gone through this process of brokenness in your life and ministry? What have you learned through these times?

Are you as open to God's breaking in your life now as you once were?

- Paul uses the analogy of *recommendation letters* (2 Cor 3:2-3) to describe the open life of the believer. What is meant by *life message*, is that we minister to others from *who* we are as a person and not just words and untried truths.

- The degree to which our very lives can be a *message* that effectively ministers to others is based upon the degree to which we allow God to break us, molding us into the person that he wants us to be. We must be able to join with John the Baptist in saying, "I must decrease, He must increase."

- In order to produce fruit in others' lives the "kernel of wheat" of our life must fall into the ground and die (John 12:24). This is often a painful process as our *old self* (natural man), with its own ambitions and desires, must die. Yet it is only through this process of *dying to self* (1 Cor. 2:1-5) that our motives are purified so that we can effectively minister to others.

- As we are willing to go through these times of brokenness, we become a vessel that God can use to minister to others. However, without this process we will only be serving out of self-strength, vain ambition, and position.

- Called, broken people do not minister out of self-strength, rather they see themselves as a living sacrifice, yielded to the Master, to serve as he desires.

Disqualification for Service

- If we do not continually allow God to break and mold us, we can eventually even be disqualified from service. This does not happen immediately, as God's initial intention is to draw us to repentance through his kindness and goodness (Rom. 2:4).

- We see an example of this during the initial stages of Samson's disobedience. His effectiveness was not immediately diminished, though the seeds for his downfall were being sown. However, his continual disobedience began to affect his call, and eventually his actions invalidated his ability to accomplish God's purpose for his life.

How difficult do you think it is to be disqualified for ministry? Is it always (never?) possible for someone to be restored in vocational ministry?

- When someone takes the path of Samson, there are always inevitable consequences for their life and ministry. While personal reconciliation and even ministry reconciliation can occur, scars always remain. Depending on the circumstances of the failure, the potential level of ministry may never be achievable (ie. David was forgiven, but it was left to his son to build the temple; Moses saw the promised land but never personally entered it).

- In Elijah's case, he had just come from the greatest achievement of his life defeating over four hundred false prophets (1Kings 19), only to be sent running by the threats of Jezebel. He ends up tired and alone in a cave. Though he had experienced God's power as few others had, he was on the verge of burnout having lost his keenness to hear the still small voice of God's leading. He had become isolated and had developed a martyrs' complex. He needed a reminder that his service (ministry) was not about him (there were 7000 others who had not bent their knee), but about God.

- Just as with these biblical examples, it is also a temptation today, in the heat of the battle, to forget that it is not *our* ministry, but that we are mere servants. If we lose connection with God as our source, then all our service is meaningless and bears no fruit (regardless of the initial authenticity of our call).

- The eventual consequence of this attitude can even be the inability to continue at the same level that God intended for us ("go...and anoint Elisha to succeed you").

Necessary Preparation

- To grow in our personal relationship with God is essential if we are going to fulfill our call. Service (doing) is never a substitute for relationship (being) with God (which will be the focus of our discussion in Chapter 2.1).

- In order to prepare for service it is also important to be committed to becoming a life-long learner, pursuing balanced education (at whatever educational level and method is appropriate) and continually reading quality books.

- Along this journey of preparation, it is also important to be faithful in a variety of ministry situations in your local church and/or ministry. Spend time with a mature Christian or Christian leader, in order to develop ministry and leadership skills, so as to be able to practically apply knowledge.

- It is also crucial to find a mentor with whom you can regularly share with and someone to whom you can be accountable for your personal and ministry growth. If at all possible, seek opportunities in which to participate in ministry together. The introductory material to this manual, as well as Chapter 3.3, discuss the importance and details regarding the mentoring process.

- Finally, there must be a continual commitment to prayer as we develop in our relationship with God and seek him to confirm his call in our life. Allow him to prepare you for the role that he has for you and seek out those who will commit to pray with and for you.

REACHING OUR POTENTIAL

Potential Roles

- The *roles in ministry* can also be described as the *spheres of service* or the context within which we express the call of God on our lives.

- This is applicable for all believers, to the degree that we all are called, yet there is also specific application to those called to vocational-type ministries.

- As previously described, our personality, gifts, abilities, motivations, desires, and experiences all combine to give us a unique expression of God's call through our lives (a life message).

- Particularly at the beginning of our development and our initial understanding of our call, the specific *role* or *unique expression* is not as clear as it becomes later in our lives (of course there are exceptions, as some know very early the exact direction God desires them to go, but this is usually the exception and not the norm).

- In most cases, the particular role usually unfolds over time as we discover our personality, leadership style, our gifts, as well as our understanding of our particular calling.

    Along this journey of discovery and confirmation there are several tools that can help in this process.

Evaluation Tools

■ Evaluate Personality and Temperament

- As we began in Chapter 1.1, it is helpful to have a basic understanding of the natural personality styles and their various strengths and weaknesses.

- Once we have an understanding of this, it is helpful to evaluate what kind of ministry/work environment best fits us and how we best work and interrelate with others.

Sidebar notes:

As you have grown in ministry, have you continued to take steps to keep up your relationship with God?

If you are just beginning in ministry, what opportunities have you taken to serve others within your own church? Discuss with your mentor practical steps you can take to begin serving others.

Consider your personality style, gifts and calling. With this in mind, what role or sphere of influence do you seem best suited for?

- The key to understanding personality, is to learn to be versatile and adapt in our interaction with others and how we minister to them. Having this attitude enables us to appreciation our differences and mitigate potential personality conflicts.

■ Determine Spiritual Gifts

How does your particular gift combination, as you understand it, affect your potential sphere of service?

- As we saw in Chapter 1.2 understanding our gift combinations can also help us to determine what our *sphere of ministry* may be, for our calling is usually related to the gifts that God has given us.

- Our particular gift combination is often confirmed through our ministry experiences, as we observe where we are effective in service.

- Asking ourselves the following questions can help us evaluate how our gifts apply to our calling: *What ministry brings us personal satisfaction and fulfilment? Do we perceive special needs or problems beyond that of other Christians? Where have we been effective in our ministry involvement thus far? What ministry activities do we find easy to do? What trends do we see in our life?* and *How have others in the Body confirmed and encouraged us in ministry.*

■ Recognize Motivational Patterns

- Our particular motivations are also interrelated to both our personality style and our gifting.

- Many view and label some of the gifts listed in Scripture as our *basic motivations*, as opposed to *spiritual gifts*. However, whichever view is taken, experience indicates that each person has certain kinds of ministry or tasks that really motivate them (ie. giving, serving, hospitality, administration, discerning, etc).

- What motivates us is most likely a combination of our spiritual gifts, as well as our abilities and interests.

- The important issue is that we take the time to evaluate what motivates us and look for clues by how God has used us in the past.

■ Identify Spiritual Passion

What is your passion? What motivates you?
Begin to formulate a personal mission statement based on what you have learned of yourself and God's direction in your life.

- Having a passion or interest for a particular group, need or area, though not a universal indicator, can be a very clear indication for some as to their *role* or *ministry*.

- It is important to note that this *passion* is often divinely inspired and serves to complement our personal motivations and spiritual gifts. God's ways in our lives are not always directly opposed to our interests (which he has given us after all).

- However, care must be taken in order to temper this passion, not allowing it to carry us even beyond God's will for us. To do this we need to keep a proper balanced understanding of our universal biblical responsibilities, as well as keeping in touch with the real needs of others (as opposed to just *our need* to help them). Our ministry, however divinely inspired a passion it may be, must always remain under the Lordship of Christ.

■ Assess Life Situation

- To varying degrees, a person's stage in life also affects their particular ministry role.

- Various factors such as age, maturity (spiritual, emotional), career, social status (marital status, number of children), and education will all affect our current level of influence (see Chapter 3.2).

- While none of these factors should keep us from responding to God's calling, they will affect the level and quality of our possible input. It is important to be realistic about how our place in life affects possible spheres of ministry.

- There are several general stages of life which may be helpful to consider in this regard. While these comments can provide some perspective and context, they are not universal in experience or application, they are merely general guidelines.

  20-30 age: During this period of life it is more important to keep moving forward in our relationship with God, maintaining spiritual and life disciplines, and not be as concerned about a specific role.

  30-40 age: During this period it is important to begin to identify the most positive and negative ministry activities we have been engaged in and take time to evaluate our current ministry role, identifying both the positive and negative and determining ways we may need to adapt. It is important to be open to God's new directions and timing during this period of life and learn the lessons he has for us.

  40-50 age: By this period or stage of life it is crucial to identify and move toward your *ministry role,* as God makes the direction more clear and opens the doors. During this stage we learn to adapt our current role to fit what we know about our motivation, personality, and gifts.

  50-60 age: By this period, if we are not a new believer or new to leadership, we have most likely been serving within a role that best fits who God made us. Our goal should be to continue to move further towards our life-purpose, effectively serving others and multiplying our efforts by investing in the lives of others.

- Of course, the age we were when we came to Christ and our current maturity in the Lord, will affect how our development coincides with our age grouping. Important to remember, however, is that though the level of our influence with others changes throughout our life, at any given stage we do influence others.

■ Identify Our Emerging Role

- Reflecting on the above will help us in discovering what *role* or *sphere of influence* God has called us to fulfill.

- Taking some time to reflect on these issues may not yield immediate answers, but will assist us in our lifelong journey of discovering God's unique sphere of ministry that he has designed for us – discovering the ministry that will be personally fulfilling as well as bear lasting fruit for the Kingdom.

A Personal Time-Line

- Another tool that can be helpful in focussing God's purposes in our lives is a simple *Timeline* (A sample and template have been provided in the "Resource Material" at the end of the manual).

- When the children of Israel crossed the Jordan River on dry ground, God instructed them to take twelve stones from the middle of the Jordan as a reminder of the miracle that he had done for them. Regularly looking over our life can help us remind us of what God has taken us through and the lessons that he has taught us. Through these personal memorial stones, we can see his faithfulness and gain strength to face the unknowns of the future. [We have written a book retracing God's faithfulness in our lives titled, *This Pile of Stones.* If you are interested in reading the *Introduction* and receiving this resource go to www.thispileofstones.org or use the Canadian address].

Sidebar notes:

How does our individual calling affect our marriage relationship?
Discuss this with your mentor.

Assess what stage of life you are in and how this affects your particular ministry. What steps can you take to improve your effectiveness?

Write your own personal testimony (ie. How God spoke to you, Personal experiences when called, God's provision, Special scriptures, Challenges/fears, Steps already taken, etc.)

Using the form provided (in Resource Material), develop your own Timeline.

- A *Timeline* is a exercise that helps us to reflect on God's faithfulness and retrace that which he has already done in our lives. Just as crossing the Jordan increased the confidence and faith the Israelites had in God, so reflecting on our *pile of stones* can help us face the purposes God has for us with new courage and faith.

- The process of doing a *Timeline* helps to outline the key events in our life, the main developmental stages/transition points, the lessons learned, and identify the key people who have influenced us. However, it is more than just recording a chronology of our life, it is the process of retracing God's dealings with us.

- Here are some practical helps to fill out your own *Timeline* using the provided template:

  - The actual dates can be filled in on the line itself.

  - The descriptions on the far left will help in organizing the various components of the chart.

  - V*alues/Lessons* learned refers to which lessons we have learned doing the various periods of our life.

  - *Major Roles* refers to the role we have had during seasons of our life: ie. son, father, husband, pastor, CEO, etc.

  - *Sphere of Influence* refers to those who we have had the greatest influence upon, from family, employees, pastoral team, church members, leadership team, etc.

  - *Development Phase* are broad descriptions or titles referring to the various broad segments of our life (perhaps a decade), such as "Beginnings," "Life/Ministry Foundations," "Life/Ministry Development," "Ongoing Maturing" etc.

  - *Key Incidents* can be itemized as Family/Personal or Ministry/Professional and refer to specific events that occurred that were key turning moments, times of crisis, or watershed experiences in our life.

  - *Influential People/Mentors* refers to those who have been influential in our life – either for a short time or perhaps over many phases of our life.

Discuss with mentor your Timeline. Where is your emphases? According to your stage in life, where should it be?

Emphasis during Ministry Stages

- While doing the *Timeline,* it is important to realize that during various periods of time in our life, varied emphases are natural.

- For instance, as we progress from early conversion to early ministry experiences, and then onward to maturing ministry and developing our unique contribution, the emphasis in our lives and ministries change.

- While developing character and integrity are crucial at every stage, during the beginning and mid-stages of our life/ministry it is predominant. During the mid-period we are often busy developing basic ministry skills and we begin to be aware of the need to determine what ministry strategies are most important for our particular ministry.

- Then as we are in longer term ministry roles and become more comfortable with who God made us and the sphere of influence that he has given us, our emphasis naturally shifts from developing ministry skills to an increasing focus on being more strategic in our efforts.

Potential Kingdom Contributions

- Our goal in fulfilling our calling is not just to run the race, but to run our race *well*. Running the race well means that we pass the baton to the next generation, leaving a legacy that they can follow.

- Each generation should be given a start with help from those who have gone on before them. They should be able to stand on the shoulders of previous generations; seeing horizons that their mentors only dreamed of.

- As we each find our unique place, making a lasting contribution for the Kingdom, we must not loose sight of the fact that it is also our task to lay a foundation that will enable others to make an even greater contribution upon our foundation.

- Potential lifetime contributions are varied, ranging from modelling a Christian lifestyle within the marketplace that can impact whole companies and segments of society, to reaching others with the gospel and seeing quantitative and qualitative growth in the Kingdom.

- Further contributions could include launching new organizations, churches, institutions, beginning a movement, introducing new paradigms, originating new concepts, methods or technologies, or contributions in the area of research and writing.

- In the area of ministry developments, kingdom contributions could include organizational expansion, initiating change, or influencing others in the area of mentoring and leadership development.

SUMMARY

- We have seen that every believer has been called to be a *minister of reconciliation*. God has uniquely created each of us and has given us gifts to fulfill his purposes here on this earth.

- God has also given every believer a sphere of influence or role in which to participate in his purposes here on this earth. Within the Body there are varying gifts and roles, and though our function may vary in intensity and influence, each believer has equal value and worth.

- To effectively fulfill God's purpose and make a Kingdom contribution is attainable for all believers, regardless of vocation. The key is to have God's heart for the world wherever he has planted us – each doing the part he has called us to do.

- In Section 2.0, we will focus on the inner character qualities and disciplines which are necessary in order to fulfill God's purpose in our lives. While a person may be highly gifted and called, without becoming a *Disciple,* we will never be able to reach our full potential.

What could you dream could be your Kingdom Contributions?
What would you like to be remembered for?

Are you already actively mentoring others so as to leave a legacy?

Discuss with your mentor what you have learned from this lesson and what areas you are still working on.
Give your mentor permission to hold you accountable in these areas in the weeks and months ahead.

Your Foundation: The Personal Disciplines

Mentoring
thru
Intentional Relationships

Chapter
2.1

Your Foundation: The Personal Disciplines

2.1

INTRODUCTION

- In the first three chapters we have looked at several key attributes of who we are as a *Person*. In the next three chapters we will be focussing on some attributes of us as a *Disciple*. This will include some of the basic spiritual disciplines necessary to be effective, as well as some of the potential pitfalls along the way, and finally focussing on hearing from God and how to be led by him.

- In the last section we began to understand the interrelation between our personality style, our spiritual gifts, and our calling. Yet understanding this is just the first step in reaching our full potential, for this must be within the context of who we are as a disciple of Jesus. Without a foundation of being a disciple of Jesus, these first three aspects of our personhood will lack focus and meaning.

- In order to be a *Disciple* there are several spiritual disciplines that are crucial in order for us to take practical steps towards our goal of realizing our full potential for the Kingdom. While many spiritual disciplines could be discussed, in this first chapter we will focus our attention on four main areas: *Prayer, Bible Meditation, Fasting* and *Lifelong Learning*.

What in your view is the purpose of the Spiritual Disciplines?

A Negative Connotation

- In many languages and cultures, "discipline" has more of a *negative* than *positive* connotation.

- It can be perceived as a duty or obligation, rather than activities that bring personal freedom. However, instead of just being an intense activity, they can provide a joy and freedom for our lives.

- The reality is that these spiritual disciplines are not just intended for special, gifted people, but for all believers – regardless of our personality, spiritual gifts, or calling. Yet regardless of a person's potential, based upon their gifts and calling, without developing these foundational disciplines, our effectiveness for the Kingdom will not be reached.

What is your reaction to the idea of "discipline"? Is it a positive or negative one?

Spirit versus Flesh

- The practice of the spiritual disciplines is by nature a spiritual activity, not a physical one. They are not just religious duties in efforts to *make* us acceptable to God, they are activities which demand a participation of our whole being, including our physical being.

- However, it is not enough to just have the willpower or self-discipline to practice these disciplines, these activities are spiritual graces and, as such, the focus must always remain on God, not the disciplines.

- Focussing on the disciplines, and not God, will inevitably lead to legalism and duty. But this is not their intended purpose, for practiced with the right motivation they can prepare us to receive God's power and grace in our lives.

- The key to their benefit has to do with what is our focus, for that which becomes our focus eventually controls us. If God is our focus, then he controls us, if the discipline itself becomes our focus, then it will master us and drive us to greater legalism.

A Balanced Life

How can you keep the spiritual disciplines from becoming legalistic and mere obligations in our life?

- To reiterate again, the purpose of practicing these disciplines is so that we may be formed into the image of Christ. While they often begin with outer activities, their focus is on the inner work of the Holy Spirit in our lives.

- The Pharisees had an external righteousness (Matt. 5:20) which was based upon their religious activities, for they had turned the spiritual disciplines into a law, which bound them instead of freeing them. Worse yet, they then became intent on putting these same burdens on others. This is always the result of a legalistic application of the spiritual disciplines: We put burdens on others we ourselves cannot even carry.

- Instead of a closer walk with God and the character of his Son developed in us, we become full of pride, self-strength and drift away from a personal, intimate relationship with God. The ultimate result being death and not life (2 Cor. 3:6).

- The *letter of the law* breeds death, but the Spirit – God's Spirit – is what gives life. If while practicing these disciplines we are not seeing the fruit of life and freedom, we need to reevaluate our motivation and focus.

Evaluate if you are focussed and balanced in this area of your life.

- The book of Hebrews focusses on us entering *his rest* and what this means for the believer. Our focus on the disciplines must never become a form of works or disrupt this *rest* that we have in Christ. We can have a contentment and practice these disciplines from a position of rest.

- With the right focus and motivation, the fruit of the Spirit can become a part of our life (Gal. 5:22,23). Instead of having to strive in our natural strength for these, they will actually become a part of who we are. This is the goal of the spiritual disciplines.

A Lost Art

- However, in most cultures in the 21st Century, taking time to practice these spiritual disciplines has become somewhat of a lost art.

- While the disciplines should never become mechanical, or have just a physical focus, they do often begin with the posture of our physical being, be it the posture of prayer, taking the time to meditate on God's Word, or the physical aspects of fasting.

What habits have you formed which have helped you keep a vibrant relationship with God?

- Practicing the disciplines has to do with forming healthy habits. Habits are powerful for they can provide a framework and motivation for maintaining activities, even when our emotions do not "feel" like it. Positive habits can take us even further than our desire.

- In this chapter we will discuss several principles that have helped spiritual men and women throughout the centuries practice these disciplines. The treatment of each of these disciplines in this chapter will be introductory at best. They are intended to assist the mentoree and mentor address these issues and learn from each other. Further reading listed in the last section of this manual, or provided by the mentor, will be helpful to give greater insights into implementing each of the mentioned disciplines, as well as those not mentioned here.

PRAYER

A Process

- Prayer is really the most direct communication we have with our heavenly Father. Of all the disciplines, it is central in terms of both speaking to God and hearing from him.

- Though as simple as talking to a friend, prayer is something even many believers do only when in a crisis or pressing need. Yet prayer is intended to be so much more.

- While as simple as conversation on one hand, it is a discipline which will require growth throughout our whole life. Fortunately, God takes us from where we are to where we need to go, in our prayer life. Learning to pray is a process (Luke 11:1), which will continue till the end of our earthly life.

- Through Jesus' life, we see that prayer was not just an act, but was rather a lifestyle (Mark 1:35). Jesus regularly and consistently spent time with his Father.

- This pattern is also illustrated throughout the Old Testament with such examples, such as King David (Psa. 63:1), and throughout church history in lives such as Martin Luther, John Wesley, Andrew Murray and many others.

- Without exception, those who have reached any measure of influence for the Kingdom have achieved a measure of consistency in the discipline of prayer.

Misunderstandings and Extremes

How does our understanding of our partnership with God affect our prayers? What is our part, what is God's part?

- However, if prayer is reduced to only asking God for things, it will not achieve its intended purpose in and through our life. Prayer is more than petitioning God to do things on our behalf and the behalf of others.

- Another false assumption is that the universe is a closed system and that God has so predetermined all things that prayer is not really necessary, or at best it is only for our own good. Yet throughout Scripture we see men and women praying to God with the obvious expectation that their prayers did matter and that they were co-laborers together with Him. Prayer is more than a formality or merely "going through the motions."

- There has also been much misunderstanding surrounding the issue of faith. Much could be said regarding this, but suffice to say at this point, that the lack of an immediate answer to prayer does not necessarily signify a lack of faith or the wrong use of words. Prayer cannot be reduced to formulas and verbal repetitions.

- The danger with prayer (as depicted by the Pharisees) is that it can so easily become a legalistic activity and lose the very life that it is intended to produce. If reduced to a mere activity preformed at a particular time, it very quickly can become mere human striving which does not bring life.

What do you do during those times when you do not feel like praying?

- Alternatively, another extreme is the approach that prayer must always be accompanied by the euphoria of spontaneous feelings. This approach de-emphasized the need for a regular, disciplined approach, for this is viewed as legalistic. Yet developing a life of prayer is, to a large degree, developing the habit of prayer.

- In the final analysis, it is not the regular practice of prayer that produces legalism, but rather the wrong motivation for such prayer.

Principles of Prayer

- As it is practiced regularly, the discipline of prayer begins as a habit, but then becomes a lifestyle.

- Yet without consistency, prayer never becomes a habit, and without forming a habit (a regular, consistent event), prayer is usually reduced to a mere good intention, usually dependant upon the need for good feelings and circumstances.

- To help this discipline become consistent, having a regular location is helpful. It is good to have a place where distractions can be avoided and there is privacy.

- One of the greatest hindrances to prayer is insincerity and hypocrisy. God desires honesty, even above a detailed understanding of theology. Honesty (with ourselves and God) in prayer is a prerequisite. To this end it is important to use common language instead of religious or church language. It is rather senseless to just repeat meaningless phrases or restating the obvious, just to make our prayers "sound good."

A Pattern for Prayer (ACTS)

- As with other disciplines, prayer is a walk of faith. It is not a formula or just a pious activity, but should reflect an authenticity which is consistent in every area of our life.

- While there is no formula for prayer, the following pattern in the form of an acronym has been helpful to many in their prayer life. This A-C-T-S guide is helpful as it highlights the key attributes and priority in prayer:

  Adoration: At the beginning of prayer we begin with worship and focus on who God is.

  Confession: Next we spend time to hear what the Lord wants us to confess, this is more than just a confession of all sins generally, it is specific things he shows us.

  Thanksgiving: This relates to more than just a grateful feeling, but are the specific attributes and actions that we are grateful to our heavenly Father for.

  Supplication: Finally our requests, those petitions that we bring before our Father. Notice that this is last in order of priority, contrary to our natural tendency and practice.

Journaling

- Journaling can be a helpful tool in prayer life (as well as in our Bible meditation).

- It can help us reflect on our prayers and God's dealings with us. Journaling provides the opportunity to reflect in order to avoid repeating the same mistakes in our lives. It forces us to slowdown and reexamine our lives.

- While there are various ways of doing this, the main purpose is to write down our thoughts, feelings, both the highs and the lows. It does not have to be eloquent or profound and need not take long – just five to ten minutes a day.

Why Prayer is Inconsistent

- Most people will pray during a crisis, but once the crisis is over, the level of prayer intensity also subsides. But prayer is more than crisis management, it is to a be a lifestyle which fosters a relationship with our Father.

- Prayer that does not become a part of our routine is usually prayer that is very inconsistent and at times even non-existent. It must be part of our daily habit for it to become consistent.

- Any unconfessed sin of which we are not aware causes us guilt and shame and can even cause us to avoid our time with the Lord. If not dealt with, our prayer

How do you think it is possible to be in a constant state of prayer?
How does this differ from having a specific prayer time?

Divide sheet in four quarters and use the A-C-T-S method to write your prayers. Which of these four (A-C-T-S) do you least often implement?
Begin a prayer journal.

Has your prayer life become inconsistent? If so, what steps can you take?

life, and eventually spiritual life, will grow cold. But as 1 John 1:9 states, we can deal with this situation and need not allow this to happen.

- Another reason for inconsistent prayer is unanswered prayer. Yet though we do not have all the answers this side of eternity, we need to continue to pray, for this is our vital connection with God and the key avenue which he seeks to speak with us. The focus of prayer is relationship and as we maintain that relationship, we will gain greater clarity in those areas of uncertainty in our lives.

A Direct Connection

- Prayer is a direct connection with God. God desires and will speak to us, for he tells us that he is a rewarder of those who seek him.

- In order for prayer to not just be an infrequent activity, it must take a central place in the disciple's life, cultivated as a habit that becomes a lifestyle.

- Prayer is a means of practicing times of solitude, a necessary attribute of all believers and particularly those who are called to be servant leaders with others.

- True strength of character does not come from more activity – even good activity – rather it comes through intimate times spent with God in the closet of prayer.

Commit with your mentor to daily spend time in prayer, as well as take time to regularly pray with your mentor.

MEDITATION

Christian Meditation

- Meditation is more than just reading the Bible, it is a reminiscing or "chewing" on God's Word. While it includes listening and reading God's Word, it is reflective in nature, seeking to come to a personal application of the text.

- Christian Meditation is the ability to hear God's Word and obey it; its purpose is to enable us to hear God's voice more clearly through the unchanging voice of his divinely revealed Word.

- It is a passive discipline in that it focusses on reflecting and listening; allowing God's Word to affect and change us. Yet its ultimate purpose is not passive, but active personal life application. While it is as simple as allowing God's Word to speak to us, it can take a lifetime to learn.

- God longs to be with us, to speak to his children and biblical meditation opens the door. As we allow his Word to go deep into our being, we will then be changed forever.

Why is it important to keep your meditations biblically focussed on the meaning of the text?

How is biblical meditation different than biblical study or reading?

Biblical Precedent

- The main goal of meditation is obedience (Psa 119:97, 101, 102), to become more like Christ.

- Throughout the book of Psalms we see meditation emphasized (Psa 1:2; 63:6; 119:48) and then throughout the New Testament we continually read of Jesus pulling away for a time of solitude and quiet (Matt 14:13).

- Throughout church history those who have carried responsibility and influence in the Kingdom have taken the time to meditate on God's Word. In the words of Dietrich Bonhoeffer, "I meditate because I am a Christian."

Misconceptions

- Some Christians may become uneasy with meditation for they believe it is synonymous with *Eastern Meditation.*

- Yet the two are not one in the same. Eastern meditation focusses on emptying one's mind, while biblical meditation on filling one's mind – specifically, filling it with God's Word.

- Eastern meditation typically focusses on being detached from the world, losing one's personhood and individuality, while biblical meditation on being attached to reality and who we are in God. While biblical meditation is a time for pulling away from the busyness and confusion of life, it is in order to live a *real* life before God and others.

- Some may also have the perception that meditation is too complicated and only for spiritual giants. Yet the simplicity of meditation indicates its universal availability for all believers.

- Another misconception is that it is impractical and leads to unhealthy isolation from the real world, yet true meditation only has meaning as it is rooted in real life. While meditation begins in solitude and reflection, its focus is personal application that relates to everyday life.

What has been some of your experiences in Bible meditation?

A Personal Discipline

- As with all the spiritual disciplines, to reap their benefits requires effort on the part of the participant.

- Meditation is by nature a personal activity, not a corporate one, so while the insights are often a blessing when shared with others, the main purpose is personal growth and change.

- Often instead of personally communing with God and receiving from him, we can tend to rely on someone else's insights and the relationship which they have developed with God.

- While we can and should learn from others, we cannot reach our full potential in Christ by relying on other human mediators, through which to develop a relationship with God. We must take the time and make the effort to learn to *Practice his Presence* ourselves, through the discipline of meditation.

Discuss with your mentor any insights they may have regarding this discipline.

Some Practical Issues.

- We learn meditation by meditating, it is not a discipline that can be learned from a book.

- Biblical meditation takes time. We need to set aside regular times to which to meditate on God's Word. As with any of the disciplines, just *putting in the time* does not ensure success, but without regularly taking the time, none of them would occur. Biblical meditation helps to bring balance to life, for it requires a pulling away from the busyness of life in order to refocus our attention on God.

- This requires a quiet place that is free from interruptions and is a relaxed setting. This quiet setting is important for it is often so hard to shut out the things of this world, something which is necessary in order to hear from God.

- The central focus of meditation is Scripture. It is not an emptying of the mind, but a filling of the mind with the thoughts of Christ through his Word. Yet biblical meditation is not primarily biblical exegesis (the meaning of the text), but rather the personalizing of the passage for our everyday life.

- Unlike Bible reading, meditation focusses on less scripture rather than more.

Often this means reminiscing on a verse or portion of a verse, during the time set aside as well as throughout the day or coming days. This *chewing* on the text with the intention of personal application, is that which makes Bible meditation so personal and effective.

- As one begins to practice Bible meditation, patience is required for in the beginning it may seem not many insights are being gleaned and there is the temptation to become discouraged. Yet this is a growth process and the long view must be taken. As you look back over time you will see God changing you through meditation in his Word.

- As you begin to meditate on a passage it is important to first have a basic understanding of the context and meaning of the teaching or passage.

- The next step is to begin to ask questions of the text that focus on personal implications for your life, not only what did or do the words or phrases mean, but what does this mean for me today?

- The goal is to *ruminate* or *chew* on the meaning of the passage so that you will see issues in your life that are similar, new ways to apply the truth, and areas of personal growth and change.

Develop a daily Bible meditation plan and be accountable to your mentor for its implementation.

A Way of Life

- Meditation is not just a single act, but a way of life. It begins with becoming centred on Christ and having him become our focus. While profound insights may not be the daily occurrence, we will begin to experience God speaking to us through his Word in ways we have not previously experienced.

- Throughout the process, it is important to be sensitive to the confirmations of the Holy Spirit and begin to use Journaling as a way to record our insights and applications.

FASTING

The Purpose of Fasting

- Fasting is the abstaining from food for spiritual reasons, it is not a hunger strike or diet, as both of these have differing objectives. The primarily purpose of fasting is to assist us to focus on God. If fasting is not unto God than its main purpose has been missed.

- Aside from its primary purpose, fasting helps us to reaffirm our source as God and helps us keep balance in our lives. Other purposes could include intercession, guidance, etc.

Share with your mentor, or small group, your experiences with fasting.

- Fasting signifies our intention to focus on God and hear from him. However, as with the other disciplines, we must be careful so as to not create a form of legalism whereby we use fasting as a *badge* or *proof of spirituality*.

- Fasting is something that God calls the believer to, it is not imposed by others, either directly or through indirect manipulation.

- Proper fasting is never a form of self-punishment or a way to impress God or try to change his mind. It is also not a form of manipulation and should not be motivated by the desire for personal blessing.

- While insights are often gleaned through fasting and greater spiritual sensitivity achieved, these also are not the main purpose of fasting.

Biblical teaching

- The Old Testament has many references to godly fasting. From the Historical Books to the Prophetic Literature, fasting is practiced as a spiritual discipline. Some examples can be found in Judges 20:26; Ezra 8:21-23; Esther 4:3; Isa. 58:3-7; and Dan. 6:18.

- But this was not just an Old Testament practice. Jesus, in the Sermon on the Mount (Matt 6:16) says, "When you fast," making the assumption that this would continue. Other New Testament Scriptures include Matt.17:21; Luke 2:36-37; Acts 9:8-9; 13:1-3; and 2 Cor. 6:3-6.

- The indication in Matt. 9:15 is that Jesus expected his disciples to fast throughout the Church Age, until he would physically return.

Types of Fasts

- There are several different types of fasts, none of which are more spiritual than the other. God calls us to different types of fasts, at different times for different reasons.

- The decision to fast is a personal one between the person and the Lord. Our freedom in Christ means that we do not put burdens on others, or even ourselves, regarding fasting.

- Fasts can vary from missing one meal to abstaining from food for one day, several days, or up to a maximum of forty days (at which time a fast must be concluded for health reasons).

- Other variations include abstaining from all food, but not from water (Luke 4:2), or a *partial fast* of eating only certain foods, or missing particular meals (Dan. 10:3).

- The so-called *Esther fast* or *absolute fast* (Esther 4:16), refers to abstaining from both food and water, the maximum duration of which is three days and should only be done if physically healthy.

- Another type of fast is a *regular fast*, which refers to a fast of one day a week, or a particular meal each day, or any other regular schedule of fasting.

- While fasting is usually a private matter, there are times when a group of people can take part in a *group fast* for a specific purpose (Ezra 8:21-23).

- Fasting is a discipline which requires growth and so it is important to begin with shorter fasts, or even partial fasts, before attempting longer fasts.

Practical Considerations

- Preparations should be made before beginning any fast, such as eating lightly (fruits, vegetables and drinking liquids) and using a light laxative (natural if possible). The longer the intended fast the more important this is.

- During the fast the senses are at a heightened state and so it is helpful to avoid filling our senses with media input etc and instead just to focus on God. While this may be difficult at first, it will become easier and more enjoyable.

- During the first three days of any fast, one typically feels tired and weak as the body is ridding itself of toxins. Physical symptoms of this are a coating on the tongue, bad breath and headaches. Hunger pangs after only a few days of a fast is not real hunger, merely the stomach reacting to conditioned eating habits.

- During this period it is important to adjust and move slower and rest more. Note also that throughout the fast some people have a tendency to feel colder. Usually

What have you learned about fasting from this lesson that you can implement?

after six or seven days of a fast you will begin to feel stronger and after nine or ten days you will often feel little hunger and have better concentration. Physically, this is the best part of the fast.

- Real hunger pains return sometime between twenty-one and forty days. At this point the body reserves are used up and during this time the fast should be broken.

- As when beginning a fast, a fast should be broken by eating small amounts of easily digested food. Again, depending on the duration of the fast, the need to do this will vary, but one of the benefits of fasting is to learn to have a disciplined intake of food. While God created food for us to enjoy, our ultimate fulfilment for our soul needs to come from God and not from food. Fasting helps us realign these priorities.

- While fasting is normally not a health risk if these guidelines are followed, diabetics, pregnant women, and heart patients should not fast. Those who are concerned about their particular health issues related to fasting should first consult their physician.

Fasting as a Lifestyle

- The key purpose of fasting is to sensitize us to God's voice and focus our attention on him and what he has to say to us.

- Yet a side benefit of fasting is learning moderation and balance in life, particularly in the area of diet, but also in other areas of life.

- Other fasts could include a fast of solitude, away from others, perhaps a media fast, including telephones or e-mail, or even an intentional fast from a materialistic lifestyle (note that one does not need an overabundance of things to be materialistic – it is a matter of the heart).

- In all of these, the point is to see God as our source and not use other things in our lives (even good things) to fill what only he can fill. As we have balance and discipline in our lives, we will have a lifestyle that not only pleases him, but is conducive to hearing his voice and growing spiritually.

If you have never fasted begin a short fast or even a day-fast. Discuss any insights with your mentor gleaned from this time.

LIFE-LONG LEARNING

Continued Growth

- In a fast-paced culture it is increasing difficult to develop the discipline necessary for continued growth.

- Ongoing growth and learning can take many forms, such as reading and personal study of the Bible and other books, seminars, tapes etc. Perhaps more than at any other time in history, there are many such opportunities today for quality personal study.

- Yet, ironically, many believers who attend church and even serve in ministries, never move ahead in their spiritual maturity and Christian walk. In large measure this can be traced to their failure to apply themselves to the discipline of personal study.

- A personal commitment to the discipline of ongoing learning is the only way to grow spiritually. No one else can do this for another individual; it must be a personal decision.

- As with the other spiritual disciplines, the goal should not be just increased knowledge, or understanding, but life change.

What steps have you already made to continue growing and learning? Discuss these with your mentor.

Reading

- In our digital era, reading has almost become a lost art, yet it is vital to

Are you committed to a Bible reading and study plan?

continually have the input of others and not plateau in our growth.

- Of course the most important place to start is by regularly reading God's Word. Yet it is also important to read other influential authors – both contemporary and classics. These give one a broader perspective of what God is saying to the Church, as a whole, as well as on a personal level.

- To gain further insights regarding personal study of the Bible, the reader will find Howard and William Hendricks' book (*Living by the Book*) very practical and helpful.

Studying

- As with reading, studying begins with the Bible, but should not end there, as there are many other worthy books by those who God has given insights.

- Unfortunately, once our formal education is over, few continue to study. Yet it is this discipline which helps to keep the mind sharp and facilitate ongoing growth. What we study or focus on will determine who we become.

- Studying is not a *carnal* or merely academic exercise, in itself it can be spiritual in nature. While meditation is devotional, study is analytical. Study is objective and creates a framework whereby meditation can function more successfully.

- Study not only takes discipline, but also humility. We must have the posture of a learner and have a teachable spirit. While an accumulation of information does not necessarily produce wisdom, with the right perspective and attitude, knowledge that is applied to one's life will result in greater wisdom and stature. This is the goal and purpose of study.

- Studying a book effectively is a learned skill, as it involves more than just reading. It involves understanding (what is said), interpreting (what is meant) and evaluation (is the conclusion correct).

- The discipline of study also includes reflecting upon our own experiences, as well as productive discussions with other spiritual people knowledgeable in their field. Very often truth is revealed as we share one with another. So by *study* we do not mean just an academic activity or "bookwork," it must encompass all of life.

- As the men of Issachar of old, so should we be students of our times and society, so that we may accurately know the days we are living in. This involves asking the right questions of ourselves, the Bible, and our culture. We will then know how to apply the lessons gleaned from our study. This truth applied in the lives of our generation has the power to set them free.

Discuss with your mentor study habits which they have acquired over the years that they have found helpful.

Attributes of Studying

- Repetition is a powerful tool in order to create habits of thought and action. Creating positive inner and outer habits can be a powerful tool in ongoing learning and growing.

- In cultures where success is judged by speed and quickness, the ability to concentrate and focus on a particular subject is diminishing. Most cultures do not value the ability to concentrate to the degree that they once did.

- It takes the discipline of studying, over a period of time, in order for comprehension to occur. This is not a easily attained result, but requires a commitment to this discipline. Study can lead us to insight and discernment in every area of life.

- As with the other disciplines, the discipline of study and ongoing learning should lead us to personal life-change. Studying need not just be an academic exercise, but truly a spiritual discipline.

Biblical Study

- Of course the most important book to read and study is the Bible (2 Tim 3:16), with the goal being inner transformation, rather than merely acquiring more information.

- The Scripture encourages us to *study to show ourselves approved*, so that we do not have to be ashamed when we handle the Word of God (2 Tim. 2:15).

- Studying Scripture includes both *exegesis* (what the text means) and *hermeneutics* (what the application is for us today). We need to know what the text means before can apply it to our own lives. Daily devotional reading is not enough, the believer who wants to really grow must be prepared to dig deeper.

- While the Scripture is simple enough for a child to understand, the nature of Scripture is that its eternal relevance is wrapped in historical settings written over a span of fifteen hundred years. This presents a problem for students of the Word, for they must first understand what the intent was for the original reader, before being able to then apply the truth into their contemporary setting.

- A further challenge for the student is that God chose to speak through many different genre of literature, ranging from *narrative history, poetry, proverbs, prophetic, parables, letters,* etc. The student must be aware of this and interpret each according to relevant principles. This means understanding the historical and literary context, as well as issues regarding content, such as the meaning of words, etc.

- Study is required for we are not free to make the Bible say whatever we want it to. Proper study, guided by the Holy Spirit, helps us keep true to the original meaning and then helps us apply this to our current situation. Further reading on this topic is necessary in order to understand some of the issues involved , as well as learn some of the necessary tools required to rightfully divide the Word of Truth. (see *How to Read the Bible for all its Worth*, Stuart & Fee, *Understanding and Applying the Bible*, McQuilkin and *Living by the Book*, Hendricks)

Are there other books which your mentor would recommend that you read? Be accountable to your mentor throughout the year of the books you read and study.

Read a book (or two) on Bible study and interpretation (hermeneutics) in order to more effectively read and study God's Word.

SUMMARY

- Each of these disciplines is fundamental to reaching our full potential and fulfilling God's purposes in our lives.

- While talent, ability, spiritual gifts and even knowing our calling are helpful, in and of themselves they will not ensure that a person will reach their full potential.

- The key to becoming all that we can be begins by our attention to the disciplines discussed in this chapter. Without developing these spiritual disciplines we will remain stunted in our spiritual growth and fail to be the positive influence God intends us to be.

- While each of these disciplines may at first be difficult to implement, with practice and a disciplined commitment, they will begin to produce fruit in the our life.

- In his classic book, *Celebration of Discipline*, Foster outlines additional disciplines such as *simplicity, solitude, submission,* and *service,* as well as what he calls the *corporate disciplines*, which include *confession, worship, guidance* and *celebration*. If the reader has access to this book, he will be greatly blessed by the truths highlighted in each of these areas.

- As we move into our next chapter we will focus our attention on those major pitfalls which can derail our growth and hinder us from reaching our full potential in the Kingdom.

Find an accountability partner (mentor) with whom to keep one another accountable these areas of spiritual disciplines.

Mentoring
thru
Intentional Relationships

Chapter

2.2

Your Challenges: The Big Three

INTRODUCTION

- In the last chapter we have looked at several key spiritual disciplines and their importance in the life of the disciple.

- While it may seem that the issues covered in the last chapter (prayer, Bible meditation, fasting) are inherently more *spiritual* than the themes to be covered in this chapter, this is not the case. The reality is that it is the very topics of this chapter that are most often the battleground for the believer. The degree to which a believer masters these three areas, is the degree to which their Christian character is either forged or undermined.

- As we shall see, these three topics are not inherently evil, rather it is how we deal with them and our mastery of them that determines if we control them or if they begin to control us.

- To this end, the last chapter has a direct effect upon the themes of this chapter, for they cannot really be separated. Our lives cannot be compartmentalized. Yet so often there is a struggle, for while we are seeking to implement the spiritual disciplines, we are losing ground and failing to gain mastery over greed, lust and the pride of life, the *Big Three*.

- The battleground for these three is manifested most clearly in our handling of our *money,* our *sexuality,* and *power.* Of course there are other subjects that could be dealt with, but these are where the primary battles occur in the life of the believer.

- While it may be more appealing to evaluate our spiritual growth by our prayer life, Bible meditation and other more *spiritual* activities, the reality is that the verdict on our life and ministry will most likely be passed according to how successful we are in handling these *Big Three*. Failure to succeed in these arenas of life will not only distract the believer, but has the potential to cripple, or even fatally wound, their spiritual growth and Kingdom effectiveness.

- To discuss these topics will require a painful honesty at times, on behalf of the mentoree and mentor. Yet without honesty in these areas, with ourselves and others, victory will remain illusive and the Christian life a facade. Honesty begins by admitting that none of us are above the temptations these areas represent and that we all, in varying degrees, have had our own struggles with the *Big Three*.

- So as we begin, let us acknowledge that, in and of themselves, these are not evil, rather each has the potential to be a positive influence in our lives and our society. While many cultures are mastered by their negative characteristics, we as Christians, however, have the opportunity to allow Christ to show us how to live as people of integrity in a world that has fallen so far from his original design.

Do you think these three areas are the key areas of temptation and struggle? Why or why not?

Reflect and evaluate which of these areas you are strong in and which are a greater temptation. Discuss this with your mentor or mentoring group.

MONEY

- Second only to the topic of the *Kingdom of God*, Jesus spoke the most about the topic of *Money*.

- It would be simpler to just view money as completely evil and something to be shunned, but the Scripture does not present it in such a black and white manner. The reality is that money can be a blessing or a curse.

• Money can be used for Kingdom purposes or it can even become a threat to our very relationship with God (Lk. 6:24, 16:13, Matt. 6:19, 19:24).

The Power of Money

How does your view of money affect your faith and prayers regarding God's provision in your life?

• As with other material things, money can become a negative factor as the believer transfers his security from God to money. At its root, it is a matter of who one trusts.

• This is often not so blatant in the believer's life or even consistently one or the other. At times we may do well in our handling of money and at other times it may begin to master us.

• Foster in his book, *The Challenge of the Disciplined Life*, makes the case that money is never "neutral," or just a *medium of exchange*, rather that it has a power in and of itself.

• Though perhaps overstated, his point is well taken, for we all have experienced how money can take on a value far beyond its particular currency value. This is true in both affluent and developing societies.

In your view, is money merely a neutral form of exchange or does it hold a power all its own?

• The classic Scripture regarding money is 1 Tim. 6:10, which states that, "the love of money is the root of all evil." While it is true that the "love of money" and not money itself is the root of all evil, we do not need to scratch too deep below the surface of any society to realize how widespread the love of money is. (Materialism is not the monopoly of wealthier nations, for even those with little, can be caught in the downward spiral of materialism that always desires more).

• If we are honest, we would have to admit that in most societies it is the majority who are grasping for it, trying to acquire it, or think their life would be better if they had more of it.

• Contrary to Foster's view, most stewardship teaching points out that money, in and of itself, is neutral and merely a medium of exchange, the value only being determined in how it is used. Yet whichever view is closer to the truth, the power that money can wield for good or evil is indisputable.

• The reality is that it seeks to be put on the same level as God. In Matt. 6:24, Jesus clearly teaches that no one can serve both *God* and *Money*. He indicates that money can take on a power all of its own in that it can become a focus of worship.

God and Money

• Of all the biblical teaching regarding money, one truth is clear: Having money is not a sign of God's blessing and a lack of it is not a sign of his displeasure.

• The Scripture also does not teach that money is evil. It is powerful, can seduce, is able to do both good or harm, yet is not evil in and of itself.

Evaluate your use and attitude towards money. As you reflect upon the notes, what changes do you think you need to make?

• In the Old Testament we see men such as Abraham, Job, and Solomon, all of whom had great wealth. In the New Testament we have further examples of Zacchaeus who gave generously, wealthy women who helped the disciples, and Joseph and Nicodemus who used their wealth for service to Christ.

• The foundational principle from Scripture is that God owns all the wealth (Exod. 19:5-6; Ps. 24.1) and ultimately all blessings are an outflow of his grace. He cares for his children as he does the *birds of the air and the lilies of the field.*

• For the Christian the money issue is not so much the amount we have, but what governs our lives. The deciding factor in the economic decisions of every disciple of Jesus is whether God, or Money, controls that decision. For example, if God asks us to step out in faith in an area and trust in him, do we obey, or do we allow money to be the determining factor? Alternatively, do we evaluate our purchases solely according to our financial ability, or do our priorities determine our lifestyle, even if we have the means to afford the items.

- The answer to these questions are indicators of who we are really serving: God or Money.

The Grace of Giving

- Giving money to God is more than a duty or obligation, it is an act of worship. Through giving we show our love to God, for we do not easily part with that which is so close to us, namely our money.

- Giving also helps to free us from the bondage that money can hold over us. As we give to God we are declaring that we trust in him more than in money. He is our God, not mammon. It is the key weapon to defeat the control money can have in our lives.

- In the Old Testament we see that the tithe (10%) was a minimum which belonged to God and then in the New Testament we gain a deeper understanding that everything we have belongs to God and it is our privilege to give back to him in proportion to our means.

- While a detailed teaching regarding giving is beyond the scope of this manual, it is clear from Scripture that God will challenge us to give generously in both tithes and offerings. This does not mean neglecting our obligations to our family, but seeking his Kingdom first means obedience to God with the fruit of our increase. This of course includes all areas, not just our finances and goes beyond a ten percent tithe.

Money and Kingdom Purposes

- Money is not something to be shunned or avoided by believers, but rather to be used for Kingdom purposes.

- The tragedy with the concept that it is better to be poor, is that opportunities are lost to redeem the riches of the world for Kingdom purposes (Luke 16).

- While God is generous and desires to bless his children, his ultimate goal is for his children to be conduits of his blessing to others. His blessings are not so that we can consume them on our own lusts, but that we may use them in the furtherance of the Gospel.

- This is often where the struggle develops for the believer, for it is so subtle in nature. It often comes in the form of the choice between investing in Kingdom purposes (often in the form of others), or in ourselves and selfish purposes.

- This does not necessarily mean that we must give all of our money to the poor, though Jesus did ask one young ruler to do this. It is more often a matter of daily obedience and gaining mastery over what God has made us stewards, rather than being mastered by material and financial means. The challenge usually is in the form of the many lifestyle decisions required, in order to properly use the resources God has entrusted to us.

Money and Business

- The potential for money to be evil and used for wrong purposes should not cause us to avoid money altogether (by living as poor as possible), but rather to be faithful as God entrusts us as stewards of that which we have.

How do you make economic decisions? Is God or Money the deciding factor?

Evaluate your giving principles before the Lord. Are you using your finances for Kingdom purposes or selfish ones? Are you open to the Lord challenging you in this area, regardless of your economic level?

- This also means affirming not only the necessity of work, but also its inherent goodness. The curse of Genesis 3:19 was not work in and of itself, but rather that it would be by the *sweat of our brow*.

- As we saw in Chapter 1.3, we each have a calling regardless of our career or if we are even vocational ministers. We all need to find our "calling" in a vocation.

- God has promised to bless the work of our hands and if this results in gaining great wealth, it becomes our gift *and responsibility* as to how that is used for Kingdom purposes.

- Making money through honest work and ethical business practices is not wrong or contrary to godly principles. In actuality, some have the very calling to have positions of influence in the business world. Business and work is not contrary to the spiritual life, rather can be an expression of how to live out the spiritual disciplines.

- For the vast majority of believers their *calling* is expressed by being faithful in a job. The spiritual nature of this calling, is to see all that we do as service unto the Lord and to fulfil our potential through serving God, not Money, by keeping our job in proper priority.

- God's purposes always supercede mere economic considerations, for he is the Lord over every area. Not having enough resources is never one of his primary considerations, just as it should not be ours.

- We must not compartmentalize our lives as to the *spiritual part* and the *business or work part* (non-spiritual). Our whole lives are to be a worship and service unto God, first and foremost. With this priority, we will have the right attitude towards others and deal with them in business with integrity, for the accumulation of money will not be our top priority.

Money and Ministry

- Many a vocational minister has been distracted by money – by either trying to acquire more of it or not having enough of it.

- Yet all that has been discussed to this point, also particularly applies to those in vocational ministry, those who also gain a living from the ministry.

- Being in full-time service does not make one immune from the deceit of riches. Often due to the ever-present financial struggles, it can even accentuate this battle. If the minister does not keep his focus and proper priorities, the power and deceitfulness of money has the potential to lead him astray – away from his calling and even away from fulfilling his purpose in the Body.

- However, forced poverty (by himself or by others) is also not the answer. The Bible teaches that he who feeds others spiritually should also have enough to live (1 Cor. 9:9; 1 Tim. 5:18). Yet in an imperfect world, where the minister may not seem to have his needs met, he must keep the right priorities and not shift his trust and source from God to money.

- While many leaders would like to be *independently wealthy*, so that they can *independently* fulfill God's visions, God purposes usually involves others in the Body in order to emphasize our *interdependence* upon each other and he as our source.

Facing the Challenge

- If we have much of it or little of it, money has the potential to distract us from our calling and reaching our full potential.

- The deciding factor is not even the amount we have, but our attitude towards it: Are we the master of it, or does it master us?

Do you master money or does it master you?
What steps do you think you need to take in regards to dealing with money?

If you are in vocational ministry, evaluate your principles of raising money for the ministry.
Discuss these with your mentor.

- If this is an area of struggle for you, a helpful first step would be to study the Scriptures and read other books regarding this topic. Then intentionally commit to God your allegiance to him and ask him to help you in this area.

- Often a further step is necessary and that is accountability with others. With either your mentor or some other accountability group of peers, be honest with your struggles and seek their assistance in helping you with your blind spots and weak areas.

- Through your regular giving consciously transfer your trust to God and not financial wealth. Consistently choose people and value them over money.

- Finally, evaluate your lifestyle and make choices that reflect a simplicity which has a Kingdom focus, as opposed to a lifestyle which is lived for selfish and personal goals.

Kingdom Purposes

- It is possible to use money and not be controlled by it. It is possible to have financial means and not serve it, but rather have it serve God and others.

- While money has the power to distract and keep us from the center of God's purposes for our life, it also has the potential to be used for Kingdom purposes. Through the Holy Spirit and the Word, the latter can become a reality in our life.

Study these steps and begin your personal mastering of money. Share successes and failures with your mentor. As a mentor also share your victories and struggles in this area.

SEXUALITY

- As with money, improper expressions of our sexuality can have a devastating impact on our personal lives, our families, and our Kingdom potential.

- Also, as with money, it would be wrong to conclude that sex and sexuality is inherently evil or wrong, for God created it and called it "good." Yet it too can be holy and redeemed, even though it has been perverted within most societies.

- However, not mastered, it can master us and be a cruel taskmaster, that can eventually inflict destruction that can affect every area of our lives.

The Bible and Sexuality

- Fundamentally, our maleness and femaleness is somehow related to our creation in God's image (Gen. 1:27). After the Creation God said that all of his creation was *very* good, including his creation of humans as sexual beings.

- God created us as sexual beings and the relationship between male and female was to be a human expression of man's relationship with God.

- Man and woman were created by God and were interrelated right from the beginning (Gen 2:7). They were naked and not ashamed, with a sexuality that was an integrated part of their whole lives (Gen 2:25).

- The fall did not create *eros* love, it only perverted it. Also perverted by the fall was the domination of women by men (or vice versa!), as this also was not part of God's original design (Gen. 3:16).

- A poetic tribute to pure sexual love is found in the *Song of Solomon.* The Bible is not ashamed, nor does it blush at the topic of human sexuality, for after all it had divine origins as part of God's original design.

- Jesus also touches on the subject of marriage and sexuality as he confirms the leaving and cleaving principle of Creation in Matt. 19:6 (as well as other topics elsewhere). He affirms the original design of marriage as the merging of two individuals without destroying the personhood of either.

Do you have a positive or negative attitude towards your sexuality? Respond to the statement that as believers our sexuality cannot be separated from our spirituality.

- Paul in his writings further affirms the Old Testament passages, as well as affirming both the inherent value of the single life, as well as the ideal of mutual sexual fulfilment in marriage (1 Cor. 7:3).

Historical Errors

- The biblical teaching is clear that our sexuality is connected to who we are as spiritual beings. As with money, we cannot compartmentalize or separate our spiritual and humanity dimensions. God has designed us as integrated beings.

- Yet throughout church history, often in an attempt to be more "holy," the spirit was seen as godly, while our humanity (the *flesh*) was seen as evil. Consequently, the *flesh* was to be shunned and suppressed. This led to a wrong understanding of human sexuality, which instead of leading towards holiness, bound burdens upon Christians that God never intended them to bear.

- The historical teaching which viewed man's humanity as evil, postulated that all sexual pleasure was bad and that sexual intercourse was only for procreation.

- Since God created men and women as sexual beings and designed them to enjoy the gift of sex within the context of marriage, this distortion led further away from godliness.

Sexual Pitfalls

- The Bible celebrates our sexuality as it was designed and intended by God, but it also provides some limitations and warnings.

- As with money, if we do not master it, it will master us. These pitfalls can not only consume a person, but can also invalidate our witness and effectiveness for the Kingdom.

■ Lust & Pornography

- While noticing the beauty of the human form is not lust in and of itself, it can lead to a constant uncontrollable passion, which will lead to an impure thought life and worse. Lust differs from the momentary acknowledgement of beauty, which is common to us all as sexual beings (which of course we all deny); it is the dwelling upon and improper fantasizing which can occur.

- Though this is at times a fine line, noticing beauty need not progress to lust. Living a life of integrity demands understanding and practicing the difference.

- In Matthew 5:28 Jesus condemns lust for it cheapens the purity of sex and human relationships as the Father had designed. It is an uncontrollable sexual passion which consumes and whose focus is to possess another.

- The subtlety of lust is that it becomes a substitute for warm relationships, which leads to sexual obsession and illicit behaviour.

- The good news is that the imagination can be disciplined (Rom 7:15,17) and that with God's grace and power, together with Christian support and fellowship, it can be mastered.

- Unfortunately, as long as we are isolated from each other, hiding behind the guise of false *spirituality*, we cannot get help or be a help for others. We can only offer healing to one another by being honest and accountable with each other and praying with an attitude of grace for one another regarding the area of sexual fantasy.

Evaluate your particular weaknesses in the area of sexuality. Those areas which are a particular battle for you submit before the Lord and then find an accountability partner to help you in this area.

■ Pornography

- Lust is the engine that drives the desire to view pornography in its many forms.

- The problem with pornography is that it limits sex to only the physical realm and trivializes it; its real danger is that sexuality loses its deeper meaning as an expression of love between those committed to a lifelong relationship.

- Pornography, by its very nature, cheapens and dehumanizes, it does not lift and ennoble. Both the subject and the viewer function on a level below that which God intended for his sexual creation.

- In practical terms, its danger to relationships is that it creates a fantasy world of perfection that no one can attain to. Those addicted, seek to escape from reality into a dream world, with all the relational problems and flaws. It eventually becomes a substitute for developing real relationships.

- As with any addiction, participants are driven to become more involved in order to receive the same level of excitement.

- While it may seem harmless enough in the early stages, it eventually holds those in its grasp with a power that is hard to break.

- As with the other challenges, however, while the power of the Holy Spirit and the Word are necessary to break its hold, often an accountability partner or mentor is also needed in order to break free of its grasp.

■ Self-gratification

- First it must be said that the Bible does not directly deal with this issue and there are no medical indications that it is physically harmful.

- Though this is often a tabu subject in Christian circles, many suffer from guilt and may not be reaching their full potential in the Kingdom, due to the condemnation they experience regarding their involvement in this activity.

- While it is usually considered adolescent behaviour, it is not an activity limited only to youth. Due to the high numbers who admit to engaging in this activity in society at large, it is likely that it is an issue that believers also deal with. But what is to be our response considering the apparent silence of the Bible?

- Views range on this topic from those who feel it is always wrong to engage in this activity, to those who view it as a harmless way of releasing sexual tension during adolescence, at a time when the individual may be physically ready for sex, but not ready for the responsibility of marriage (Dobson's view). For those later in life it can be seen by some as a means to provide a healthy outlet when sexual intercourse is not possible, or as a mutually enriching experience for married couples.

- While severe condemnation is probably not warranted regarding this subject, the reality is that if it is not mastered and under control, it can become an addiction whose fruit is not healthy. The fact is that as it becomes combined with sexual fantasies and pornography, it becomes a snare that can dominate a person's life. If it becomes an obsession, it can be very destructive to the person's self-esteem and emotional health and even cripple one's spiritual life.

- The real danger is in the lustful thoughts and desires that often accompany this activity, not just the act itself. In any event, God will not suspend someone's sexual desires through prayer and fasting, as with other physical appetites, this is a discipline that must be learned. Together with the power of Holy Spirit we must learn to control our passions.

- Being obsessive about quitting is also a danger which can lead to further despair. The vicious cycle of condemnation can even lead to further isolation and bondage. As believers we should be agents of God's grace (truth and power),

If this has been a weak area for you, what steps can you take to discipline your thought life. Make yourself accountable with someone in this area. Begin to then live a life free of condemnation.

even while someone may be struggling in these areas of their life. They need to see who they are in Christ and the availability of his power to live a godly life.

- As believers we must be gracious one with another in some of these areas, instead of creating the illusion that none of us deal with these same issues. Through healthy teaching and positive relationships we can help others rise from what otherwise can be a downward spiral.

- Finally, we need to be aware that due, in part, to personality, background, upbringing and many other factors, each person has a varying intensity of sexual desire. Each person needs to be aware of their own needs and weaknesses and allow God to personally deal with them in each of these areas.

■ Sexism

- Sexism is the desire to dominate and control another person. This has typically been directed towards women by men.

- Yet female inferiority and hierarchical structures, due to their gender, are not biblical – God created men and women equal.

- Man's domination was a curse as a result of the fall (Gen 3:16), not God's original intent.

- This teaching has caused confusion and great harm for the Kingdom, as it has even resulted in women being wrongfully invalidated in their expression of their God-given calling.

- Further treatment of this topic is beyond the scope of this manual, but for a deeper understanding of this issue a good place to start is, *Beyond Sex Roles* by Gilbert Bilezikian and *Why Not Women* by Loren Cunningham/David Hamilton.

Singleness and Sexuality

- Particularly in many western societies, traditional marriage between one man and one woman is no longer the norm. This has led to the breakdown in the family unit, which will inevitably result in the majority of adults in western societies being single.

- In dealing with this reality, it is important to realize that singles, Christians included, are created as sexual beings and have sexual needs.

- Yet it is possible for a Christian single to express this in healthy, non-sexual expressions of affection. We must recognize that singles need emotional connection and fulfilment, even while being committed to reserving sex for marriage.

- It is not only possible, but important, for singles to be able to love and be loved and receive and give affection, within caring relationships which do not end in sexual expression.

- In a changing culture, the church needs to provide support and opportunity for this to happen in healthy ways.

Controlling Passions

- It is possible for singles (and those married) to accept and control their sexuality. While seeking a mate, it is possible to have caring relationships and remain pure. Sexual intercourse is a want not a need – we can live without it.

- As intimacy grows in a relationship, so must the commitment to one another. This is why sexual relations, the ultimate expression of intimacy, is reserved for the

What are the sexual and family norms in your society?
Which of them do not line up with God's Truth and how do these differences impact you as a believer? As a leader?

If you are single, discuss with your mentor, or accountability partner, your level of success in controlling your passions. What practical steps can you take to grow in this area?

ultimate expression of commitment, which is marriage. Promiscuous sex violates this spiritual aspect of our bodies.

- Frustration in relationships occurs when the intimacy level is greater than the commitment level. While we should not deny the existence of passions, we must realize the power of these passions and the need to control them.

- This fact should lead the Christian single to set guidelines for their relationships. While not denying their humanity and inherent design as sexual beings, parameters need to be set so that this passion does not overwhelm their good intentions.

- To stay pure, at the very least the erogenous zones of both the male and female should be avoided, as well as being aware of how other expressions of affection can lead to improper expressions of affection.

- For those engaged to be married it is advisable that the engagement period is not too long, for during this time in the relationship the commitment is high, which puts added pressure on the couple for greater intimacy.

Pre-marital Sex

- In an increasing post-modern world, the idea of abstaining from pre-marital sex seems outmoded at best, irrelevant at worst. The fact is that those who hold to no absolute truth, will also find biblical references on this topic irrelevant.

- However, more recently, believers have also been affected by popular culture and are expressing varying degrees of confusion regarding this subject.

- While the term *pre-marital sex* is not found in the Bible, the Greek word, *porneia* carries with it the definition of not only the actual act of intercourse, but also other sexual activity reserved for within the marriage commitment.

- This Greek word has been translated in the older King James Version as *fornication* and in the newer translations as *sexual immorality*, yet the meaning from the original is the same, to engage in sexual activity outside of, or before, marriage (a sampling of these scriptures include: Matt. 15:19; Acts 15:20; Rom. 1:29; 1 Cor. 5:1, 9, 11; 6:9, 13, 18; 7:12; 10:8; Gal. 5:19; Col. 3:5 Heb. 12:16).

- Sexual intercourse before marriage is forbidden for it produces a "one flesh" bond (1 Cor 6:16), which is to be reserved only for the person that we are to be joined together with for life. The union is more than just a physical and emotional one, it has been designed by God to be spiritual in nature.

- The current relativism found in many societies regarding sexuality is not a new phenomena, though it is perhaps more widespread now than ever. In both Jewish and Christian teaching and culture, the practice of sex before marriage was a foreign concept, though practiced by the pagans around them. Scholars point out that in the Graeco-Roman world, sexual relations outside of and before marriage, was commonplace and accepted. This would explain the many scriptures in the New Testament regarding to refrain from this practice.

- STD's (sexually transmitted diseases) and pregnancy are not the only reasons to avoid sexual relations before marriage. The main reason being that due to its spiritual nature (the mystery of "one flesh"), God has reserved it as an expression of a life commitment which joins two individuals. It is to be a living analogy of God's love relationship with man. Even if participants are not aware of this, pre-marital sexual relations does damages this "one flesh" reality, the results of which participants carry with them long after the act itself.

- Having said that, there is also grace available for those who have failed in this area. Though there are consequences, the spiritual effects of premarital sex are not irreversible, but they do require God's healing touch. Even after marriage, it

What are your standards for your relationship with the opposite gender?

If you are a leader, what are your guidelines and standards in your interrelation with those of the other gender?
Are there changes that you need to implement to avoid even the "appearance of evil?"

What is your view of pre-marital sex? Consider how you can articulate this for those in your culture.

is important to not avoid what happened and seek counsel and prayer, especially if someone was in a long term pre-marital relationship.

Singleness by Choice

- Before making the decision to marry, we must be aware that marriage requires much time and effort for it to be successful. While it is desirable, it is not to be entered lightly or as a matter of course.

- On the other hand, it needs to be acknowledged that vocational celibacy is a valid choice (Matt.19:12; 1 Cor. 7:32-35). As a church we must make the effort to accept those who choose this lifestyle and not treat them as if they are second-class members, or somehow not normal.

Marriage and Sexuality

- While sex and romance may be part of the decision process in getting married, it should never be the only consideration.

- Particularly Christians should consider other issues such as questions of vocation and calling, the good of others, and how their marriage could potentially advance or hinder the work of the Kingdom of God.

- Ideally, these would all be dealt with before the marriage, but in reality this does not always occur. Often ahead of the marriage there is not always wise counsel available in order to help in determining the answers to these issues, or the time taken to fully understand our own motives.

- Yet in God's grace, he can take us from where we currently are and restore and rebuild, even the very foundation of our relationship if that be necessary. He is always the God of the second chance and new opportunities.

The Act of Marriage

- The decision to marry is so important for it is a life commitment that demands our best energies and efforts.

- While we often prioritize the spiritual disciplines on a higher level than the efforts to improve a marriage, the effort expended for our marriage is very important. For just as we serve Christ through prayer, Bible reading and fasting, so the actions we take to preserve our marriage can be a service for Christ.

- Many have neglected the disciplines to keep a healthy marriage and have not only lost their marriage in the process, but even more tragically, their faith in God. It is impossible to overestimate the importance of the marriage relationship, as its demise has the potential to touch every area of our lives.

- Fortunately, God's grace reaches down and touches us even in the midst of the pain and tragedy of marital breakup. While scars remain, he is the God of restoration and the second chance, in even hopeless situations (As with many topics along our Mentoring journey, a detailed teaching on marriage is beyond the scope of this manual, if this is an area of need, speak with your mentor and get the help you and your spouse may need).

- As with other areas of married life, a couples's sexual life is not automatic, but requires much communication, as well as daily give-and-take. Couples must be aware that men and women respond differently, and while the basics can be learned from books, we need to be a learner of each other to find out how we can best please our spouse.

- Generally, women respond to sex in terms of relationship and sharing, so it is the

If you have fallen short of the biblical standard, having repented, receive God's grace and forgiveness. God has healing for you. Next, take necessary steps in order not to repeat moral failures in this area.

Discuss with your spouse your reasons for marrying and establish new expectations (if necessary) of how your marriage can be a positive influence for the Kingdom.

110

man's responsibility to know his woman and take time for her. This is how he shows love to her, both in and out of the bedroom. Typically, women need a loving caring relationship to experience fulfilling sex, while men open up emotionally through the act of sex.

- Though not always easy for most couples, it is helpful to talk and pray about their sex life together.

- Understanding the rhythms of fulfilling sex within a marriage takes a lifetime, which is why marriage is to be for life. Sex becomes boring when it is only seen as "the act of sexual intercourse." It is of course so much more; it is the sharing together of two people for life.

Marriage Defined

- In many so-called post-modern societies there has been a growing confusion as to what constitutes a marriage. This confusion has also become evident in the culture of the church. Though this is not an in-depth study, a few thoughts regarding the very definition of marriage may be helpful.

- In Scripture, and early societies, marriage actually began with the engagement period. The engagement period leading up to the marriage had a much more prominent role than we see today, as preparation for marriage in both the Old and New Testament.

- The Engagement was a beginning of the contract which was often sealed with the payment of a bride price, which was like a down payment (but not to be confused with the dowry, which has become a burden in many cultures even hindering couples from getting married). The bride price was a payment by the future husband as a guarantor of his intentions. It was also an insurance for the woman should she be defiled during the engagement.

- The engagement was an important process towards marriage and had many of the obligations of married life, yet without the couple having physical relations (if this were to occur the man would lose the bride price and the bride's father, together with the bride, had the choice to continue with the marriage or break it off).

- The wedding itself was more than just a festivity, but was a time for others to publically speak a blessing on the pair and welcome them into the society as a married couple. It was a right of passage. However, in some cultures where there is an expectation of a large, expensive wedding, it has even caused some believers, who are not financially able, to avoid the wedding and marry secretively, of course missing out on this public blessing and confirmation.

- Churches should assist families in these cultures understand the true purpose of the wedding for the marriage, and not force them to choose between going into marriage with a huge debt, or bypassing the wedding completely, opting instead to just "live as married."

- While a wedding certificate, in and of itself, can never make a good marriage, Paul encouraged (Rom. 13:1-7) believers to uphold the law of the land and if this is a component of marriage in your country (in whatever form), it would seem to be consistent to have this tangible symbol of a inner commitment. Interestingly enough, a legal document signed by witnesses is required for any financial contract to be legally binding in most countries. How much more should this be the case for those entering a life-long commitment of marriage, which is so much more than a financial transaction.

- If for no other reason than to symbolize what has taken place (particularly in cultures where written contracts are used for every other commitment), it would seem reasonable that this societal norm be supported by believers for something as important as the life union of two individuals as one.

Spend some time discussing your sex-life with your spouse. Are you satisfied, frustrated? Read books on the subject and become a student of your spouse. Consider ways that you can better meet the needs of your spouse.

Think through the changing values and views in your culture regarding marriage.
Do further study regarding what constitutes a marriage and be able to communicate a biblical view regarding marriage.

- In Genesis 2:24 we see the picture of a contract as the two being *stuck* or *bonded* together. Breaking this covenant actually broke a covenant with God (Prov. 2:16-17). The marriage bond is actually a model of our covenant with God and may indicate why marriage and the family unit is so under attack in many societies today.

- So what constitutes a marriage? Is it just two people who love each other and decide to stay together, until the state gives them the label of "married"? While this may be the trend in many western nations, we as believers need to uphold the standard of the biblical foundation, as well as the applicable societal norms (those which do not violate biblical principles), which confirm the divine institution of marriage. It is more than conjugal rights, a private commitment, or a private promise based upon the best of intentions. From biblical principles we see that it is a contractual joining of a man and woman to become one flesh, witnessed before God and human witnesses, only to be dissolved by death.

- As mentioned previously, stating the ideal and God's pattern is never to condemn or in any way communicate that with God there are no second chances. God forgives and at times we must accept his grace for our errors (and the hardness of others) and move on in the face of situations that are far less than ideal. While a study of divorce and remarriage is beyond the scope of this manual, if this is an issue that touches you, speak with your mentor for additional reading and help with your particular situation.

For the Married

- By definition, marriage is monogamous; it is a lifelong pledge to love and be loyal.

- Of course the path of marriage is not without its difficulties, such is the reality of life. Yet disagreements should be handled fairly and never lead to physical violence or emotional abuse.

- Every marriage is worth fighting for. When conflicts arise that cannot be dealt with alone, it is a wise couple who seek wise godly counsel in order to help repair the marriage and provide direction towards a resolution.

- While any sexual expression outside of the marriage bond damages the marriage, there should be a healthy sexual liberty within the marriage bond. Christian couples should enjoy the varied sexual intensities and seasons of married life and give of themselves to each other. Marital sex includes self-disclosure, vulnerability, and spiritual union, however, it is also to be fun and pleasurable.

- While expressions of affection from others needs to also be controlled (1 Cor. 6:12), couples need to give each other room so that their spouse can also receive from others through healthy non-sexual relationships. Yet it is not appropriate to be spending regular personal time alone with someone of the opposite sex, for we eventually give our hearts to those we spend time with. Even with same sex relationships, we should never allow time with others to take away from time with our spouse or deplete emotional energy that should be reserved for our spouse.

- Increasingly it is becoming more a challenge to live a pure sexual life, as either a single or married. The path of God's purposes is lined with those who have failed to rise to this challenge. Many have succumbed to the various sexual pitfalls along the way and never reached their potential.

- This area of our sexuality is often avoided in church circles for a variety of reasons and yet it is this very issue that has caused so many to live less than effective Christian lives, or at worst lost their faith completely.

Together with your spouse, evaluate your marriage as to your communication level, ability to deal with conflicts, common goals and expectations, as well as your level of intimacy.

Be honest with each other and if need be seek a mediator or outside help (counsellor, friend, seminar) to improve your marriage.

POWER

- Another major potential pitfall is the area of a lust for power, which has a root of pride.

- Just as with the issue of money and our sexuality, power is not inherently evil, as it can be used for positive or destructive purposes.

- More space will be devoted to this important topic in Chapter 3.1, *Servant Leadership*, and so it will only be introduced here.

Drive for Power

- Almost universal in our world is the desire for Power – from political, military, economic, and virtually every arena of life.

- Unfortunately this desire and lust for power can also be found in the Church. As a minister and leader this is a particular temptation that needs to be mastered.

- The improper desire and exercise of power in any arena of society is destructive, but within the form of religious power in the Church, it can be particularly damaging. For those who seek to find solace in the Church from the manipulation and impure motives in the world, only to find spiritual leaders motivated by the same spirit of power, the results are often devastating.

- Religious power can destroy others like no other power can, for if someone is convinced that what they are doing is for the Kingdom of God, then all who oppose them, or have another point of view, must be against God.

- The danger in experiencing and witnessing God's power through our ministry, is the subtle shift which can occur as we begin to assume some of God's power as our "own."

What is your motivation to lead others? Ask the Lord to show you your heart.

Pride

- If a leader begins to believe that he is infallible and working on behalf of God, then virtually any action and attitude can be justified due to the righteous cause. This sense of "rightness," based upon pride within a leader's heart, often means that the leader is accountable to no one.

- Pride was at the root of Satan's fall from an angel of God, to an angel of darkness. Scripture compares pride to the practice of witchcraft, for it has the ability to deceive even the very devoted.

- This combination of pride with power is a deadly combination, for pride makes us think we are right and having the power enables us to force this "rightness" on others.

- But God will share his glory with no other and if the leader (or person) does not recognize this deception and repent, God will deal with them.

- Individuals or ministries who have fallen into this pit of pride, have often begun with pure motives (see Chapter 4.1), but over time began to believe that their success was due to their own ability and not due to God's grace.

Have your mentor discuss with you how they have dealt with the temptation of power as their ministry or influence has grown.

Accountability in Leadership

- As with the other pitfalls, having relationships with which to be accountable can be the difference between victory or defeat in this area.

- Yet those with this drive for power tend to want to be alone and not in relationship with others. Yet it is crucial that the leader have those with whom they can honestly share.

- The leader needs those who they can confide in and with whom they have mutual respect. They need to have those who they give permission to speak into their lives.

- It is important to establish these types of relationships before they are needed, for once pride and power have a foothold, it is very hard for others to gain access to the leader. These relationships need to be established before success, so that they can keep the leader in touch with reality as his ministry grows and is successful.

- The potential for self-deception cannot be overestimated. To counteract this a leader must maintain a sober self view, enabling them to remain humble.

Humility and Servanthood

- The more we are used of God in other's lives, the greater is our need for humility.

- Throughout Scripture we see God, in his faithfulness, developing this character quality in his servants.

- As Paul had a *thorn in the flesh* that kept him in a state of dependence on God, so did many other leaders from Scripture have a unique *messenger* that forced them to have an proper estimation of themselves. These apparent *weaknesses* or *thorns,* in whatever form, are meant to keep leaders in dependence upon God as the source of their power.

- In later chapters we shall discover that true leadership is *serving* and *developing* others from a position of vulnerability and love. It is a laying down of one's life, just as we saw our Master lay down his life for others. Jesus, the greatest leader of all time, layed aside his power and position and became a servant and we are to follow his example.

- Leadership can be defined as having influence. This being the case, the greater one's influence the greater the need for humility and meekness.

Dying to Self

- Without exception, this quality of humility is developed in the servant's life through difficulties, wilderness times, failures and disappointments.

- The leader must be willing, however, to be led into these wilderness times. In John 12:24, Jesus teaches that unless a kernel of wheat falls into the ground and dies it bears no fruit. This is a process which often occurs *in the dark hidden places.* Yet being willing to enter this process, will determine the degree to which we follow in Christ's footsteps as servant-leaders.

- It is in this process that our own ego and desire for reputation is crucified with Christ; it is in these wilderness times when we are weak that we learn to rely on his strength.

- These preparation times, as with Moses or Paul, occurred when they were hidden from view and had very little influence and no leadership title or position. This is why it is important to not be in a rush to be thrust into positions of influence before God has molded us.

Identify those events or attributes in your life which God has allowed to teach you humility and keep you from pride. No longer ask him to remove these.

Do you have those who you are accountable to? Are they free enough to be honest with you? If not, begin to seek out such relationships.

Is your ministry and life characterized by servanthood? Look for those around you who seem to have learned this and, if possible, spend time with them in order to learn this attitude.

- Jesus learned these lessons, as we see him in perfect submission to his Father. Learning this same submission is what helps us receive from others and not mount the pedestal that keeps us separate from others; to not take that first step towards pride and the potential for a mighty fall.

- We never see Jesus using his place of influence to overrun others, control them, or try to use them for his own purposes. Out of respect for others, he even limited doing what may have seemed good in the eyes of others, but what he knew was not the will of the Father (Matt. 4:5; Jn. 6:26; Lk. 4:16-27).

- Having influence also necessitates being willing to walk alone at times. This is often the price of spiritual power – to be willing to wrestle alone as a Jacob with our own angel.

Serving versus Position

- The lowest form of leadership is from position, yet this is the predominate pattern of the world (see Chapter 3.2).

- Position does not guarantee influence or spiritual power, for this is something that is earned through serving others, a concept completely opposite of worldly leadership.

- Jesus modelled this for us and then delegated his ministry of *power* to us (Lk. 9:6; Jn. 14:12). A power that came from serving. The disciples did not have human authority, only a divine confirmation. This is in contrast to those who had official authority, yet had no real spiritual power and authority.

- It is this type of positive power that restores relationships and can set people free, in contrast to seeking to lead by manipulation, pride and control of others.

- Spiritual leaders must be aware of the dangers of power and the many temptations there are to abuse it, particularly with other believers.

- Only through vigilance and the power of the Holy Spirit will we be able to avoid the double pitfall of pride and power.

Have you had your time in the desert or wilderness? What did you learn that has helped you in your life and ministry? Discuss this with your mentor or mentoring group.

Universally Applicable

- The potential to positively use power and influence is applicable in every area of life, from our personal life, to our family, to our job.

- It is so diametrically opposed to the world's way of leadership, however, that it takes divine strength and courage in order to implement it. Living like this is impossible in just our own self-strength.

- Exercising power and influence as a servant leader in every area of life helps to nurture confidence and not subservience; it enhances communication not isolation; it inspires faith and does not try to control and manipulate others.

- In every area of life, it seeks to encourage and develop others, not push others down in order for self-exultation; it seeks to enable others and foster their growth. It is at the very essence of living a mentoring lifestyle.

SUMMARY

- Each of these areas have proven to be major pitfalls in the life of believers over the centuries. Those who do not heed the warnings of previous generations do so at their own peril.

- While not each of these areas will hold the same level of temptation for us, each of us have our weaknesses. The purpose of this chapter is to help us honestly face ourselves – often the hardest person to be honest with!

- Yet each of these are not inherently evil, but can be redeemed for Kingdom purposes, if we learn to master them, rather than being mastered by them.

- Hopefully by this time you will have developed a level of trust and honesty in your relationship with your mentor so that you can share your struggles, as well as learn from the experience of your mentor.

- In our final chapter in this section we will focus on how to hear from God and be led of him as his *Disciple*.

Together with your mentor, evaluate any of the areas in this chapter that you need to improve or make changes. Commit with God and your mentor to take the practical steps necessary.

Disciple

Chapter

2.3

Mentoring
thru ————
Intentional Relationships

Your Direction: Being Led of God

INTRODUCTION

- In this section we have been discussing some of the necessary spiritual disciplines as a foundation for our lives and ministry and in this chapter we will be discussing the connection between the spiritual disciplines and our being led and guided by God.

- We will look at some of the practical issues pertaining to understanding God's will in our lives, so that we may be directed by him with confidence. Being led of God need not be a mystery, rather it flows from a personal relationship with him.

- By practicing the spiritual disciplines, we grow and mature and being led of God becomes more and more *natural* in our daily lives. God desires to lead his people and has given us the ability to hear him, yet to hear from him we must believe and expect that he will lead us.

Extreme Positions

- In our desire to be led of God there are two extremes that we can fall into, both of which led away from God, rather than towards him.

- One extreme is to look to God for guidance in those areas in which he expects us to use the common sense and wisdom that he has given us. It is not that God is not interested in the mundane and even the smallest detail of our lives, but there are matters (such as the daily selection of our clothing), that he expects us to use the wisdom that he has given us.

- This *over spiritualization,* needing to hear a voice from God on every issue, can sometimes be merely an excuse for not wanting to take responsibility for making our own decisions. In this extreme, everything is "prayed about" and yet no decisions are made. This can often lead to strange behaviour that does not bring personal growth or glorify God.

- Another extreme is to undervalue the supernatural leading of the Holy Spirit. Perhaps due to past hurtful experiences, manipulation by leaders, or even false teaching, we can tend to focus entirely on the rational and logic of human reasoning in determining his direction in our lives.

- While God does not expect his children to disengage their minds, there are times when his leadings will seem to not make sense according to our limited human thought and perspective, and we must take that step into the apparent unknown.

- But we must find a balance between these two extremes. On the one hand we need to be aware that God wants to lead us in every area of our lives and yet, on the other hand, we need to come to a place of maturity so that we are not always seeking a *spectacular* answer.

- There are obvious challenges in attempting to follow God's leading in our lives and ministry. Often we can find ourselves asking, *Are these my desires or God's?* and *How can I determine between the two?*

- Throughout Scripture the pattern we see is that God does clearly lead his people. He desires to bring clarity and understanding to his people, not confusion. As we

Which of these extreme positions do you tend to lean towards?

What struggles do you have in attaining balance in this area of your life?

From the previous session on Spiritual Disciplines (2.1) what have you applied in your life that has assisted you in hearing from God and his leading in your life.

grow in maturity we will begin to understand his ways in leading us.

Principles not Formulas

- While there are principles and guidelines to follow, being led of God cannot be reduced to simple formulas. Knowing his voice is based on a relationship with him; the better we get to know him, the better we will understand his heart and his ways.

- This requires regular times of quietness and solitude, learning to live in the reality of his presence through the exercise of the spiritual disciplines (Session 2.1).

- We see this pattern throughout Scripture. Jesus regularly spent time with his Father (Mark 1:35 and others), as did such personalities as King David, Isaiah, Peter, and Paul to name just a few.

- So while there is no formula, learning to hear God's voice first begins with a our desire, but then we must also be intentional in developing the disciplines necessary to hear from him.

GODS LEADING

- God has provided the means by which we can hear from him and learn of him. In Chapter 2.1, we discussed several of these keys, such as spending time with him through prayer and his Word, and so will not devote as much space to them here.

- While each of these ingredients to hearing from God are listed separately, in reality they cannot be separated. Just as the individual ingredients of bread must be correctly mixed together in order to produce a loaf of bread, so each of these by themselves (Word, Prayer, His Spirit) is only one aspect of hearing God. They all need to be functioning together in balance, in order for us to be led of God.

Nice pix

God's Word

How has God led you through his Word in the past? What adjustments do you need to make in order to more effectively hear from God through his Word?

- We see in Jesus' ministry that he learned of his Father through the revelation of the Old Testament Scriptures. This focus on the Scripture for revelation and direction continued in the early church, as Christians relied on the Old Testament, as well as the emerging sacred writings of the early apostles.

- What we have in God's Word is more than just a book of good teaching, morals, or even principles, it is the revealed will of God, for all time and eternity. It is not just letters on a page, for the Holy Spirit takes these words and makes them alive in our spirits, as we take time to meditate on them.

- Of course this takes time and effort, for we must apply ourselves to read and meditate upon God's Word (as discussed in Chapter 2.1). Those who know the voice of God have learned to exercise their spiritual ears.

- In order for the Holy Spirit to speak to us through God's Word, we must take the time to hide it in our hearts. Often we want to be led of God, but we do not take the necessary time in order to learn of him and discipline ourselves to know and understand his Word. Yet the fruit of this discipline is a clarity and confidence in his direction in our lives.

- Being led through God's Word is often as simple (though challenging) as accepting its truths and obeying its precepts. At other times it may seem as if the Holy Spirit "speaks" directly to us through a specific passage. ("Speak" does not necessarily refer to an audible voice, but rather the inner impression or direction that the believer begins to perceive as the *voice* of the Holy Spirit).

- As we memorize and know more of God's Word, it becomes a inner resource that God can then use to lead and guide us.

Prayer

- As with Bible reading and meditation, prayer is not so much a certain activity (though it does include this), as it is a continuous communing with God. Throughout the day we can learn to be aware of his presence and be communicating with him. It is two-way communication, for though we talk to God, more importantly, he talks to us.

- Prayer could be considered the most direct contact with God. Though it is usually perceived as the vehicle to get answers from God, the focus of prayer is most often personal change, rather than trying to change God's mind on a matter.

- As mentioned in a previous chapter, to hear from God we must spend time together with him in prayer. The simplicity of this is often complicated by our schedules, obligations, and wrong priorities, yet it is only as we discipline ourselves to become quiet enough to listen to the Father that he will be able to speak to us. Those who seek him with all their heart, are the ones who hear his voice.

- As we commune with him, he takes the truths from his Word and confirms them to our hearts. Learning to do this is a process which takes time, but this discipline can become a lifestyle for the believer which provides a consistency of walk and peace of heart in even the most stressful situations.

- Prayer and Bible meditation cannot be separated. God uses his Word to speak to us while we are in prayer and then as we prayerfully meditate on his Word, we hear from him.

- However, hearing from God can be hindered through unconfessed sin in our lives (Isa. 1:15; Ps. 66:18), not being in right relationship with others (Matt. 5:23-24; 1 Peter 3:7), or not obeying God's previous directives to us.

- A further hindrance to hearing from God occurs when we reduce prayer to a mere formula or religious ritual. Those who hear from him must come to him in spirit and in truth.

- When we pray we must have faith that God will answer. We must also then be spiritually sensitive to perceive how God is answering our prayers. This means making the connection between our prayers and the events in our lives. It is as we begin to actively seek God with expectation, that we will begin to see him work in our everyday lives.

Indwelling Holy Spirit

- God is a Spirit and he relates with humankind through his Spirit. We often speak of this as the *inward witness* or *inner leading*, and it is made possible through the indwelling of the Holy Spirit.

- In the Old Testament, God's Spirit came upon individuals primarily to do a task (Judges 6:34; 1 Sam 6:13) and often the manifestation of God's Spirit was a physical one (ie. Glory in the Temple, Pillar of Fire in the wilderness, etc.).

- Then at the beginning of Jesus' earthly ministry, we see that the Holy Spirit came upon him in the form of a dove – a physical manifestation of an inner reality (Luke 3:22). Later, we see the disciples receiving this same Holy Spirit at Pentecost (Luke 24:49; Acts 1:8), which ushered in a new era.

- In the New Covenant, hearing from God directly is not limited to just a chosen few or even through just spectacular physical manifestations. Instead we see

Reflect on how God has led you through times of prayer recently? What adjustments do you need to make in order to more effectively hear from God through your times of prayer?

Are there specific areas in which you need God's direction? Are there any hindrances in your life that you know of in hearing from God?

Do you live in the awareness of God's indwelling Holy Spirit?

God desiring to speak to each of his children by his Holy Spirit.

- The promise in John 14:16 is that after his (Jesus') departure, the Holy Spirit would lead and guide all believers, just as he led Jesus.

- As Jesus returned to the Father he promised to send the Holy Spirit to fill every believer (Acts 2:1-21; 1 Cor 12:3; 12-14; Eph 1:13-14). Instead of a one-time event, this filling was to be a continual activity of living in the Spirit (Eph 5:18). One of the key purposes of the Holy Spirit is to indwell the believer and reveal truth to us (1 Cor. 3:16), enabling us to be led of God.

- Further titles which help to explain the nature of the Holy Spirit include, the *Spirit of Conviction* (Jn. 6:44), the *Spirit of Truth* (John 14:16-17), as well as *Teacher*, *Helper*, and *Guide*.

How can you practice the presence of Christ more consistently in your daily life?

Walking in the Spirit

- The external law of the Old Covenant could not provide the power to follow the law. It was a foreshadow of things to come. With the coming of the New Covenant through Christ, the inward power of the Holy Spirit is ever present to help the believer live as God desires us to live (Gal 5:16). While in the Old Testament God's Spirit was characterized as *coming upon*, he now desires to *live through* every believer.

- There is no longer a need for another mediator between us and God, for the Holy Spirit indwells us and will lead us into all truth, we have direct access to God. He abides within and desires this intimate fellowship in order to reveal Christ in every area of our daily lives.

- While the Holy Spirit indwells all believers, to the degree that we surrender our will and way to him, he will be able to lead and guide us into all truth. He is available, but we must give the Holy Spirit permission to work in and through our lives.

- To be led of him we must daily practice the awareness of God's presence in our lives through the spiritual disciplines, for if we are not attune to him, the reality that he is ever present will have only a minimal impact on our lives.

Visions and Prophecy

What place do prophecies, visions, etc play in your life? Do you place too much value on them? Do you not place enough value in them?

- God's people throughout Scripture have had visions and dreams and have prophesied. According to Joel 2:28, God will continue to pour his Spirit out in this manner.

- In both the Old and New Testament we find saints having both visions and dreams (ie. Paul's Macedonian call), yet as Paul later teaches, even these need to be tested as to their source. This is accomplished through a combination of the inward witness of God's Spirit and his revealed Word. Without this balance we can be susceptible to believing any dream or vision as being from God, when in fact it may only be our imagination, or perhaps worse, the influence of the enemy.

- While the primary function of prophecy is to exhort and encourage God's people, it can also serve as a confirmation relating to what God has already been speaking to the believer. Through the Word, prayer and the counsel of others, we are admonished to evaluate the word of the Prophets according to the Word of God.

- The good news of Jesus' death and resurrection is that the separation between man and God was forever removed. Each believer is not dependent upon someone else to act as a mediator between them and God. In all areas of life, including finding direction, we may go directly to God as our source.

- The real danger is that visions and even prophecies can be easily manipulated by others and even by the enemy, which is why it is so important to rely on God's Word as the "more sure word of Prophecy."

- God may use prophecy from someone else as a confirmation of his leading, or as an exhortation, yet his primary desire is to develop a personal relationship with each believer so that they may hear his voice directly.

- Our goal should not be to seek after the sensational, but develop an intimate relationship with God, whereby he can lead us by his Spirit. This will bring a stability and consistency in our walk with him as we seek to fulfil his purposes in and through our lives.

Testing our *Leadings*

- Being led by the indwelling Holy Spirit means that the disciple must learn to hear his voice. As mentioned, this *voice* or *inner impression* is most often not an audible or physical voice, but a impression in our heart or spirit.

- The challenge in being led of God is learning to discern between the voice of God speaking to us, our own ideas and thoughts, and thoughts or impressions that could even originate from Satan (though they may come in the form of an *angel of light*.)

- The fact is that Satan is real (1 Tim 4:1, Rev. 16:14, Matt 24:24) and that he is seeking to deceive even the believer.

- Though Jesus defeated the enemy at the cross, he seeks to exert his influence in our lives, which is why we must be on guard and prepared to engage in the fight of faith (Eph. 6:10-18).

- This battle is often won or lost in our mind, as Satan comes to plant thoughts that are contrary to truth and seeks to discredit God. This is the battle of faith and spiritual warfare, knowing God's truth from his Word and rejecting the lies of the enemy (ie. as Jesus did in the wilderness).

- To be led of God we must test the spirits (thoughts) to determine their origin (1 John 4:1). Yet this is not merely a subjective exercise, there are several criterion which can help us test these inner leadings.

  - First, God's inner leadings will never contradict his revealed Word. The Apostle Paul teaches that even if an angel of light were to come and teach something contrary to God's Word it would be false.

  - God's leadings are also usually consistent with our gifts and his previous leadings in our life (which is one of the benefits of doing the Timeline in Chapter 1.3). His leadings line up with how he has designed us, confirming our interests, abilities and gifts.

  - God often asks us to do something that stretches us beyond our comfort zone in order that we may grow, in this his leadings usually require a step of faith. However, we need to be careful to test these leadings (as described in this chapter) to be sure that they are from him, not just something that will be a distraction.

  - Finally, God's leadings are never self-promoting or self-serving, for he will always lead us towards servanthood, not greater personal power. He is always more interested in building his Kingdom, rather than our temporal kingdom.

Further Cautions

- While the following points do not necessarily indicate that a particular leading is definitely *not* from God, if some of these are present it may be advisable to spend more time with the Lord in order to be sure we have discerned his *voice*.

What have you learned about discerning between God's voice and your own desires?
Discuss with your mentor your understanding of your desires and God's desire for you? Are they similar or different?

Discuss the criteria given for testing our inner leadings as well as the other cautions given. Do you agree with all of these? Why or why not?

- Extra caution should be exercised if the decision requires that we need to make a huge life change within a very short period of time. This is often not the way God operates, he is not in a rush or under time pressure. If there are decisions that have to be made quickly, if it is God's direction it is always accompanied by contentment and faith.

- Also, if the decision will mean going into debt or will place someone else in an awkward or vulnerable position, it is most likely not a divine leading, or at the very least we did not hear clearly what he said. Again, more time should be taken to test the leading.

- Seldom will God's leading require breaking family relationships or close friendships. While following God as a Christian can mean a separation of family relations due to our faith, in terms of God's direction, we are referring to embarking on specific decisions that would cause tension in our close relationships. If this is the case, we should be cautious in proceeding with the course of action.

- Another indicator that caution should be exercised, is if the leading we have produces unrest or unease in the mature Christian friends and counsellors whose judgement we value.

- If one or more of the above characteristics are present, more time should be spent seeking God's direction and greater caution should be exercised.

The Body

- The New Testament emphasizes the truth of the *priesthood of all believers*. This teaching means that there are not two levels, or classes, of Christians. All believers have direct access to God and do not need to go through any person or group as a mediator in order to approach God; through Christ's death on the cross we all have equal access.

- Yet though we tend to emphasize this individual, personal nature of God's leading in the believer's life, the reality is that we have also been grafted into the Body of Christ, which by its very nature signifies interrelationships one with one another (1 Cor 12:27; Eph 4:12, 15-16).

- We see this evident as the early Church began functioning as a community (Acts 2:42, 44, 46-47). In terms of direction, in Acts 13:1-3 we read that the church fasted, prayed and worshipped together in order to hear God's heart on the issue of sending out Paul and Barnabas. Later at the Church Council of Acts 15, the early church had a difficult decision to make regarding the future of the Church. As they gathered together, the Spirit directed their joint decision making process.

- This was not so much a democratic model, but rather of a common clarity which came from their mutual unity, as each sought to be individually led of the Spirit and then came together to confirm with each other what God was saying. Unfortunately, this model for direction in the church became more of an exception than the rule throughout subsequent church history.

- Yet even today as a Body, we are to mutually *interdependent* with each other. What we lack, others can give us and we can offer our gifts to others as they have need. God has placed each of us in the Body and we need each other.

- This requires a high level of mutual submission in order to allow those with other gifts and perspectives to speak into our lives as if God were speaking through them. It is within healthy Body relationships that we can learn to listen to one another and value God speaking to us through other members of the Body. He has placed us as members in his Body and has given us a unique, specific role to play in the Body.

- However, this does not mean that some members in the Body are mediators or

Do you agree or disagree with the cautions given here? Explain.

What do you think of the statement, "Apart from the Body I cannot fully understand God's purposes for me in and through the Body?"

professional "listeners of God" for others. We each still have a responsibility to hear from God and to test the spirit ourselves. This principle of body ministry becomes unhealthy as others are allowed to control and manipulate others (directly or indirectly) and this is not what is meant by learning to listen to one another. A warning sign is if it becomes one-directional – always from the same individuals toward others. Mutual submission in the Body means that there is both giving and receiving by everyone in the Body.

- This also does not mean that leadership does not have a role to play in the Body. Their role, as servant leaders, is to be developing and encouraging all members of the Body (see Section 3.0).

- God desires believers to mature and grow as members of the Body are in mutually accountable relationships with one another (1 Cor. 12:12, 14-15, 19). These relationships are also a gift through which God desires to provide a safety and direction for his people. God has placed each one of us in the Body, his universal Church, in order to fulfill his purposes in the world through us.

Are you open and accountable to a local body of believers to hear from God through them? Discuss with your mentor your current situation and any concerns you have regarding this.

Limitations

- As with other means of direction, several cautions and guidelines are necessary.

- Obviously, this only functions as leaders are operating according to biblical principles. Unfortunately this is not always the case and many use their position and authority to manipulate and control others in the Body. Each member of the body must be valued and respected in order for the Body to function as God intended.

- There is also a danger that people will hinder the initiative of their leaders and their freedom to exercise their gifts. While they are to be accountable, leaders also need the freedom to lead, for this is their gift to the Body.

- A further caution is to recognize that even the majority can sometimes be wrong. Even if a majority group of believers agree on a course of actions, if it does not line up with God's Word and according to biblical principles it is not God's leading, for he will never lead contrary to his Word.

- Finally, we must recognize that given our human limitation, there are times in the Body when we must agree to disagree – and yet to do so agreeably! Even in those cases where separations do occur, it is possible for this to happen within an atmosphere of grace, kindness and blessing others.

Discuss experiences you have had where you were led by circumstances and not God and the consequences.

Circumstances

- To some degree, our circumstances will always affect our understanding of God's leading in our lives, however we must be careful to not rely too much on our circumstances in determining the direction or decisions God would have us take.

- It is also important to not rely on our past experiences in determining God's direction for the future. Our interpretation of our past experiences may be misleading, or may even contradict Scripture and the direction God wants to lead us.

- Also, being led by "open and closed doors" can often lead to confusion. Constantly "putting fleeces" (as Gideon did, motivated by his unbelief) before God, or relying on our physical senses to determine his direction, is not an ideal or desirable pattern to rely upon for leading. As with any form of external leading, these can be manipulated by the enemy and others.

Are putting "fleeces" before the Lord a valid biblical pattern of God's direction?

- Open doors are not necessarily from God, as they need to be evaluated to determine if they are really from him (Moses' *open door* to kill the Egyptian led to forty years in wilderness and Saul's *open door* to offer the sacrifice without the

How have you dealt with the "open" and "closed" doors in your life? What steps do you have to make in order to be led by God's inward Spirit, instead of circumstances?

prophet cost him the kingdom). Often, seemingly closed doors can actually be God's way to lead us to his open door. As with an over emphasis on seeking prophesy for direction, so the use of *open or closed doors* can seem right, yet God's purpose is for us to know his heart and be led by him through an intimate, personal relationship.

• God will not always supernaturally *close the door* if a direction is wrong and all *open doors* are not always positive indicators of God's will. Instead, we need to be led by God's inward Spirit, his Word, and prayer. When circumstances do not align with these, then we need to pause until God gives us clearer direction.

A Caution

• There are times when our circumstances do not seem to be in line with God's Word and events around us seem to be out of control. In this state of confusion we often do not know what direction to take.

• At these times it is first important to reaffirm our faith in *Who* God is, in his character. It is crucial that we do not try to understand who God is through the filter of our circumstances. We need to gain his perspective on our circumstance, instead of trying to discover God's character through our circumstances.

• Also, we need to recognize that God wants to lead us specifically. During this time it is best to spend time with God, focussing on him more than on the decision that must be made. In the absence of clear direction, it is usually best to not make a hasty decision. It is during these times that we can learn patience and waiting on God's timing.

• If we have been faithful to do our part and God has still given no direction, it often can mean that we know all that we need to know regarding the matter, or we may need to wait for the correct timing. Though we may at times feel that God has not given us clear enough direction, if it is God's will, he will always gives us enough faith to take that first step, as we endeavor to keep our heart soft towards him.

• Being led of God does not mean always *feeling* his presence. We need to learn to walk with Him without necessarily "feeling" his presence. As we mature God expects more from us, so that he can entrust us enough to put us in difficult situations which he desires that we positively influence.

• If we are always governed by the external, or the need to constantly sense his presence, we will remain immature and not as usable for the Kingdom. Maturity means that we learn that even during the most difficult of times, God is with us by his Spirit and is leading us to bring his Kingdom rule into the situation.

Reflect on a "wilderness" time you went through and what you learned during this time? If you are currently within one of those seasons, discuss this with your mentor and evaluate you attitude during this time.

The Wilderness or Silent times

• As with Job and other biblical examples, there are also those times in our lives when it seems that we hear nothing from God and that he is silent at best, or against us at worst. While there may be no hindrances that we know of on our part, we may sense a divine silence and no inward sense of his presence.

• During these times we need to learn to function on the foundation of already revealed truth. The first one being that God is still interested and concerned, however for reasons which will be clearer one day than they are now, he has chosen to lead us through a *wilderness* or *silent* time. Though we may not sense God's presence during this time, by faith we must affirm within our heart (not our feelings) that he is still with us (he promised never to leave us) and is actively working on our behalf.

- While sin can cause this apparent distance between us and the awareness of God's Spirit, if this is not the case, then we need to still continue with the disciplines to maintain a vibrant relationship with God.

- Another possible explanation is that this is a time of the testing of our faith. God is preparing us for that which he has for us in the future. This time can be a time God is teaching us to walk by faith and not physical senses or even spiritual feelings. It is during these wilderness times that we can learn spiritual truths that we can learn no where else.

Memorial Stones

- During these wilderness times it is often helpful to reflect and meditate on what God has already done in our lives and how he has helped us in the past.

- In Joshua 3 - 4 we see the Israelites taking twelve stones from the Jordan River as a reminder of God's faithfulness in bringing them through the Jordan on dry ground. For generations to come they were able to walk by that pile of stones and reminisce about God's faithfulness and goodness.

- Similarly in our lives, we too need to reflect upon those stones of remembrance which point to God's faithfulness in our lives. These are reminders of how God has helped us in the past, but they also can help to provide faith for the future.

- During times of major decision it is a helpful exercise to reflect back on these key times – back to events for which we have had the benefit of time to see the faithfulness of how God led us.

The Life of Faith

- Foundational to the life of faith and being led of God is the need of a personal encounter with God and maintaining a personal relationship with him.

- Being led of God does not always mean there is no risk in taking the next step – actually quite the opposite is true. At greatest risk is not our peace or joy, but our own comfort, personal desires, and expectations.

- Even at those times when we may be somewhat confident that we know the direction God wants us to take, there is usually still enough faith required, until we see the answer. During those times we need to rely on what we sense God has said to us more than our natural sense or sight.

- The Christian walk is based on faith not sight (2 Cor. 5:7), for without this unreserved trust in God, and who he is, it is impossible to please him (Heb 11:6). Stepping out will always require faith on our part, a faith that believes that we are accurately responding to God's leading and direction.

- As we continue with the last half of the program, may we have the faith to trust God to change us into his image, so that God may be able to touch many through our lives.

SUMMARY

- In this section we discussed the spiritual disciplines necessary to maintain a personal relationship with the Father. We have also discussed several pitfalls which can sidetrack us in our pursuit of fulfilling God's purposes in our lives. Practical steps have been offered to help the disciple be all that they can be in Christ.

Reflect on a recent circumstance in your life that you still do not understand or that you struggled with. Through scripture and prayer allow the Holy Spirit to reveal God's character in these situations and show you God's perspective. Share this with your mentor.

Reflect on some of the "memorial stones" that you have in your life. How have these built your faith and how can God use these to guide you in the future?

Discuss with your mentor your understanding of God's leading and what you have learned in this session. What changes in your thinking and understanding do you think you have to make?
How will God's truth regarding how he wants to lead you affect your future decision making process?

- Finally, in this chapter, we have looked at some principles of being led of God and how he desires to lead us and how important this is if we are going to reach our full potential and effectiveness.

- With this chapter we have reached the halfway point of our mentoring journey. Thus far it has been a journey of self-discovery as well as self-development. We have seen who God has made us and the requirements necessary to be his disciple.

- This has been a foundation upon which the last six chapters will now build. In the next section we will discuss issues of leadership and how God wants us to influence others. Then in the final section, we will conclude with looking at God's Mission on this earth and his desire to partner with us to see this accomplished.

Leader

Chapter

3.1

Mentoring

thru

Intentional Relationships

Your Foundation: Servant Leadership

INTRODUCTION

- In the last two sections we have looked at aspects of who we are as a *Person* and as a *Disciple*. In Section 1.0, we discovered our personal mix of personality, spiritual gifts and calling and then in Section 2.0, the need to develop spiritual disciplines in order to reach our full potential.

- In this section we are going to focus our attention on being a *Leader*.

- We are going to discover that leadership is not a position or title, but that at its core it is the *ability to influence others* – something we all do to some degree. This definition is assumed in this chapter, but will be discussed in greater detail in Chapters 3.2 and 3.3.

- While we all influence others, these chapters will help us do this in a more intentional manner. We will discover the biblical pattern for leadership, as well as acquire attributes necessary to move others towards Kingdom priorities and values.

THE FOUNDATION OF SERVANTHOOD

Substance not Style

- As we have discussed already, each of us have a particular personality style from which we most comfortably operate. We also have looked at the gifts that God has given to us in order to serve others.

- So when we speak of servant leadership we are not talking about style or even gifting – it is more fundamental than this. At a foundational level we are all called to exemplify servant leadership, regardless of our personality style, gifts, or calling.

- Servant leadership is also more fundamental than the experiences we have gleaned from our education or our job. Actually, the degree to which these experiences have been contrary to a biblical model of leadership, is the degree to which we may need a paradigm shift in our thinking. Our values, priorities and perspectives may need to change in order to pattern our leadership after Jesus' teaching and example.

- Just putting the word "Christian" on an existing leadership pattern, or bringing it into the church does not necessarily mean it conforms to a biblical model of servant-leaders. Unfortunately, *Christian* leadership often does not vary much from worldly forms.

- The potential for leaders to cause harm is even greater within a Christian context for, in their attempt to seem more *spiritual,* leaders can try covering their our own ego and insecurities with spiritual forms and language.

Leading by Power

- Our values, assumptions and principles of leadership can indicate if we are leading from a *power* or *servant* perspective.

What is your current leadership philosophy? Have you developed this intentionally or unintentionally?

Is being a servant-leader compatible with other leadership models? Explain.

What characteristics do you see in your life and ministry that reflect you are leading by power and not servanthood?

- The key question in determining our basis for leadership (power or servanthood) is, *"Are we helping to equip and release others to fulfill their God-given purpose in this world, or does our leadership inhibit them from moving forward?"*

- Leading from power or position is based upon power, authority, and control. Often this leads to a focus on *doing,* or activity, rather than *being.* The tendency with this pattern of leadership is to use *service* or *activity* as an indicator of *spirituality.* This leads to a competitive spirit, and service out of duty rather than love.

- Production or producing becomes the bottom line. While Scripture does emphasize the importance of fruit in the believer's life, we must be careful to accurately define success and not reduce everything into *bottom line* terms. The apparent success of "bigger and better" is not always the measure of Kingdom success.

- Similar to the idea of success being defined only in terms of the *bottom line*, is the tendency to see everything from a totally pragmatic point of view. It is dangerous to reduce all decisions to the criterion of "whatever works must be right." We must be prepared to take the longer term, biblical view of success.

- While progress and "accomplishing for the Kingdom" is obviously not wrong, as a leader, our motives must be more than just based upon "the end justifying the means." In reality, this concept can be quite dangerous when applied to spiritual matters.

- Perhaps the clearest indicator of positional leadership is the desire to control and even manipulate others. Within Christian settings this is most dangerous, for the reasons for control can seem quite noble: World Evangelization, Discipleship, etc. However, achieving these legitimate goals through the means of control and manipulation is a dangerous combination, particularly since people may even be willing to be manipulated and controlled, due to their own insecurities and wrong understanding of true leadership.

Do you see areas in which you manipulate others with whom you have influence?
Are you willing to change these patterns of control?

- Yet the ultimate fruit in peoples' lives is not righteousness, but disillusionment and bitterness. Very often the root of this bitterness, can be traced back to leadership that was wrongly motivated.

- Disillusionment occurs in people as leaders have the belief that they alone *speak for God* and that the people are just there to support *their* vision.

- This, of course, is reminiscent of the practices of the Medieval Church, with its authoritarian structure where only a few elite could speak for God. These "leaders" ignored the possibility that they could be wrong and were not open to correction from anyone, let alone the laity.

- This will be further discussed for, while more subtle today, these forms of control and dominance are still evident in Christian circles and need to be addressed.

- In Chapter 2.3, we briefly discussed the temptation of power. For the leader this is perhaps one of the greatest pitfalls that limits ultimate growth for the Kingdom.

- The subtlety of those who succumb to this temptation is that they may not always recognize that this has become their motivation. However, it becomes evident in that they increasingly need to be the focus of the ministry and begin to enjoy being the center of attention.

- The evidence in their ministry is usually their inability to develop others with a resulting high turnover as people leave their ministry, after being hurt and abused. Given the choice, no healthy person desires to be manipulated, irregardless how noble the vision.

- This power-based leadership style is based upon control, position and title.

Leading by Serving

- In sharp contrast to leadership based upon position and power, is leadership which is based upon a foundation of servanthood. While most would agree that the Christian leader needs to serve out of humility, the day to day reality of this is often a challenge to apply.

- Being a servant-leader is contrary to the tendency of our *natural* man. It goes against our desire to be seen and recognized. In the natural, we see humility as the first step towards being taken advantage of and this fear stifles the freedom of being able to serve others.

- Servant leadership flows from a security in our own identity, knowing and accepting who we are in Christ. This is why it is so important to know who we are and how God has uniquely gifted and called us (Section 1.0), for only then will we be able to serve others without trying to be something we are not; only then will we have an accurate estimation of ourselves.

- Yet this proper self-perspective can only be attained through an accurate perspective of God. He is the one that has called and commissioned us and so we do not have to strive to be something that he has not intended us to be.

- Our motive can then be a pure one, to serve God first and not a position or role. Next, we can serve others selflessly, instead of using them to reach *our* goals and *our* visions.

- Servant leadership focusses on equipping and developing believers to be all that they can be according to their unique gifting and calling. This frees people to be who God made them and develop into the areas of service that he has for them.

- It is not just goal-orientated or just focussed on the *bottom line*. Its focus is on the needs of others and God's direction as to how to best meet those needs. As others are developed in ministry, they then need the freedom to explore and grow in various expressions of ministry (Chapter 1.2), having the opportunity to first express their gift in perhaps smaller, "safer" settings than in a large, public setting. By providing this opportunity, we can help others grow *into* their gifts.

- Having the freedom to be able to grow in ministry is also applicable to the personal life of the servant-leader. A servant-leader who is secure has the freedom to step into those new areas that God would have for him. The leader is then free to take risks as God directs, instead of only being concerned about needing to achieve the appearance of success.

- The servant-leader's source of influence is based upon his life-message (Chapter 1.3), living an open and vulnerable life that is an open book for all to read (2 Cor. 3:2). This authentic style of life is virtually impossible for those whose focus is merely power or position.

Biblical Foundation

- Though the actual word "leadership" not used much in scripture, we can trace godly leadership values and principles throughout the Bible.

- The most profound example, is that of Jesus' life and ministry. In Mark 10:43-44, Jesus seems to affirm that to be great in the Kingdom is a valid and desirable goal, yet it was Jesus' definition of *greatness in the Kingdom* that was so revolutionary. To be really *great*, meant to be the servant of others, just as he came to serve. Though the very Son of God, he most often described himself as the Son of Man, a servant of others.

- The clearest example of this was when Jesus took a towel and washed his disciple's feet (John 13:1-17). "Jesus knew that the Father had put all things under his power....so he got up from the meal ....and began to wash his disciples'

What is the fruit of those who you are influencing? Are they being released or stifled?

Is your leadership characterized by servanthood as described in this chapter? If not what changes need to be made?
Discuss this with your mentor.

feet." He then teaches his disciples that this was to be an example for their ministries. The central characteristic of someone who is great in the Kingdom is to serve from a heart of humility (Matt. 23:11,12).

- The real power comes from God, not our title, position or strength of personality (Matt. 23:9-10). Very early in the first century church, the apostles had to deal with this issue as some tried to elevate them about others (ie. "I am of Paul, I am of Apollos" 1 Cor.1:12). However, in the New Testament paradigm, ministries built upon personalities or position do not exemplify Kingdom values. It is God who raises up those of influence and we must learn to exercise this in humility.

- Even the greatest apostle of all time, Paul, did not see position or authority something to misused. He did not lord his authority over others, but desired their best (2 Cor. 1:24). Peter, another key figure in the early church, confirms this same attitude, "not lording it over those entrusted to you, but being examples to the flock." (1 Pet. 5:3).

- Leadership in the Kingdom is to be relational and not hierarchical or organizational. As depicted by the disciples, power struggles at their very root destroy relationships, though it is to be these very relationships that bind us together in the Body.

- Yet, while there is an equality in the Kingdom, every believer has unique roles and contributions (see Section 1.0). Throughout the Pauline Epistles we see this principle of *unity yet diversity*, in the Body. The very use of the human body as an analogy indicates the nature of the Body of Christ as an organism, rather than an organizational structure.

- Further, building our own kingdom actually hinders the advancement of the Kingdom of God, for as spiritual leaders we are to point others to God's Kingdom not our own.

- The focus of our message and of our method must be Christ. As leaders we are mere bond-servants (2 Cor. 4:5). This picture does not elevate the leaders above others, but reverses the typical pyramid structure of leadership. We even see a plurality of accountable leadership under the headship of Christ, each having a different function, yet an equality of value.

The New Covenant Paradigm

- As we observed in our discussion concerning being *Led of God* (Chapter 2.3), Christ's life, death and resurrection had a profound impact as a new paradigm was inaugurated where the Holy Spirit is accessible for every believer.

- In the Old Testament, we read of God's Spirit coming upon particular individuals (ie. the prophets and kings) and how they were the link between God and the people. We see men such as Moses, Joshua, and David who spoke for God during Israel's theocratic period.

- However, after the day of Pentecost, and the dawn of the Church Age, the Holy Spirit abides in every believer and all believers have equal access to God.

- The term "church" (*ecclesia* or "called out ones") referred to the early group of believers, those who had acknowledged Jesus as their Lord and Saviour. This new movement was not a new *organization,* but a vibrant growing *organism.* The disciples, as key leaders of this new church, were ordinary people who were not to be elevated above others. We see this throughout the New Testament, as the early Christians looked to Christ as their model for leadership, rather than an Old Testament, patriarchal model.

- Unfortunately, throughout subsequent church history the term "church" came to mean an *organization* or *institution*, rather than the *people of God.*

Study and meditate on Jesus' ministry and particular his role as servant. Discuss your new insights with your mentor.

God's People

- This new concept of the *people of God* was a radical one. But without fully appreciating its implications, it is impossible to understand and live the principles of a servant-leader.

- We are bound together in the Body of Christ by relationship (Jn 13:35, Jn 17:23), not hierarchical structures. While this does not mean that there are not those that God has called to positions of leadership, this *leadership* is completely different than any models we see in secular circles.

- There is a completely new basis for these relationships one with another, including those who have the gift and function of leading.

- Unlike the pattern of the religious leaders of the day, Jesus warns those who would lead in this new Kingdom that he was establishing, to not take on special titles (Matthew 23:8). They were to show by their words and actions that they have only one Master and that in the Body all are equal brothers and sisters.

- The family illustration is continued in John 15:15. The relationships in God's Kingdom are to be those of a spiritual family. Members of the Body of Christ were not to be employees, rather they were to be co-laborers, working together in unity, though with a diversity of function.

- As we discovered in Chapter 2.3, under the New Covenant the Holy Spirit came to be our primary guide, there is no longer the need for individuals or groups to function as mediators; each believer has both the privilege and obligation to be led of God.

- This eliminates the need for an elite model of leadership as was more common in the Old Testament. God has called and equipped every member of the Body for a purpose and function within the Body.

- Christ as the *Head of the Church* desires to lead and direct every member. The role of the servant-leader is to help develop and equip others to fulfill the role that God has for them; they are to help others reach their full potential.

- This, of course, is impossible to accomplish if the leader continually must reinforce images of power and position over those he has been called to serve. Instead of the use of intimidation and manipulation, however, servant-leaders can lead others through mutual respect.

- With this attitude and perspective, the power of the Holy Spirit can be released through God's people, as was clearly evident in the early church.

STRUCTURES THAT FACILITATE SERVANTHOOD

Form and Function

- In order to better understand the implications of servant leadership it is helpful to understand a few key principles regarding structures.

- In terms of form and function, function refers to the substance or internal reality and truth, while the form is that which helps to facilitate this function.

- This principle can be illustrated through the analogy of the old and new wineskins of Matthew 9:17. New wine is not put into old wineskins, for as the new wine expands it will burst the aged, hardened wineskins. This can also be a good analogy of the need for form and function to correspond.

- The message of the Gospel is always relevant and never changing (new wine), but often the forms to express it can become old and not as effective. The challenge is to keep our forms relevant so that they may be usable vessels for the new wine of the gospel, which is always current.

How does the concept of the priesthood of all believers apply to the Church as an organism rather than an organization?
What direct application is there for your leadership?

How has the concept of a "professional" clergy limited the mission of the Church?

- Forms, in and of themselves, are not wrong. All aspects of Christian life and spirituality have need for some forms within the human experience. For example, forms have developed to facilitate worship, though, over time, they have varied in different churches and cultures. At one time Martin Luther's hymn, "A Mighty Fortress Is Our God" was considered too unruly to be sung in church.

- While the need for forms never ceases, over time we often need to change our forms in order to maintain their relevancy as vessels for the function the are intended for. The issue of headcoverings and meat offered to idols are examples from the First Century, while other issues such as worship styles, church governance, proper attire for preaching (to name just a few), may be more common today.

- The danger is that the form itself can become even more important than the function for which it is a *vessel*. Because it is so easy to confuse form and function, congregations have even divided over issues relating to *form*, not *substance*.

- All ministry functions within certain forms and thus it is important that we understand the difference between form and function and evaluate if our current forms, or structures, are enabling us or hindering us in our goal of being vessels of the new wine.

- While it may seem that forms are neutral or *mere* vessels (as in the analogy of the wineskins), they have the potential to either conserve or waste the new wine. Forms either inhibit or enhance function. The common phrase, "We have always done it this way!" has stifled many a fresh, innovative idea. Yet instead of fostering stagnation and hindering growth, the right forms can actually cause healthy growth to take place.

- Though forms are not neutral in their affect and are necessary, it is also important to remember that they are not inherently spiritual in and of themselves. They are not able to bring about real change on their own. The real power for changes is the substance of the function (new wine), not the structure itself (the wineskins).

- Structures are tools that can help or hinder ministry. Spiritual life itself does not come from the structure, it can only be enhanced or hindered by it. This explains why ministries that were once effective can lose their impact, for in time their forms or structures are no longer aligned with their function.

Leadership Structures

- If our ministries have structures that, by their very nature, are based on power and position this will negatively affect the fruit of the ministry. Instead of releasing people, they will seek to control. This has particular application in the mentoring process (see Introductory chapter).

- In power-structures, the leader is the one that "hears" from God and becomes the focus; demands are then usually made upon the people to fulfill the leader's vision. Instead of God being served and people blessed, people end up serving the leadership and even worse, the structure itself. The form takes on more importance than even the function and eventually questioning leadership can become seen as questioning God.

- The biblical teaching of the *priesthood of all believers*, where each member hears and responds to the Lord, is a protection from this stifling structure. Ministry that relies on power structures tends to emphasize roles and position over gifting and calling; its focus is controlling and limiting not equipping and developing.

- The leader's understanding of the nature of the Body and the role of the members of that Body will determine (intentionally or unintentionally) which

How does the relational model of Church structure, as opposed to a hierarchical one, affect the style of leadership? What part of this concept do you struggle with?

structure a leader emphasizes or patterns his leadership after. If a local body is a pyramid-structured organization, with the leader at the top and others beneath him, then it may seem permissible for leaders to control others and use them to accomplish their tasks. However, if the members of the Body are seen as fellow members (ie. *priests unto God*), then the attitude of the leaders will be more one of equipping others to reach their full potential in Christ.

- Structures can be a positive influence as they serve the Body, rather than something that we must serve. With a structure that encourages servanthood, the leaders and people learn to discern the mind and will of God together. They can then adapt the structure so that it better facilitates the work of the ministry. This results in the continual adapting of the structures, instead of people having to continually change to fit structures that has become outdated and ineffective.

- As leaders, our challenge is to create an environment where God's people are equipped to do *works of service*. Our forms and structure should not become more important than the function which they are there to serve.

- Appropriate structures are required in order for others to be released to minister. Structures that have a relational focus and an emphasis on the leading of the Holy Spirit from a team approach (ie. "and it seemed good to us and the Holy Spirit"), will best foster an environment that builds up the whole Body of Christ. Flexible structures facilitate the equipping of other servant-leaders.

The Solidification of Structures

- Left to their own, however, structures become hard and unmoving (as in the wineskin analogy). Over time, a form that may once have effectively facilitated function, can outlive its usefulness. This is due to the changing needs, cultural and societal realities, as well as many other possible factors. Throughout history this process has been occurring and is still evident in the Church today.

- This *hardness of the wineskin* is usually a gradual process. The initial fresh wind of new ideas and goals is accompanied by simple faith and obedience. As these simple efforts produce fruit, our human tendency to build an organization and structure around this new life (which in and of itself is often necessary). Yet what often then occurs, is that the structure itself must be served (cleaned, maintained, oiled and watered) and people rely more and more on the "professionals." The final result is often the decline of individual spiritual freedom and ongoing innovation.

- As the emphasis on the *priesthood of all believers* further declines, more and more power and authority becomes vested in the leader's position. There can then become a greater distinction between laity and clergy and eventually the people of God are content to watch vocational ministers (or *professionals*) do the work of the ministry.

- Finally, assets, property, and traditions need to be protected and all that remains is the structure, with little of the new wine, which has usually by this stage sought out new wineskins. At this stage, the reversal of the solidification process is virtually impossible to reverse within the same structure. The wineskin has been neglected for too long and cannot be brought back to a point of flexibility.

- Understanding the need to keep our structures fresh and flexible can assist us in ensuring that this process is not inevitable within our sphere of influence. Creating structures that empower and divest power should be the goal of the servant-leader.

Are you releasing and equipping others that you have influence with or is your leadership more characterized by a pyramid-structure?

Do you think forms can remain flexible, or is it inevitable that they become inflexible? Discuss the ramifications for leadership.

What steps can you take in your current sphere of influence in order to maintain forms that are flexible?

PEOPLE NOT POSITION

Gifts and Calling

- Soon after the First Century, a "professional" clergy developed, motivated in part by a desire to keep the faith pure.

- There was the subsequent development of two classes of believers, where those who had certain gifts were given prominence and those with less noticeable gifts were sidelined.

- This development of a vocational clergy became a stifling structure in which gifts were not encouraged and developed and even the very concept of "calling" became misunderstood.

- Yet the biblical perspective is that each believer has been given gifts to be used for the furtherance of the Kingdom (discussed more thoroughly in Chapter 1.2 and 1.3).

- Returning to our definition of leadership as, *someone having influence* (rather than a position or title), it is then the gifts that each believer has that gives them the sphere of their influence.

- In this regard, every believer has a sphere of influence (a leadership role) which is made possible through the gifts that God has given them to use for the benefit of the whole Body. Likewise, each believer is also a *follower,* as they defer and receive from the gifts of others.

- It is important to remember that service, or ministry, is not primarily a task , but is an act of worship towards God (Rom. 12). This is why all believers have the same value, regardless of our function, for it is the Head of the Body who has given us our gifts and it is to him that we are faithful.

Gifts and Spheres of Ministry

- While it is true that our gifts make room for us, we usually need a *sphere of ministry* in which to express these gifts.

- For each gift there are multiple services possible and varied results (1 Cor. 12:4-6). These *different workings* can refer to the varying *degree*, or *sphere*, of ministry (ie. some minister to tens others to tens of thousands). While it may be the same gift, there are varying expressions of that gift.

- God has assigned a field (sphere of influence) to us and it is here that we will be most effective (2 Cor. 10:13). For example, the gift of teaching may be within a small group, a large group, or mass media. Also, different teachers may use different methods directed towards different audiences, yet it is the same gift of teaching. Maturity is not only understanding our gift, but learning to be content with the sphere of influence that God has prepared for us to use that gift.

- Gifts and spheres of ministry are given by God and recognizing them can help us stay focussed and not become covetous of others, or feeling condemnation thinking that we should be doing tasks that God has not called us to accomplish.

- As discussed in Chapter 1.2, the gifts of Ephesians 4:11 could be described as specific *spheres of ministry*. Over the centuries, these gifts in Ephesians have been seen as referring to official "offices" (or positions) in the church. Throughout Church history various of these gifts have been emphasized over others. Yet regardless if they are seen as official positions or not, they are given as gifts to the whole Body for the purpose of building up the whole Body.

- Each of these gifts listed in Ephesians – apostle, prophet, evangelist, pastor, teacher (or pastor/teacher) – have a different role or sphere of ministry within the Body, yet they need to operate in balance in order for the Body to be built up and

Take steps to develop your area of gifting and ministry and seek ways to express this in the local body of which you are a part.

Reflect on your particular spiritual gifts and sphere of ministry.
Are you frustrated or finding fulfilment at this time in your life?

released to do those *works of service* that God has purposed for it.

- The danger is if these gifts are only seen within the context of *professional* or vocational positions in the Body. Another danger is if the rest of the Body sees those with these gifts as having the exclusive right to *do the ministry,* instead of having the role to equip everyone in the Body to do the work of the ministry.

- While these equipping gifts may tend to lead to a vocational position, this may not necessarily be the case. For even if a person has one or more of the equipping gifts, they are to have the attitude of a servant-leader and use their gift to serve the whole Body.

Servant-Leadership

- Servant-leaders free people to be all that God has called them to be, rather than put expectations on them which they cannot bear. A leader (an *influencer of others*) helps others find this right fit for them in the Body. This requires structures and forms that are freeing, not stifling or condemning.

- Servant-leaders help each member find how they can best make their contribution – *preparing God's people for works of service.* They need to equally value all the gifts and their place in the Body.

- Servant-leaders are willing to be used by God to raise up others who will have even greater influence and greater spheres of ministry. Instead of stifling this, they will encourage it by developing forms that will be vessels for the *new wine* God produces.

- Servant-leaders realize that they are not on the top of an organizational pyramid, but see themselves as partners together with all the members of the organism of the Body of Christ.

Do you have a plan to equip and develop others in your ministry?
Can you think of others who are doing a good job of equipping and releasing God's people for ministry? What can you learn from them?

Challenges of Servant Leadership

- Paul's example in 1 Corinthian 1:26 - 2:6, highlights the challenge to live with a servant attitude, even though our natural tendency is to have greater power and take control. We must resist the temptation of our sinful nature and through the indwelling power of the Holy Spirit follow Christ's example (this is not to negate the natural tendency of the *High D* personality style, though their tendency must be under God's control, see Chapter 1.1 regarding this topic).

- We must resist allowing our ministry or gifting to become synonymous with who we are as a person. To be balanced, we must make a distinction between *our ministry* and who we are as a child of God.

- We must also resist the temptation to have our ministry develop into an organization that must be served, instead of our organizational structures serving our ministry purposes. This can only occur as we are willing to allow the Holy Spirit to keep our wineskins pliable.

What are your particular challenges in living as a servant-leader? What steps can you take to align your leadership with the biblical pattern.

- We must finally resist the temptation that comes from others who, due to their weakness or false understanding, want to be led by a human personality that will satisfy their ego (ie. "We want a king!"). As servant leaders we must not allow others to force us into the mold to become the type of leader who will think and choose for them. Our focus must be to help them grow into maturity.

- The reality is that while we are maturing, at times our leadership may be motivated by more of a power structure and at other times a servant model. Our goal is not perfection, but moving towards the high calling of consistently influencing others as servant-leaders. This is a growth process which requires regular doses of grace, by God, others, as well as ourselves.

Discuss with your mentor steps you want to take in order to become a better servant-leader?

How would the current structures around you have to change in order to facilitate this?

SUMMARY

- In this chapter we have laid the foundation for our future discussion regarding leadership. This foundation is that leaders are to follow the example of Christ in his role as a servant-leader.

- We have defined leadership as those who have influence and have established that we all have some measure of influence by virtue of our gifting. We all have areas in which we are leaders and therefore can apply these lessons on being a servant-leader.

- As we continue in this section on leadership, we will look deeper into the attributes of leadership and how we can be used by God to develop others to be leaders in his Kingdom. Yet as we continue on this journey, we must never forget that leadership is about serving.

Leader

Mentoring
thru
Intentional Relationships

Chapter
3.2

Your Development: Growing as a Leader

INTRODUCTION

- We have discovered that the servant-leader paradigm is the foundation of Christian leadership.

- Yet *serving* is the not opposite of *leading*, rather it is the *way* in which we are to lead. Instead of from position or power, we can help others reach God's purposes by serving them.

- In this chapter we want to consider some of the implications of this for the servant-leader. We will discuss some of the attitudes and disciplines that a leader must develop and some of the potential pitfalls that must be avoided.

DEFINING LEADERSHIP

Having Influence

- In order to maintain a proper perspective and not redefine leadership from a worldly point of view, we need to keep in focus that the Christian leader is to be a servant-leader.

- "Everything rises and falls on leadership," is how John Maxwell states the importance of leadership. Yet while there are many definitions of leadership, each with their own emphasis, leadership could perhaps best be described as *someone who has influence* (a concept used widely by others, but generally attributed to John Maxwell).

- We all are influenced by others, as well as influence others to varying degrees (which can be a positive or negative influence). This level of influence is affected by our maturity, gifts and our sphere of ministry (or role), among other issues.

- As we saw in the last chapter, leadership is not so much about having a title or position, but has to do with serving others. Power leadership seeks to do this by coercion, while servant leadership through example and service.

- The old proverb: "He who thinks he is leading and has no one following, is only taking a walk," illustrates both the need for leadership and the foundational definition: Without positively influencing others, we are only fulfilling a position.

What do you think of the definition of leadership as the ability to influence? Discuss your perspective.

Born or Developed?

- Many have assumed that leadership is something that you either have or do not have, something some are born with and others are not.

- While it is true that some people, by the virtue of their strength of personality, gifts or role in life, seem to more naturally be "leaders," this often is due to a faulty definition which believes that leadership is only based upon position or power.

- Using servant leadership as a model, it is clear that while the "born" or "natural" leader may emerge early to places of influence, to remain effective in leadership certain characteristics must be developed in our lives over the long term.

Do you think leaders are born or made? Explain.

- It is possible for each person to grow in their influence – in their leadership – if they so desire. As we noted last chapter, however, this does not mean that all will reach the same level of influence, for God has callings and purposes for each of us. Our responsibility is to serve where he has called and placed us and not strive in the flesh for *spheres* or *levels* of influence.

- So while it may seem that some people are *natural* leaders, very often the truth is that they have made the effort to learn and acquire skills and attitudes that have helped them gain influence. Those who start with advantage and position, as well as those who do not, can become true leaders (*influencers*) as they make the effort to grow in their ability to serve others.

- Some people are born with some leadership qualities and then build upon this through good models of leadership and additional leadership training. On the other hand, others have few of these natural gifts or the opportunity to grow in their leadership abilities, yet have the desire and self-discipline to become a leader. In either of these cases, it is never to late to learn and grow in the attributes needed to become an influencer of others. While natural ability and opportunity may determine the beginning point of our leadership journey, it need not determine our ultimate destination.

- So wherever we currently find ourselves in terms of leadership, with modelling, training and personal self-discipline we can increase our present level of influence.

Levels of Influence

- Regardless of their position, it is obvious that not everyone has the same level of influence. The level of our influence also varies within our different relational contacts. Yet the degree of our influence is never static or unchanging, it always has the potential to increase and decrease.

- Maxwell outlines various levels of influence and how that influence is obtained. He sees the first and lowest level of influence being that of position or rights. In this case, people follow the leader according to obligation, however, in this case there is not much loyalty or relationship.

- A higher level of influence, is influence that is obtained through relationships. This occurs as people begin to follow a leader because they have an affinity for and like the leader as a person.

- This leads to the next level of influence where people begin to follow a leader because of what they have been able to do for the organization. Those in the organization see the benefits to the organization through the leader and this motivates them to be open to his influence.

- A further stage is as a leader begins to help others grow personally. This reproductive stage is powerful for people begin to follow because of how they have personally been helped. Maxwell sees respect as the highest level of influence and occurs as people follow because of what the leader represents; they have earned the right to influence through their very personhood.

- To progress to higher levels of influence requires time and greater amounts of commitment. It also requires more growth on behalf of the leader. As a leader progresses to greater levels of influence he must be careful not to neglect the foundational levels for they also remain important.

- Finally, it is important to realize that we will not relate to everyone the same or have the same level of influence with everyone in our life or organization/ministry. A leader must understand this and, though having reached a certain level of influence in one arena, not assume that the same is true in a new or different setting.

What level of influence do you have in your ministry, job or organization? Evaluate how this differs with the various people that you are in relationship with.

Which of these stages describes you?

Spiritual Leadership

- Leadership, or being a person of influence, implies movement or direction – taking people from where they are to what they can become. Blackaby describes spiritual leadership as moving people on to "God's agenda."

- It is having an understanding of where people are at, what God's heart is, and then how to help people move closer to his desires. The most effective means of doing this is through servant leadership, not power or manipulation.

- As mentioned in the last chapter, this requires being led by the Holy Spirit and having the right attitude towards others, valuing them as joint members of the Body of Christ.

- In this regard, our definition of leadership goes beyond that of just a good manager. While good leadership eventually requires good management, these are not one in the same. Management could be described as the process of ensuring that programs and objectives are implemented, while leadership has to do with the casting of vision and motivating people. The need today is for better leaders and not just better managers, for most people want to be led and not just managed.

PREPARATION OF THE LEADER

Development Necessary

- If leadership and influence is something that can be developed, and not just a skill or attribute we are born with, then to grow as a leader we must first grow as a person. Maxwell states, "When we are foolish, we want to conquer the world. When we are wise, we want to conquer ourselves."

- Those who positively influence others over long periods of time have taken the time to prepare themselves spiritually and mentally. Though we may not see it, their influence has not been by chance. While we can be *given* a position, we must *earn* influence. And to do this we must continue to grow.

- The spiritual disciplines already discussed in Chapter 2.1 are foundational for the preparation of the leader. To lead others the leader must first be under God's guidance. A further key in the development for the person who wants to lead with authenticity and openness is allowing God to take their own experiences and use them for the Kingdom.

- These experiences form the *life message* (see Chapter 1.3) of a leader and give us the context from which to influence others. In order for these life experience to benefit others, we need to understand and deal with our particular issues (and we all have issues), such as our home life, crises, struggles, failures and hardships. Prayerfully reflecting upon what God has taught us and how he has shaped us through the unique experiences we have gone through is essential in God using these for his glory. Doing a *TimeLine* (Chapter 1.3) will help in this process.

- As we grow in our level of influence, we develop through stages of maturity. Robert Clinton outlines the various stages of a leader's growth and development beginning with our dealing with the realities of our family upbringing, with a focus on our inner character growth and development.

- The next growth stages occurs during our early ministry and then move towards a greater maturity as God begins to work *through* us and not just *in* us. As we mature, ministry and life experience begin to combine to produce maximum effectiveness as we see others beginning to build upon our efforts.

- This requires a commitment by the leader to continue growing and changing. As discussed in Chapter 2.1, life-long learning is a prerequisite for all believers, and

What steps have you taken to develop yourself? Reflecting back over the last two sections in the manual, which areas have you grown the least in? The most in?

What steps have you taken to become a life-long learner?

this is particularly relevant for those who would influence others, for as we have seen, the first means of influence is by example.

- To become a mature leader requires disciplined on-going learning, both formally and informally. As those in other professions must continue to read and grow, so must the Christian leader if he desires to be an influence in the Kingdom.

- Billy Graham is undoubtedly one of the greatest spiritual leaders of the last century. But when asked what he would do differently if he could start over, even he said, "For one thing I would speak less and study more."

LEADERSHIP QUALITIES

- It is a sad fact that most leaders who fail, fail due to inner issues, not external issues.

- The first requirement of leadership then is to be able to lead oneself; a leader's first responsibility is for their own personal discipline and growth. We as leaders must learn to master ourselves.

- Perhaps the greatest leader of the early church, Paul outlines for his mentoree the necessary qualities of a spiritual leader (1 Timothy 3:2-7). At the top of his list was, being above reproach, morally pure, and of sound judgement. Oswald Sanders (*Spiritual Leadership*, 1967), a spiritual leader of the last century, includes further qualities such as, a sense of humour, patience, friendship, tact, power to inspire, some administrative ability, a listener, and able to do correspondence.

- With this overview, we will discuss in greater detail only a few of the key attributes that someone of influence must develop in order to reach their full potential.

Purity of Life

Review some of the decisions you have made or need to make in light of some of the Scriptural principles outlined here.

- To live a life above reproach is a prerequisite to be an effective leader. Being extremely talented and gifted will not compensate for moral deficits of a leader. Being above reproach, was central to Daniel's life (Dan 1:8) in the Old Testament, as well as for Timothy (and others) in the New Testament (2 Tim. 2:19-21). This was discussed in some detail in Chapter 2.1, as we looked at some of the potential pitfalls for the leader.

- Purity of life is dependent upon choices, yet not all decisions are a clear choice between right and wrong. Being able to determine between difficult moral issues requires maturity and integrity.

- Yet how do we make decisions when the outcome is not known and the issue is not a clear moral, right and wrong one? While there are no easy answers, the Scriptures outline several principles in helping to determine if an activity is right or wrong; beneficial or detrimental.

- In 1 Corinthians 6:12 we see that, while everything may be *permissible*, the real question is if it is *beneficial*. In making the right choice, when the matter is not a clear moral one, we must ask ourselves if the activity in question is *beneficial*, not just if it is *permissible*.

- Additionally, though it may be permissible, is it something that has the potential to addict or become a taskmaster (1 Cor. 6:12). We must ask themselves if the activity could potentially gain mastering in our life.

- A leader must also determine if the activity in question will cause a weaker person to stumble in their faith. Though we may have the freedom to engage in an activity, do we love others enough to refrain from the activity, in order to avoid even the appearance of evil (1 Cor. 8:12-13).

- A final principle is to determine if the activity in question will ultimately glorify God. While it may be difficult to determine this about the most mundane activity, at the very least the activity should not in any way bring disgrace to God or his purposes (1 Cor 10:31).

Integrity

- Integrity is about who we are and not what we do. It is the beginning place of all our decisions and actions. It is the consistency of our inner motivations and thoughts with our actions and words. Integrity has to do with the leader being morally consistent, both publically and privately.

- Leaders lead by example and not just through words. Ultimately, leadership has more to do with *being* than *doing*.

- Integrity is developed during the developmental stages in our life, often in the anonymity of darkness when no one else is looking. But though it is developed in the shadows of anonymity, it is tested in the open, where the stakes are high.

- Externally, it may seem as if a leader has greater freedom to do as they want, but the reality is that a leader must have even higher standards than those they influence and this often limits their freedoms. As we increase in influence, our rights decrease and our responsibilities increase.

- While we no longer have the same freedoms as others, our responsibilities may increase. Leaders are often required to give up virtually every one of their rights (1 Cor. 4:9; 6:12; 8:12-13; 9:15-18), though few of their responsibilities.

- *Integrity* differs from *image* in that integrity remains the same regardless of who we are with. Image is more concerned that a decision will benefit us, and less concern as to how it will affect others. It is more likely to take credit, rather to recognize the contributions that others have made for our success.

- However, integrity results in greater influence, the trust of others, and a good reputation, not just an enhanced image. The foundation of servant leadership is integrity and not image.

Are you a person of integrity?
What steps do you need to take in order to better live a life of integrity.

Focus

- Having talent and abilities are not enough for a leader to reach their full potential. Even having spiritual gifts and calling alone do not ensure that a leader will complete life's race with integrity. It is our discipline to remain focussed and on target that will determining our effectiveness.

- Being focussed goes beyond just not being lazy and inactive, the result of which is rather obvious. Being focussed, means that our efforts must be towards the right goal, as opposed to working hard towards *any* goal.

- Another common enemy of maintaining focus is for the leader to try and do just a little bit of everything. While this is a more common mistake during the developmental stages of our life and ministry, if the trend continues as we age, we will never fulfill the purposes that God has for us as leaders.

What is your focus as a leader?

Self-Discipline

- Self-discipline begins with spiritual disciples. Without a spiritual focus our discipline can become nothing more than legalism that does not produce life in our lives or others.

- As with other qualities, self-discipline is dependant upon the leader. By nature, some leaders are more disciplined than others, yet regardless of our natural tendencies, all who desire to be effective leaders must learn the art of mastering oneself.

- In addition to the mastering our personal life – spiritually, emotions and physically – as a leader we must also learn to establish priorities, manage our schedule, and evaluate our activities.

- Other practical helps would include, prioritizing our schedule, doing projects one at a time, as well as understanding our personality type and working according to our natural style (see Chapter 1.1).

- There are no universal systems that work for everybody, the leader must experiment and establish ways to organize their lives. If this is an area that you struggle with in your life, there are many good practical books that you will find helpful for time and personal management.

Would you characterize yourself as self-disciplined? Why or why not?

Accepting Responsibility

- While accepting responsibility would seem obvious enough to not need mentioning, the fact is that some leaders have as much struggle with accepting responsibility as those they lead. However, often due to their position or role, they can avoid their responsibility by passing it on to others.

- The effective servant leader is one who accepts responsibility for who they are and what they do. This includes accepting responsibility for what they have received as gifts and calling.

- With a proper perspective of others (as members of the Body) and a sober judgement of themselves, a servant-leader is also accountable to others. Accepting responsibility includes valuing others enough to have the integrity and humility to admit error and times of lapses in judgement.

- It has been said that successful people are willing to do what unsuccessful people will not do. Those who are effective, learn to be motivated by God's Spirit and strength of character and not their own emotions. Doing what we have to do, not what we like to do, is what causes growth and success in us and others.

LEADERSHIP AND VISION

Visionary or Vision

- Being a *visionary* is not the same as being a *person of vision*. A visionary has many dreams, but seldom can convert them into reality, while a person of vision, not only has the dreams, but knows how to make them a reality.

- To be effective, a leader must progress from being a *visionary* to becoming a *person of vision*. The source of vision for the spiritual leader is not self, but divine revelation. It is more than just a great idea, it must be God-inspired.

- This is crucial for a leader to learn to distinguish, for when our resources and strength come to an end we need to know that God was the source of the dream or vision.

Discuss the difference between being a visionary and a person of vision. Are your visions based on God's vision?

God's Vision

- Having a dream is fundamental to being a person of influence for it is what others look to us for ("Where there is no vision. . ." Prov. 29:18). Leaders who have not learned God's priorities by listening to him can wrongly motivate others to sacrifice and work for *their* vision, instead of for God's purposes.

- God has a plan and purpose and he has called us to join him in this mission (see Chapter 4.2). God's call is to those who will develop and equip others to fulfill his purposes. We must evaluate our vision according to God's will and direction (see Chapter 2.3) and learn to effectively communicate this to those whom we have influence (discussed more fully in Chapter 3.3).

- For others to buy into the vision and sacrifice for it, we must have integrity and a level of influence greater than can be achieved by mere position and power.

Wrong Vision

- Just as we discussed the need to differentiate between our voice and God's voice (Chapter 2.3), so must we be able to distinguish between God's vision and what is merely our dream or idea.

- Just because the challenge presents itself in the form of an *open door* does not necessarily mean that it is God's vision (Chapter 2.3). We must evaluate if it is only vanity and personal ambitions that is motivating our vision.

- While leaders are called to serve others, vision must also not be based solely on the perceived needs of others. It can be deceptive to determine goals and direction completely on market-driven criterion. The leader must be able to distinguish the real needs of those they serve.

- Not even the availability of resources can always be taken as a clear indication of direction. Having the resources does not necessarily mean we should take a course of action and *not* having enough resources does not necessarily mean that God is not in a particular course of action.

- As leaders our visions need to originate in God (Isa 55:8-9). Particularly as we grow in influence, care must be taken as to not abuse people's trust and lead them towards a wrong, or merely personal-driven, vision. As leaders we need to be careful as to what we ask others to sacrifice and work towards, for it is only worth expending the resources of the Body of Christ on divine purposes.

> Consider a time when you were led by a wrong vision. What did you learn through that experience?

LEADERSHIP AND PRIORITIES

Managing Priorities

- Learning to manage priorities is another one of the keys to effective leadership.

- The first step in ordering our priorities is spending time with God and understanding his purpose for our lives, for without clear purpose there are no criteria for determining our priorities.

- As discussed in Chapter 2.1, the leader must first prioritize his schedule so that there is time to practice the spiritual disciplines. Second to this, is time spent with family and maintaining margins in life, so that mental, emotional and physical health is fostered.

- Effective leaders do not allow life's demands and daily pressures to control their schedule or priorities, instead they take initiative to plan ahead so that they are not always just reacting to the urgent.

> Reevaluate the priorities you currently have in your life. Discuss these with your mentor.

Priority and Time

- Determining priorities usually has to do with issues of time. Prioritizing our time is perhaps the greatest challenge.

Evaluate ways in which you could better manage your time.

- Time wasters are many and varied. Idle conversations can waste large amounts of time (not referring here to meaningful conversations that build relationships), as can disorganization in both our data and our schedule. The leader must also guard against new forms of media (internet) and other technology which can steal much of our time, particularly before we master the new technology.

- The key to being a leader is being able to manage three or four high priorities at the same time. This means differentiating between not only what is a priority, but the urgency of that priority. Those activities which are both a high priority, as well as urgent, need to have top priority, while those tasks which are not important, as well as not urgent, should be a low priority, or may not need doing at all.

- Learning what we must do and what can be delegated to others is a matter of setting priorities. Particularly as we increase in our sphere of leadership, it will not be possible to effectively do all that we once did. To continue to be effective means not doing more, but rather deciding what are the most important things to be doing.

- Determining priorities is usually difficult, for choices have to sometimes be made between equally important tasks, however, some things always need to be neglected in order to reach our goal.

- Priorities are not static but dynamic, they are always changing; requiring constant evaluation. Determining the *top priority* from *good priorities* is the difference between effectiveness and ineffectiveness.

The Pareto Principle - the 80/20 Rule

- A tool that has helped many leaders reevaluate their priorities has been understanding the Pareto Principle.

- It states that, 20% of our priorities will give us 80% of our production IF we spend our time, energy, money, and personnel on the top 20% of our priorities.

- However, if we reverse this and spend the majority of our time on those things that do not yield a return, or with the wrong people, we will not be effective.

- Other examples of this principle include:

    20% of our time produces 80% of the results.
    20% of the people take up 80% of our time.
    20% of our work gives us 80% of our satisfaction.
    20% of the people give 80% of the money.
    20% of the people will make 80% of the decisions.

Discuss the Pareto Principle and its ramifications for your leadership.

- While this holds true and can be very helpful, a word of caution is in order. Our priorities should ultimately be determined by God's purposes in our lives. Where we invest our time and energy cannot always be clinically determined by empirical data, as this principle seems to indicate.

- Particularly as relates to others and where we invest our time in developing others, we need to be careful as to not violate other relational principles by implementing the Pareto Principle. As we saw in the last chapter, other criteria need to also be taken into consideration.

- Having said that, the Pareto Principle can be particularly helpful in evaluating if we are currently investing our time and resources in what we have determined are our top priorities.

PERILS OF LEADERSHIP

- As in Section 2.0, when we discussed the possible pitfalls (money, sex, power) to practising the spiritual disciplines, there are also several inherent pitfalls or perils as leaders grow in their influence and effectiveness for the Kingdom.

- While there are more perils than those that are listed here, these are representative of some of the main dangers that the leaders must avoid.

Unwillingness to Change

- Leaders must always be willing for personal change, for only then can they help others change. Once we no longer are willing to adapt and change, the seeds of inflexibility are sown in our ministry or organization and the end result is an inability to contain new wine (see last chapter).

- One of the key tasks for leaders is to prepare others to go through change as they see where people are at, and where God wants to take them. This very process implies change and that we as leaders must learn how to do this (discussed more fully in the next chapter). But before we can help others with change we ourselves must first be willing to change.

- Generally, others will resist change and so the effective leader must be an example of someone willing to change. "Do as I say and not as I do," has never been an effective leadership technique. As leaders we must learn to lead by example.

Pride and Egotism

- Pride or egotism will also eventually eliminate the leader's effectiveness. Pride is the main sign of leading by power or self-strength, as opposed to through servanthood.

Are there areas of spiritual pride in your life?

- Spiritual pride is perhaps one of the most dangerous pitfalls of all, for it isolates leaders from others, often the very ones who could speak into their life. In the end leaders can even believe that they are infallible.

- Pride also makes one unteachable for the leaders see themselves above others, rather than still part of the Body and accountable to others within the Body of Christ. There is only one head of the Church and that is Christ, all members, regardless of influence, are equal brothers and sisters.

Sexual Sin

- This was extensively discussed in Chapter 2.2, but is important to mention here again.

- In a day when there is unprecedented attacks on the basic morals in most societies, spiritual leaders have not remained unscathed. The varied and many temptations around us have entangled many a promising leader. Even those who have not publically fallen need to walk in humility, realizing that they are not above such temptations.

What practical steps have you taken to protect yourselves from sexual impurity?

- Yet the leader is not helpless. Through the power of the Holy Spirit, combined with some practical disciplines, this pitfall need not trap us in its snares. Though living a life above reproach is a challenge, several key steps are helpful for us to remember as leaders.

- It is important for leaders to build accountable relationships before the temptation arises, for if we wait too long to do this, it is often too late to resist moral temptation.

- Leaders must recognize that they are not immune to this temptation and need to take the warnings of others seriously. A helpful exercise is to regularly consider the spiritual and practical consequences for one's family that would result from moral failure.

- Healthy habits are also important to develop. Controlling where we go and what we view is central to resisting temptation. Limiting our freedoms as a leader often means paying particular attention to avoid even the appearance of evil.

- If married, leaders need to not neglect the relationship with their spouse and guard their heart in all other relationships with those of the opposite sex. Singles also need to be careful to maintain purity of thought and life in their relationship with the opposite sex.

- Leaders must recognize that they are never beyond temptation in this area and should have those who pray regularly as intercessors for them in this area.

Success or Popularity

- Others have a tendency to put leaders on a pedestal. The temptation for the leader is to begin to enjoy this and even believe what others are saying about how *great* they seem. But servant-leaders need to always maintain a proper, sober estimation of themselves and not allow themselves to be unrealistically elevated in the eyes of others.

- While failure is a difficult test, success is perhaps an even greater test. Having gained greater levels of influence presents leaders with temptations and power to use and abuse that which was not available when they were merely a "shepherd on the backside of the desert."

- We can evaluate our tendency to pride by evaluating how we react when others are promoted or recognized more than we are. Second to this is to evaluate how we respond when others point out our weaknesses. The test of our servant leadership is whether we will lead others as Christ did or in self-strength, with its emphasis on power.

Cynicism or Negativism

- It is inevitable that others will disappoint us as we lead them. Consequently, the leader needs to safeguard against the cynicism about life and others which this can produce. Repeated disappointments by others can lead to the tendency to assume that everyone will let us down, which leads to bitterness and negativity.

- Leaders have an inherent weakness in this area, for we often must focus on what is not going well with our ministry/organization. It is this very reality that can begin to lead us to a negative outlook. To guard against this we must regularly go to the Lord and gain a proper perspective in order to lead others from a position of hope and faith.

- Ultimately, cynicism and negativism indicates a lack of trust in God. It poisons not only relationships, but erodes our hope in the future potential of people. It can detrimentally affect the atmosphere of our whole ministry or organization, which is why as leaders we must eliminate it from our lives.

Infallibility and Indispensability

- Regardless of how gifted and talented a leader may be, no human leader is above error, regardless of the evidence of a call, their past successes, or past fruit in the ministry.

What is you reaction with others who you lead point out your weaknesses?
What does this indicate about your heart condition?

Evaluate your own tendency towards negativism. In the future allow this awareness to bring growth in this area of your life and leadership.

- The greater a leader's influence the greater the temptation to believe that they are indispensable to the Kingdom of God. While everyone has value, leaders must discipline themselves in order to maintain an accurate estimation of themself, realizing that they are where they are due to the grace of God.

- Having a proper perspective of the Kingdom as well as our role as a servant, we will esteem others more than ourselves, being secure enough to develop others so that they will also assume places of influence in the ministry or organization.

- Having a proper estimation of ourselves also means that we recognize when it is time to step aside so that others may pick up the baton of leadership. True leadership means being secure enough to pass on the mantel to others.

Depression

- Depression is a common companion of many leaders. While many leaders have wrestled with it, victory only can occur as the leader's emotions are under Christ's lordship.

- Depression in the ministry often occurs following great victories, which is why we must learn to be on guard and even anticipates these emotional swings (ie. Elijah after the victory on Mt. Carmel).

- Related to depression, is the fear of failure which occurs at times in our lives which can paralyse us from moving forward. Though a leader may appear strong in public, many struggle with the feelings of wanting to withdraw and hide. Instead of trying to deny that these feelings exist, as leaders we need to face these and gain God's perspective on our situation, allowing the Lord to strengthen us through these times.

- As with many of the other perils for the leader, having an accountability group of those who show unconditionally care and support can be the difference between defeat or victory for the leader. However, if depression becomes a continuing cycle, or becomes clinical depression, a leader or minister should seek professional help.

If you have struggled with depression, evaluate steps you need to take in order to gain freedom in this area.
Discuss this with someone you trust.

Spiritual Neglect

- Often the very responsibilities and obligations of leadership can cause the leader to neglect his relationship with God.

- This is often subtle, for we as spiritual leaders often spend so much time "handling" God's Word and applying it in other's lives, yet we may not be spending enough time in personal application. This inevitably cuts us off from the very source of spiritual power which we need.

- We must take practical steps in order to become intentional in this discipline – regular creative new approaches are needed to keep this time with God fresh. After many years of similar routines, sometimes changing the venue, time or method of the devotional time can be helpful.

- Continuing to be effective and being able to help others develop is more dependent upon these spiritual disciplines than any other characteristics of our leadership. Conversely, spiritual laziness is a peril that will most effectively invalidate the influence of any Christian leader.

Discuss with your mentor any areas of spiritual or mental laziness. Establish a plan in order to rectify any lethargic tendencies in your life.

Intellectual Laziness ✓

- Perhaps second only to spiritual neglect in negative consequences to our leadership, is mental or intellectual laziness.

- The real danger for the leader is that it is a sign that we have stopped growing, and without personal growth it is impossible to help others grow. While the leader may be able to function for awhile, eventually neglect in this area will become evident for all to see.

- Leadership demands insightful, creative thinking, which requires input from a variety of sources. This should include surrounding ourselves with those who provide mental stimulation, as well as through other avenues such as books, tapes etc.

- While the tendency is to surround ourselves with only those who agree with us, it is helpful to also expose ourselves to new ideas from other segments of Christendom. This helps to sharpen our own ideas and convictions as well as provide an appreciation for other schools of thought.

- We need to continue a pattern of life-long learning, including formal and informal study, as well as learning to be reflective in order to glean insights from the events in our lives, and understanding the society in which we live.

Neglecting the Home

- Those who serve others all day often find it easy to let down their guard with their own family. It is possible to neglect to do the very things with those closest to us that have made us successful with others. The tragedy is that those with whom we have the most influence, by virtue of our role, are the very ones that we may end up giving the least of ourselves to.

- The first step in ensuring that this does not happen is to establish quality time at home as a priority. Keeping this as a priority will constantly be challenged by competing schedules, and other "seemingly important" obligations. The reality is that, to keep this priority, some things in the ministry or office will not get done and we must learn to accept that, for it is a matter of priorities.

- As with all other areas, developing these habits does not just *happen*, we must be intentional. This is particularly difficult during those times when things are not going that well at home and when it may be easiest to avoid the problems at home. Yet it is at these very times that we must show servant-leadership with those that God has entrusted closest to us, our families.

- The greatest honour is to have the privilege to raise up another generation of leaders from within our own families. To influence the members of our family to be all that they can be for the Kingdom and reach their God-given potential will be the greatest confirmation of our credibility.

Neglecting the Details

- Leaders who can clearly see the "big picture," yet do not take care of the small details along the way, are in danger of never reaching their goal. It is usually this lack of care to the details, particularly as related to relationships, which derails progress.

- These details can include seemingly small, insignificant organizational matters ("didn't you file the document!"), as well as hidden relational matters ("I didn't think she was offended...").

- This does not mean that leaders must necessarily be micro-managers and do everything themselves, but they need to develop those around them who can assist them in their weak areas and blindspots.

- This also necessitates that the leader does not avoid conflicts at all costs, for small things left to fester will eventually grow and become overwhelming, for them and for the ministry.

Have you done everything within your power to make your home life a priority?
Ask your spouse if they agree with your answer!

Are there small details in your life that you have neglected taking care of that have the potential to threaten your personal or spiritual potential?

COSTS OF LEADERSHIP

A Higher Price

- While everyone has the potential to grow in their influence of others and become servant-leaders in the Body of Christ (and society at large), there is a price to pay to achieve this greater influence. This greater price, is often the price others are not willing to pay.

- It may mean limiting ones' own freedoms and even being held to standards which are higher than others that do not seem fair. Yet the fact remains, that the more effective the influence of the leader, the higher the price that has been paid along the way.

- Being a servant-leader also means being prepared to share with others out of even our own weaknesses and failures, so that others may identify with us and we can serve them. It is this very *life message* (see Chapter 1.3) that gives us the right to influence other's lives (2 Cor. 4:8-11, Gal. 6:17).

Interact with the statement, "leaders are required to pay a higher price than others." What rights do you personally think you will have to give up in order to be an effective leader?

Loneliness

- Loneliness is another cost of leadership. It is often the close companion of the true leader. This does not mean that the leader does not have meaningful relationships, but there are always those times and those burdens that the leader must carry alone.

- Even Paul, perhaps the best known Christian of the first century, was often alone (2 Tim. 1:15). A more recent great spiritual leader, A.W. Tozer, wrote, "Most of the world's greatest souls have been lonely."

Fatigue and Criticism

- Another price of leadership is fatigue.

- J. Oswald Sanders penned, "Mediocrity is the result of never getting tired.." This underlines the need of the leader to learn to go to the Lord in order to gain his strength for the task.

- Criticism and rejection are further costs of leadership.

- Perhaps no pain is greater than making decisions and then being criticized and rejected by the very ones those decisions were meant to benefit. This is something that the leader who desires to serve and influence others must learn to deal with.

- Instead of defending oneself and justifying one's actions, the leader must take this pain to the Lord so as to not get bitter and spread this poison with others.

- Yet through a sweet spirit and right attitude, criticism can become a blessing rather than a curse.

Pressure and Apparent Confusion

- What seems to be a paradox is that as a leader matures and has more influence, the pressures and even perplexity seem to increase not decrease. Concerning this J. Oswald Sanders writes, "God treats the mature leader as a mature adult, leaving more and more to his or her spiritual discernment and giving fewer bits of tangible guidance than in earlier years."

Discuss with your mentor the concept that God gives less tangible guidance as we become more mature. Do you agree or disagree?

- It is this "fewer bits of tangible guidance" that seem so paradoxical. Yet God's purpose is to make us more into his image and to have us work in partnership with him. To this end we need to learn to rely more on who he is and not just on external direction and feelings. God wants us to have the faith in him to accomplish more for his Kingdom, even when there does not seem to be any tangible guidance.

- Yet it is this apparent perplexity which adds pressure to the leader's life. Hudson Taylor, the great missionary to China, wrote, "...now as I have gone on, and God has used me more and more, I seem often to be like a man going along in a fog. I do not know what to do."

- It was said of Jesus that he was willing to endure the cross, "For the joy set before him..." That joy was you and I. He was willing to endure the cross due to what it was going to achieve in us.

- So we a servant-leaders have the privilege to join in the fellowship of his sufferings and endure the price of leadership for the joy of helping others reach their full potential and become all that they can be in and for Christ.

Are you willing to pay the price necessary to become a person of influence? Prayerfully evaluate this answer before the Lord.

SUMMARY

- In this chapter we have seen that leadership is not something a chosen few are born with, but rather leadership attributes can be developed and learned. Everyone can grow in their sphere of influence.

- From a foundation of servant leadership, we have discussed the necessary qualities to develop in order that we may become a person of influence. We have also seen some of the potential perils along the way and how they can be avoided.

- As we continue with the last chapter in this section, we will focus our attention on some of the ways in which we can begin to develop others, so that they may also become *influencers* for the Kingdom.

What has particularly impacted you from this chapter?
What one or two changes or steps can you take to apply what you have learned?

Leader

Mentoring
thru
Intentional Relationships

Chapter

3.3

Your Legacy: Developing Others

INTRODUCTION

- In this last chapter of this section, we will see the potential we all have to develop others.

- As we saw last chapter, the greatest challenge hindering some from becoming the leader or *influencer* that God desires for them, is the misconception that leaders are born and not developed. Consequently they do not strive in this direction and are content to be influenced by others.

- But for those who have accepted the challenge of positively influencing others, there is another potential hindrance or obstacle limiting their effectiveness. This is the misconception that they are not yet able (due to various reasons such as age or apparent lack of wisdom etc) to mentor or develop other leaders.

- The first of these misconceptions was discussed in the last chapter and in this chapter we will discuss the issue leaving a legacy (also discussed in the Introductory pages). It would be helpful at this point to take the time to look over the introductory material.

- Both of these obstacles will not only hinder us personally, in our sphere of influence, but will also limit what God wants to do through us in developing others. God desires that we begin to mentor others, right now, not wait until we are older, more experienced or "have it all together."

- There are many who desire to be mentored and we can begin to help them on their journey, even as we are being helped on our journey.

Do you feel that you are able to mentor others? Why or why not?

LEADERSHIP IS INFLUENCE

We All Have Influence

- As we discovered in the last chapter, the fact is that we all influence others. It is not so much a matter of *if* we will influence others, but what *kind* of influence we will be.

- With some intentionality, we can have a positive influence in our world through influencing others for the Kingdom and moving them towards God's purposes.

- This is, after all, the main purpose of leadership – to develop and equip others so that they may reach their potential. As the Chinese proverb says: "If you are planning for one year, grow rice. If you are planning for twenty years, grow trees. If you are planning for centuries, grow men."

- In this chapter we want to take some first steps in learning how to grow others.

Evaluate what level of influence you have with the key people around you.

Our Influence Varies

- Though we have the potential to influence others, we do not have the same amount of influence with everyone, or even the same amount of influence within our various circles of relationships.

- It is first helpful to observe how others respond to us, so that we can evaluate what level of influence we have in their lives. For example, we have greater influence on those who think that our ideas are good and inspired, as opposed to those who do not particularly appreciate the input that we have to offer.

- To be effective, and not frustrated, we need to assess where to focus our energies according to those who we currently influence. At various times in our lives, our level of influence, as well as the particular people we influence will change, so it is worthwhile to evaluate our current spheres of relationships and ministry.

- Expanding in influence is a matter of growth. Maxwell outlines the four levels, or stages, of influence as *modelling, motivating, mentoring* and *multiplying*.

- Modelling being the way we are influenced by others from a distance, where there is no personal relationship. Motivating being more personal and not with the masses, as with modelling. Finally mentoring being a more longer-term influence, helping others reach their full potential and become influencers of others (which leads to multiplying our influence).

Why Develop Others

- Often the pressures and responsibilities of leadership leave little time to develop others. The leader's time is often consumed with responsibilities and fulfilling their visions, so developing others is put on the sideline, perhaps to be done at some point in the future.

- In addition to a priority issue, developing others can also be seen by some leaders to be a threat to their leadership.

- Yet the reality is that those closest to us will either make us a success or a failure, so if for no other reason (though there are many other better reasons), developing others around us is in our best interest. To the extent that we learn to positively develop those closest to us will determine the positive (or negative) effects on our own life and ministry.

- With this perspective, developing others to become co-leaders with us is really the best use of our time. The perspective that developing others is a threat to leadership indicates that we see leadership as positional power, not in terms of releasing and empowering others.

- Developing others is never really a threat, for even if at times someone seems to undermine "our leadership," if we maintain a servant-leader perspective, we realize that true leadership is not a position or title that someone else can take from us. Rather, it is the influence we have earned over time and which others have given us.

- Someone has said that "Followers tell us what we want to hear, leaders tell us what we need to hear." Our focus as leaders should be to begin to develop other *leaders*, not just surround ourselves with *followers*. Though this requires leaders who are secure in who they are, the benefits are worth the risks.

- Developing others who can then reproduce themselves, not only will add to our effectiveness, but will multiply it. Further, the more influence we have, the more leaders we will need around us.

- Leaders grow leaders, and those who have influence attract those who desire to influence. Growing as a leader should mean expanding the sphere of our influence.

Do you feel threatened by developing others around you?
How would a proper biblical perspective change your attitude and actions with regards to developing others?

Is developing others a priority for you?
How does your ministry and lifestyle reflect this?

DEVELOPING OTHERS

Who to Develop

- The key to developing others, is to spend our best time with the *right* people.

- Strategically selecting others to develop individually, or as part of a team, may seem rather calculated and clinical. But recognizing that we must be intentional, in no way excludes being open to those who God brings our way who may not seem to *fit* these criteria and yet who we know he wants us to spend time with.

- Though we must be open for this divine intervention, being intentional in our choice of the right type of person is crucial in order to see lasting fruit of our efforts and lasting benefit for the Kingdom.

- A top priority in choosing someone to develop is to select those with similar values and those who we really believe in. We must ask ourselves, *Is this someone who we would enjoy spending time with?*

- Of course the first key consideration is the character of the person. It is not a matter of seeking for perfection, or someone who has no failures, but rather goes to the their heart motivation. *Do they desire to follow after God and have the character of Christ formed within them?*

- Other issues to consider in choosing and developing a protege or team member is to determine if they have a measure of influence already, have a good attitude and some people skills, as well as if they have the necessary gift-combinations and calling.

- Further questions that are helpful in considering who to develop would include, *Do they follow through on what they commit to, are they a person of integrity and self-discipline, willing to take responsibility?* and *Do they take initiative and have good communication skills. Are they willing to grow and change?*

- While there are many issues that could be listed, these are crucial. However, we must be careful to not exclude those who may be underdeveloped in some area. Perhaps most difficult, is that we must also honestly evaluate if we are the person who can help them in the areas in which they have need. This is also an issue to be considered when mentoring someone else.

- The leader does not need to be a perfect model (more regarding this will be discussed below), but does have the responsibility to create an atmosphere where potential leaders can grow, modelling and motivating others by giving them opportunities to minister.

Who are some of the key people around you who you are committed to developing? Evaluate how you can better serve them.

How to Develop Others

■ People Focus

- Developing others, though not easy, bears long term fruit. Leadership is more than just achieving our goals or organizing a smooth operation, based upon performance. Rather, the true leader's success is defined by the degree to which people are being developed and released for ministry.

- As Blackaby states, our ultimate goal as a leader is to "move leaders to God's agenda." True leadership is developing others to better do what God has called them to do. We are to be partners together with God in accomplishing this.

- Developing others is all about people, not programs, tasks or achieving goals. First and foremost, it is being intentional about taking people from where they are to where God wants them to be.

- Consequently there is not a simple plan that works in every case. It is more about building relationship, learning about the person and then allowing God to

What changes do you need to make so that your leadership is more focussed on people?

positively influence them through who we are and our particular gifting.

- Crucial in this process, however, is that the leader values others and believes it is more important to walk together than alone.

- As we discussed in Chapter 3.2, the structure that best facilitates developing others is a servant-leader model with an *all-members-are-ministers* perspective. It is virtually impossible from a power or position model of leadership, for in this case developing others is always seen as a threat and counterproductive.

■ Practical Application

- Once we see this as the need and focus of our leadership, we must then learn how we can best begin to develop others. The place to start is to understand the particular needs of those we are called to develop.

- While our motivation to meet the needs of others is not in order to manipulate them, the leader who develops others must be aware of their needs and be able to help them meet those needs so that they may reach their full potential.

- As we saw in Chapter 1.1, our personality style is so fundamental to who we are and our motivations, that the leader must also take each person's unique strengths and weaknesses into account.

- It is a valid need for emerging leaders to want to be worthwhile and encouraged as such. This is not necessarily selfish on their part, but a need which should be met. Actually others will start reflecting in their own attitudes and actions the way we think of them, so as we encourage and build them up they will grow into their potential.

- Learning proper ways to motivate (as well as what de-motivates others) is also crucial for the leader. Even when someone is just beginning in a task or ministry, people usually find it motivating to be able to contribute and participate in the process. Helping them work in areas of personal strengths and reflect back to them the importance of what they are doing is also greatly motivating.

- Alternatively, people are de-motivated by public criticism, belittling, manipulation, insensitivity, as well as feeling like they are not given room to grow and develop.

- While encouraging others is vital in this process, the leader must also give others the freedom to fail as they are growing and developing.

- Failure and success are often misunderstood. Many think that success is just a matter of chance, timing, or luck. Fewer understand that it is usually the result of hard work and planning, often behind the scenes. This is something that those we develop must understand. Being open with them regarding our particular journey can help them put their own journey into perspective.

- Success is never instantaneous, rather it is a process which requires time. Our primary goal in developing others is helping them attain *true* success; not perfection or just achieving goals and tasks, but fulfilling the calling and purpose that God has given them.

■ Time is Essential

- Developing others involves determining where someone is at, where they need to go, and then what they need to get there.

- Leaders must take responsibility to initiative the type of relationships which can foster this taking place. Understanding servant leadership and the importance God places on relationships in the Body of Christ, they must begin by prayerfully choosing those whom they can develop and then begin spending time with them.

- Developing people takes time and people skills are essential. These skills usually

What have you learned about motivating and de-motivating people?
What practical steps can you take to improve in this area?

Discuss your time-priorities with your mentor. What changes need to be made in order to develop others.

must be learned, as they are seldom *natural*. People must know that they are cared for before they will give permission to be developed by someone else.

- As well as time, this type of relationship requires a certain transparency and honesty on behalf of the leader. While at times the price may seem high, requiring time taken from a busy schedule and important obligations, the dividends are immense for both the individual's development as well as for the Kingdom.

- Throughout history, well known personalities have been developed by anonymous people and have even gained greater influence than their mentors. As servant-leaders, this is both our task and privilege – to develop and mentor others.

THE CHALLENGE OF DEVELOPING OTHERS

- Being able to communicate with others and helping them through the challenges of change – which is inevitable as we move people from where they are to where God wants them to be – is essential for the leader desiring to equip and develop others.

Communication

- The leader's role is not to try to sell *their* vision through force of character, or even communication skills. Rather it is to bring others into a relationship with God. While vision and purpose is crucial in this process, the vision must have a divine origin, not just the latest idea of a leader.

- The servant-leader model speaks of a partnership which values every believer and believes that they can hear from God directly. Then as the leader submits the vision to others with humility, it is ultimately the Holy Spirit who must confirm it in the hearts of others.

- The leaders must accurately communicate who God is and teach others how to hear from him; their direction must be directed to God. The risk is that others will not see the direction as we do, but instead of this being a negative, it can help us clarify the vision we believe we have received from God, as well as provide an opportunity to help others take responsibility and learn to hear from God.

- Granted this is not a common approach taken in leadership and the goal of total unanimity is seldom achieved. As we discovered in our discussion on structure, while form is important, it must correlate with appropriate function. So this approach to communicating vision will not be successful if it just becomes another form imposed over old attitudes. Its application must be within the context of valuing every member of the Body and the confidence in their ability to hear from God.

- Our task as leader is not to manipulate or "make things happen," but meekly (does not mean to be weak) follow God as Moses did, knowing that if we heard from God, God will also confirm it with those he has called us to lead.

Change

- To help people move from where they are to where God wants them be necessitates change, and *change* is perhaps the most difficult of issues for the leader to help others through.

- Howard Hendricks once said, "If you want to continue leading, you must continue changing." So the first step in helping others through change is for the leader to also be continually willing and prepared to change.

Are you open to continual growth and change? What specific habits and routines from your life indicate this?

Discuss the challenge of "meek leadership" without resorting to manipulation and self-strength.

- Change is often resisted for it creates a fear of the unknown and disrupts routine. In addition, if the reason for the change is unclear, or if people do not have "ownership" of the change, it is also resisted.

  - The reason why change produces such fear is that people want to succeed, and change can be seen as a threat to this. They have a fear of failure so resist any change and potential personal loss. This resistance to change can be experienced by both leaders and those who they seek to pour their lives into.

  - In helping others through change, it is important to realize that there are two aspects of change: both the need for the change, as well as the timing of that change. Every decision that will require change needs to be evaluated as to the necessity of the change, as well as what is the best timing of that change.

  - Right decision, but at the wrong time will be just as unsuccessful as a wrong decision with the wrong timing. To be successful it must be both the right decision at the right time, which means having taken the right steps and time necessary to alleviate other's fears and help them process the change.

  - The leader's task is to create the right climate so that change is possible and even welcomed. This takes a high degree of trust and integrity earned through honesty. A plan which then begins a process that is accepted by as many as possible will ensure *ownership* and success of the change.

DEVELOPING A TEAM

Discuss with your mentor lessons they have learned with regard to developing and working with a team.

- Though somewhat beyond the scope of our purpose for this chapter, the following are a few introductory thoughts regarding developing successful teams or staff.

- As we have discussed under the topic of servant-leadership, this model of leadership functions best in the context of a plurality of leadership and team approach. The New Testament record seems to substantiate this with the variety of terminology being used for "leadership," with no clear hierarchical structure emerging, other than Christ being the head of the Church. Authority seemed to flow from gifts and function, rather than from title and position.

- After the First Century Church, hierarchical structures developed which were repressive, at best, and unbiblical, at worst.

- The reality is that each of us are immersed in structures today which are, to varying degrees, vestiges of past centuries. The challenge is to return to biblical values regarding servant leadership and apply these within existing structures to the best of our ability. Even when structural change is necessary, our challenge is not violating the very heart of the Gospel (such as the fruit of the Spirit and the unity of the saints) in our efforts to bring about that change (particularly applicable in Chapter 4.3).

Successful Teams

Reflecting on both successful and unsuccessful teams that you have worked on, what have you learned?

- Leaders create an atmosphere in which teams can flourish. This begins with valuing others and seeing that their needs are met.

- Effective team ministries are not developed by chance, but are developed by understanding why each person on the team is a part of the team and then defining their role, both individually and as a group. It is also then important to develop a group identity, which requires spending time together and much communication.

- To begin with, there must be a clear understanding of what the ministry (organization etc.) really needs and what the job or task requires. Only then can we determine who are the right people for the team.

- The reality is that often teams are already established, in which the leader has had no input as to the participants. This is particularly the case in volunteer settings. Yet even in these cases it is more important for the leader to value each member and help them become all that they can be. Importance must be placed on the people, not the task.

- In determining who to develop as a team member, character qualities such as integrity, teachability, having a servant's heart and a heart after God are crucial. Those who work closest to us also have to share our values, respect us and be loyal. While other qualities and specific skills may be desirable, these can very often be taught and developed, while these more fundamental attributes are more difficult to develop in a person.

- Central to developing a team is learning the art of delegation. However, many leaders fail to delegate, for they are insecure or have trouble placing their trust and confidence in others. But in order for our delegation to be effective it must be done slowly and be part of a process whereby someone does not feel overwhelmed with immediate deadlines to meet.

Discuss principles of delegation and evaluate your success in delegating.

- Helping others become acquainted with the task and allowing their input are key ingredients to successful delegation. Responsibility should be released in stages as their ability is proven. This will also help them gain confidence and not become discouraged.

- Faithfulness is a key ingredient to look for when delegating. *Has someone been faithful in small things, faithful in working with others, faithful in the shadows?* These are all indicators that they are ready to be co-laborers.

- The big picture is to see delegating as developing others and even grooming them for leadership. This underscores the importance to choose those who have similar values and a certain maturity, for there is a high likelihood that they will develop into places of influence next to us. Consequently, care should be taken in choosing who to initially delegate tasks to.

- Above all else, the servant leader should be a facilitator. This means decentralizing decision making and involving others as much as possible, not creating an atmosphere where truth and wisdom belongs to just a few, but selflessly developing others.

MENTORING OTHERS

- There are various levels of developing others. It may be as simple as delegating a task to someone and helping them achieve that goal, to developing someone on a ministry team, to a more intentional relationship, such as a mentor-mentoree.

- Yet not all relationships, which have the purpose to develop others, are necessarily mentoring relationships. Some may not be quite as intensive and focussed, or the relationship may not be as close as that which develops within the mentoring relationship.

What are your hindrances to NOT being involved in mentoring. Explain.

- While many of the same principles apply across the spectrum of relationships, whose focus is developing others, the mentoring relationship as described in this program has some unique features.

- However, it must be stated again, the mentoring relationship is just not for a few, all those who have a desire, can be involved in mentoring (though preparation may be needed). The foundational principles and goals of influencing others and help them reach their full potential are the same.

- To be healthy leaders we need both mentors and mentorees in our lives, we need to be mentored as well as be involved in mentoring others. The *Introduction* to this manual addresses most of these issues, but a few thoughts are included here from both the perspective of the Mentor and the Mentoree.

Finding a Mentor

- Due to various factors and reasons (see Introduction) there are usually more mentorees desiring mentoring than mentors willing to mentor.

- While, ideally, the mentor should seek out the mentoree (the viewpoint assumed in much of this chapter), the reality is that often it is the mentoree that must take the initiative and approach a potential mentor.

- In determining who would be a helpful mentor in our life it is important to consider if the potential mentor has the qualities of character which we admire and want to develop. Looking for a perfect mentor is pointless, for they do not exist. Integrity and honesty are better qualities to look for than perfection.

- But a mentor must be willing to spend time with the mentoree and there must be enough basic commonalities to make the time spent together enjoyable.

- Other factors to consider are, *Does this person have credibility and are others currently following them? Are they reproducing other leaders?* Also it is important to evaluate what the strengths are that they can offer us and if these are the areas we want and need to grow in.

- While there are other factors to consider these are a few beginning steps in finding a mentor.

While being Mentored

- At the beginning stages (and throughout) of the relationship it is wise to assess expectations (ours and theirs). What do we want from this relationship and what can we give?

- Then while being mentored, it is important to be asking the right questions of your mentor, remembering that their goal is not to give you all the answers, but to help give you direction in the process of discovering your own answers; the goal is improvement, not perfection.

- In this mentoring process, do not try to impress your mentor with your own knowledge and ability, but be a learner. The best motivation for your mentor is for you to put into practice that which you have learned.

- It is good to have a healthy respect for your mentor, but remain objective and think critically; the mentor is not someone to be slavishly obeyed. Mentoring is not one person exercising power over another, nor is it unhealthy discipleship that borders on "shepherding."

- Finally, be disciplined and communicate your progress. Stay persistent and do not give up. This is an indicator of your potential for leadership.

Choosing who to Mentor

- The first step in desiring to develop others must be to consistently increase our capacity to develop ourselves. This happens through personal and professional growth (see previous chapters).

- In choosing who to mentor, you must be careful to choose individuals who share a similar philosophy of life and have similar values, as well as someone who you believe in and who fits well with your particular strengths (they need what you have).

- It is also critical to start the mentoring process when the time is right and to

Consider if you spend enough time with those who you consider mentors in your life. Are there any adjustments that need to be made?

Evaluate your attitude and actions as a mentoree. Are you maximizing this relationship?

receive permission from the potential mentoree. While it is to be intentional, it is not coercive or in any way condescending, we are partners together.

The Process

- The purpose of mentoring is not to solve all of the mentorees problems – they will continue to have challenges throughout life, particularly as they become leaders. Maxwell articulates it well as he writes, "The higher people go – personally and professionally – the more complicated life gets. Schedules get tighter, money issues increase, and greater demand are put on successful people. But the good news is that if they continue to grow and develop themselves, their ability to deal with problems will also increase."

- The goal is to help the mentoree become all that they can become in Christ. Its focus needs to be on attitudes, relationships, leadership, and skills (both personal and professional).

- The mentor is a guide (not boss or parent) whose purpose is to encourage the mentoree to improve and grow in maturity; motivating them in this lifelong process.

- While intentional, this relationship must also be consistent, providing stability for growth, even through the difficult times.

- At various stages in our lives we may mentor a variety of types of people. Some may have few leadership skills or interest and may just need to be encouraged in the strengths that they already have. Others may be good at managing, but need to grow in their comprehension and implementation of the big picture, while still others may require help in seeing how they need to adopt a more effective leadership style.

- Most good leaders are already growing, but often need help to develop a systematic, intentional, personal plan for growth. Mentoring a good leader means having the privilege to provide feedback and help them stretch forward towards even greater growth.

- In each of the cases, it is the wise mentor who takes the opportunity to also learn from those they are mentoring.

> Do you have someone who you are mentoring – pouring your life into? Discuss with your mentor steps you are taking to develop others.

LEAVING WELL

How to Transition

- No matter how much influence a person has, no one is indispensable. The issue is not *if* the transition of leaving will come, but rather how we will deal with this leadership issue *when* it arises.

- Blackaby writes, "Leaders with integrity recognize when they have made their most worthwhile contributions. Then they graciously hand over the reigns of leadership to the next generation."

- This is the most basic reason for developing others, knowing that our own days are numbered.

- The issue surrounding leaving must not only be dealt with by those who need to step aside by virtue of their age, but also by those who need to move on for various other reasons.

- It is important for the leader to evaluate their motives and honestly answer why they are really leaving. If a misunderstanding is the root cause, responsibility must be accepted, or a root of bitterness and other baggage will be taken by the leader to their next assignment or position.

> Discuss with your mentor issues of "leaving well" and any insights your mentor may have from both positive and negative experiences.

- Regardless of the reason for the departure, it is advantageous for leaders to seek to receive a blessing before leaving, which of course necessitates dealing with any hurts to the best of their ability. Most departures have a "people" component and so it is critical that the relational aspects are dealt with in a godly manner.

- Finally, when it is time to leave, it is best to leave clearly and completely (stuff, people, position, perks). Not leaving completely will be detrimental to the leader as well as to the successor and will cause the ministry or organization to suffer.

Founder Syndrome

- It is particularly difficult for the torch of leadership to be passed on by those who have founded or established a work or ministry.

- Even leaders who were once great can diminish their life-long contribution by staying as the primary leader longer than they should. Often their particular gifts have helped bring the organization to its current level, but it may takes others with other gifts, who can take it to the next level.

- Often the departure of the founder is necessary, so that others can emerge and develop. Recognizing the need to leave in a timely manner (and not criticizing the successor), will ensure that the leader can continue to have a positive influence to the next generation.

- While this is a difficult time for any leader, it can be particularly difficult for a founder. When the time comes for the leader to retire from their position and job, understanding that they are just changing assignments and not leaving their calling can be a helpful perspective.

LEAVING A LEGACY

- If we believe that leaders are developed and not born, then it necessitates that they somehow be developed. Leaders are those who take the responsibility to not just lead others, but to mentor other leaders.

- Yet even this is not the end of the process, for *leaving a legacy* means that these leaders which have been mentored, in turn, are able to mentor others. As Maxwell points out, "Leaders who do not develop people will one day find themselves hitting a wall in their success. No matter how efficient and strategic they are, eventually they run out of time."

- Only as every generation continues to mentor the next generation, teaching them to then mentor the next generation, is the cycle of multiplication complete. This mentoring process is not limited to only those who are chronologically younger, or those who are similar in personality, ability and background. The mentoring process is much broader than this.

- In order to mentor others, who in turn will develop another generation of leaders, we as leaders must finish well. Then one day we will be able to say with the Apostle Paul, "I have fought the good fight, I have finished the race, I have kept the faith." (2 Tim. 4:7)

- In order to finish well we must not be deceived that the success of our ministry is due to our own skills and power, or allow success to distract us. We must remain disciplined people of the Word and prayer. We must guard ourselves from thinking that we have arrived at some point and are above the restrictions which God's Word places on others.

- A further challenge to finishing well and leaving a legacy is to not find our identity in the ministry, or our title, rather being content to be a "child of God," keeping a humble estimation of ourselves and a biblical perspective of others.

What steps are you taking to begin developing others and leaving a legacy?

Do you see any weaknesses in your life which will keep you from finishing well?
Be accountable with your mentor and take steps to strengthen these areas.

- Those who leave a legacy have also learned to deal with any destructive hidden sins or habits, before the pressures of the ministry and/or success cause these to be manifest publically for all to see.

- Though we may have mentored others, we must always remain honest with ourselves, recognizing our own vulnerability and finding peers with whom we can be open and accountable to.

- Our goal one day is to hear those words from our Master, "Well done though good and faithful servant!"

SUMMARY

- Though leadership is not for the faint of heart, we have discovered that it is not just for a few who have been born with leadership qualities – we all have the potential to become a greater influence with others.

- Though we all have the potential to influence others, we have a responsibility to continue to grow and develop so that we may become the kind of people who will be a positive influence on others for the Kingdom, helping them go from where they are to where God wants them to go.

- The foundation of all such leadership is that of a servant. Leading not from position or title, but rather developing others and, thus, leaving a legacy.

- As we transition to the next and final section, *Minister*, we will be focussing on the direction or purpose of discovering ourselves as *Person* (Section 1.0), developing ourselves as *Disciples* (Section 2.0), and growing as a *Leader* (Section 3.0).

- The purpose of our journey of discovery and growth in these last three sections is so that we may join God as co-laborers in the harvest field fulfilling our destiny as his *ministers* in a needy world.

Discuss with your mentor those truths from this Section on Leadership that have most impacted you.

Commit yourself to find mentors and to be a mentor.

Minister

Your Motivation: Being God's Person

Mentoring
thru
Intentional Relationships

Chapter
4.1

Your Motivation:
Being God's Person

INTRODUCTION

- In this last section, our focus will be on our role as a *Minister*. We will be discussing some principles and practical aspects of the *Mission of the Church*, but will first begin with the important discipline of examining our own hearts, as to our very motivation for service itself.

- For our purposes, the term *Minister* will have the widest possible scope. It will include all Christians who at one time serve others, regardless of their *sphere of influence* or *scope of ministry*. The use of the word in a *vocational* sense is also included (see Chapter 1.3) , but this is not meant to exclude those not in a vocational-type "ministry."

- There is obviously a connection between leadership and the role of a minister and in the last section we have discussed the minister as a leader and the principles that apply to leading by serving. As with true leadership, ministry is not about position, or even our particular role, it is about serving others out of a pure heart.

- To be effective in our service in the Body and in the world, the minister must be a pure vessel. While perfection is not attainable, ministering from pure motives is, so this is where we will begin our discussion.

OUR HEART CONDITION

- As Peter writes in 1 Peter 5:1-4, we are to serve, not because we must but because we are willing. Ministry is only effective as it flows from a heart that has the right motivation.

- This motivation of servanthood has its roots in our understanding of our call (See Section 1.3) and what that means for our *role* or *sphere* of influence.

- The blessing of being able to serve others and have influence in their lives also comes with a responsibility. If it is true that long term effective ministry can only originate through pure motives, we have the obligation to examine our hearts and keep them pure before the Lord.

- The minister's calling relates to our motivation. Relevant questions to ask ourselves are, *Why do we want to influence others? What motivates us to continue in our role or sphere of ministry?*

- The root of our motivation is determined by our heart condition. So to begin with we must be prepared to analyse our own hearts.

Take some time to consider your call and how this affects your motivation for what you do.

Grace Required

- As we begin this process of examining our own hearts, it is important that we have an understanding of God's grace and mercy and have experienced this personally. God relates to us on the basis of his goodness and grace, for even at our best we need to receive from his mercy, not according to what we deserve.

- The process in this chapter is not a form of works for gaining acceptance before

Prayerfully examine your heart and respond to the Lord's promptings regarding any steps you may need to take.

God, for this can only occur through personally accepting the finished work of the cross. After all, in the final analysis, all of our righteousness acts are still only "filthy rags" by comparison (Isa. 64:6).

- Examining our hearts and correcting our motivation is not a *prerequisite* for salvation or righteousness, but rather is an *expression* of us having received this finished work of Christ within. It is since we have received such unmerited favour and grace that we examine ourselves.

- There is a direct application for the *leader* and *minister*. For only as we live in this grace can we minister this same grace and acceptance with others. But in order to do this we must learn how to examine ourselves within the context of his grace – which is a work of the Holy Spirit, not an exercise of human self-strength.

- Even during our lowest times, when we see the wretchedness of our own motives, we can know that God's attitude towards us is one of grace. This means that we can approach him, confess what is necessary, and then continue on the journey without condemnation.

- As we walk in the light of obedience, even in our imperfections, God does not condemn us – and we also need not condemn ourselves.

Examination of our Heart

- While the ongoing process of heart evaluation is to be done in partnership with the Holy Spirit and immersed in grace, Scripture does admonish us to examine ourselves.

- The danger as we minister to others is that while admonishing others to examine themselves, we ourselves can forget to do the same.

- Due to various factors (which we will discuss in this chapter), our hearts can become cold over time. Wrong motivations can then originate from a heart that has become cold or somewhat hard towards God. This is why leaders need to take steps in order to keep their conscience soft and pure towards God's promptings."

Honestly ask yourself these questions.

- Some difficult questions which are appropriate to ask ourselves in this self-examination are, *What do our words reveal about the condition of our heart? Do we put others first? Are we always honest?* (Even those slight ministry exaggerations) *How do we speak of others when they are not present? Is our heart still humble, able to accept responsibility for wrong actions, words, and thoughts?*

- As God uses us to minister to others, it is easy to begin to believe that our *success* or effectiveness is due to our own wisdom or ingenuity. The minister must guard against the subtlety of this personal deceit. Cultivating the ability to have a sober view of who we really are and having the ability to be honest with ourselves, is one of the key assets of an effective Christian leader.

- Alternatively, deceiving oneself is the first step to a hardened heart, which eventually will affect the very motives of the minister.

- As we saw in the last chapter, our goal is to leave a legacy and finish well. Unfortunately, the lesson from history is that many who begin well never finish well. Some do not even finish the race at all.

- Those who regularly serve others are susceptible to this. As they discover their gifts and calling and begin to fulfill God's purposes in their lives their sphere of ministry and influence grows. Being used of God begins to then become equated with relationship with God. Not immediately, but over time they may begin to neglect the spiritual disciplines and attitudes that enabled God to use them and expand their influence in the first place. The eventual result is the ineffectiveness of their ministry or service and it all begins with a coolness or hardening of one's heart.

A Hardened Heart

- The obvious and quickest way to harden one's heart is through the entertaining of unconfessed sin and harbouring known disobedience to God. Leaders must be particularly careful to not allow the deceitfulness of sin to harden their hearts (Heb. 3:13).

- Regularly going to the cross and allowing God to reveal any disobedience in our hearts is a key for Christian leaders to remain effective in our service to others. Left to ourselves, our own hearts begin to deceive us. We need God and his Word to reveal truth to us.

- A clear sign of a heart beginning to harden is pride (Prov. 16:5; 18:12; 21:4). For those in spheres of influence, this can be indicated by the lack of openness to correction from others. Living an open, vulnerable life is not compatible with a prideful heart. One cannot, simultaneously, minister with humility and be unapproachable.

- This pride can further be expressed by taking credit for another's work and not giving other's the recognition that they need and deserve. (Principles regarding this were discussed last section on *Leadership*).

- It is impossible to have the right motivation for ministry with a heart that is not soft and open to God; a pure heart is a prerequisite for the leader who desires to have the right motivation for service.

Pray and reflect on the condition of your heart. Be open to areas in which God will reveal hardness in which he wants to soften.

Our Responsibility

- Though we recognize that it is a work of God's grace to keep our hearts pure, leaders and ministers have an obligation to guard their hearts. This is the Christian leader's responsibility (Prov. 4:23).

- As we have discovered already, Christian leaders have many responsibilities, but the first and foremost responsibility is to *keep* their heart, for ministry flows out of a pure vessel.

- The subtle process of a hardening heart often occurs gradually, in small increments and almost unnoticed. In contrast, softening a hardened heart takes a conscious choice and often great effort. While God's grace and mercy is always available for our failure and sin, there can at times be scars which remain from our actions taken when we hardened our hearts. While God forgives and restoration is always possible, there can often be some irreversible consequences for our ministry.

- It is possible that a leader may not reach the same level of influence or sphere of ministry that would have been possible. At the very least, this time of hardness and estrangement from God can result in time lost and diminished influence. Moses' unbelief, illustrated by his hitting the rock, meant that he was not able to set his foot in the Promised Land. Other examples include Samson's disobedience, or Elijah's loss of perspective, each of which had varying degrees of consequences for their ultimate task and calling.

- The effectiveness of a minister is so directly related to a pure and soft heart that this must be the top priority of the leader.

Describe ways in which you currently guard your heart in reference to other relationships, your leadership responsibilities, and your personal activities.

God's Promise

- Fortunately, we are not alone in evaluating our hearts. While we must be willing, it is God through his Holy Spirit, who has promised to reveal our hearts to us.

- God has promised to help us – not only by revealing the condition of our hearts, but also by giving us the power to change. The honest prayer to have God search our heart is a prayer which is always answered (Psa 139:23-24).

- We need God's help, for it is not always an easy matter for us to determine the condition of our own hearts. Our more natural tendency is to rationalize and justify. Even with pure motives, we are often more aware of the outward actions and results than we are the reasons and deeper motivations for our actions.

- But God is faithful to reveal our motives and heart condition, for he can clearly view our heart (1 Sam. 16:7; Heb. 4:12-13). He not only shows us what our true motives are, but he tests us in order to purify our motives.

- It is often during this testing period that we come face to face with what our real motives are and can deal with them. While we must then make the choice to change our heart, it is God who provides the opportunity through this time of testing (Prov 17:3; 21:2).

- God desires to test our hearts and purify our motives, so that we will reach our full potential for him. While it may seem *risky* to ask God to reveal the secrets and motives of our heart, once we understand his character, we can be assured that he desires the best for us and will remain faithful to us. His purpose is not to destroy us, but to fulfill his purposes in and through us.

- As God reveals our secret sins, improper motivations, hardness, or pride, he then desires to bring healing, forgiveness and restoration.

In what ways has God tested you?
What have you learned through this process?

Pure Motives

- It is possible to have pure motives. This does not mean that we do not have failures, make mistakes or even disobey God at times, but our motives – why we do what we do – can be pure.

- The foundation for pure motives is a relationship with God; knowing him personally and intimately. This is the basis and prerequisite for all effective ministry. We cannot be a positive influence with others without taking the time to foster such a relationship with God.

- Service for God which flows from proper motivation is a result of a right relationship with God. As discussed in Chapter 2.1, this right relationship is dependant upon our commitment to the spiritual disciplines. This is more than just daily devotions – though it does include those regular, quiet times alone with God – it has to do with our whole life lived as worship to God.

- This necessitates disciplining ourselves to avoid anything – even apparent *good* things – that would draw us away from God and our call or service for him (1 Cor. 6:12; 10:23). God knows our hearts and as leaders we need to continually be asking him to show us who we really are ("Search me and know my heart," Psa.139:23).

- We need to regularly ask ourselves if we are taking enough time to know God and evaluating what the focus of our heart is. If we are more focussed on our senses or circumstances, very often the keenness of our heart towards God is affected.

- We also need to reflect on our personal life in order to see if any habits, relationships, or activities are keeping us from being as close to God as we could be. If not, we will notice our heart becoming cold.

Spend some specific time in prayer this week to ask God to reveal your motives to you. Record what he shows you in your journal.

- In addition, Christian leaders need to take initiative in the area of relationships. We need to ask ourselves if we are pure and open in our relationships with others, not harbouring unforgiveness or bitterness that can so quickly harden our heart towards God and others.

- It is also crucial to have a healthy relationship with our spouse. The health of this relationship will not only affect our ministry, but our very ability to worship God from a pure heart (1 Peter 3:7).

Confirmation

- While our motives and heart condition may seem to be hidden from physical view, they will always be revealed through the fruit of our lives. Our heart condition will be revealed by our actions and confirmed by our reputation. Others will eventually know whether we have a heart for God or not.

- Regardless of our position, others will see if our lifestyle communicates a passion for God, or if we are lukewarm in our faith. The difficulties and even unfairness of life and ministry will either produce a sweet spirit or bitterness, which will be evident by all those around us.

- Regardless of our words, it is these attitudes and actions which indicate to others the condition of our heart and motives. Our actions and activities need to be consistent with what we are communicating by our words.

- Following is a sampling of some of the external criteria which can confirm the internal condition of our heart, for while maintaining a pure heart is a private matter, the results will eventually be evident for all to see.

What spiritual disciplines or activities have you discontinued due to a busy schedule and increasing responsibilities?
What steps do you need to take to get your personal life in order?

PROPER HEART MOTIVATION

To Serve

- As we discussed in Chapter 3.1, servant leadership must be the foundation of all those who desire to positively influence others for the Kingdom.

- Jesus' ministry example was that of a servant (Mark 10:45; Phil. 2), which is also the essence of Christian leadership, service to others.

- In contrast to this model, is leadership that is motivated by having our own needs met and lording our role over others; desiring others to serve us, instead of laying down our lives for others.

- If service is not motivated by love (but rather out of guilt, duty, having our needs met, etc.), then there will be no lasting fruit among those we serve.

To Impart Life Message

- *Life-message* (see Chapter 1.3) is the sum of all that we have gone through and usually manifests itself in the reoccurring themes that God uses in our lives to touch others.

- God reveals himself to each of us through his Word and his Spirit, but he does this within the context of our family roots, educational experience, and our other various life experiences, including both the good times and bad, both the setbacks and the victories.

- With a proper perspective and attitude, all of these factors can (eventually) be used to make us into the messenger that God wishes us to be. They not only help us develop these truths in our lives, but form us into the person that we are, able to identify with others and share these truths with power and conviction.

What does ministering or leading from "life message" mean to you?
What would you have to change in your ministry, leadership style, or attitudes in order to serve in this way?

■ <u>Brokenness</u>

- A life of brokenness is a prerequisite to this serving style of leadership. In order to serve the way Jesus did, "a broken and contrite heart" is essential (Psa 51:16-17).

- Some characteristics of a broken life include humility, teachability, and sharing with others with honesty. The leader who has been broken is not defensive and can receive criticism graciously.

- These type of leaders long to see others develop beyond themselves. They are not driven by increasing their own reputation or influence, but enjoy when others increase and succeed.

- God uses the sufferings and weaknesses of the minister who has learned brokenness, to bless and encourage others ("comforting others in trouble with the comfort we have received," 2 Cor.1:4). Being that "drink offering poured out" that Paul writes about is not dependent upon the response of those we serve, but is offered unconditionally to others.

- In contrast, without this brokenness of heart, Christian leaders will often blame, accuse and even pull away from the very ones that God has called them to serve. But broken-hearted, servant-leaders have the potential see others' lives changed through their influence.

- We see this attitude in Paul's ministry. The Apostle had the burden of God's people on his heart and was even willing to suffer in order to assist others achieve God's purpose for their lives (Phil. 1:7).

Do you serve from the foundation of a broken heart?

■ <u>Transparency</u>

- Living a transparent life – revealing both the good and bad times for others, so that they may grow – is a quality of character that keeps the leader from pride.

- We can more effectively help others by our honest and open manner, than by an unrealistic, overly spiritual misrepresentation of a *godly* life. Transparency enables others to see our integrity and gain practical insight into *how* to live their lives.

- A prerequisite of this type of leadership is humility of heart. It is impossible to have a proud heart and at the same time live a transparent life before others. This, of course, does not mean that perfection is required, for this is a burden no person (and leader) is meant to bear.

- Paul testified that he had ministered to the church in Corinth with an open heart (2 Cor. 6:11) and that he had nothing to hide in his ministry with them.

- We can be engaged in the maturing process, with all of our failures, and still have a purity of motive and transparency of life. This is in contrast to giving others the feeling that we have attained a level of perfection that few others will ever be able to achieve! Few will be able to identify with this type of attitude or be able to receive from God through it.

- Transparency in ministry does not mean only sharing the mistakes of many years ago and giving testimony to God's faithfulness, it also means sharing current idiosyncrasies and failures as well as challenges we still face.

- The purpose is not self-pity or even self-promotion, but rather that others will be able to identify and be helped in what they are going through. We are to be those *open books, read by all people* that Paul talks about in his epistles. But it is not just about sharing failures, but rather giving others an open view into the development of our walk with God.

Are you transparent in your dealings with others?

The Risk of a Transparent Life

- Having made the case for living a transparent life, it must be said that this style of ministry comes with a cost. The impact on others is dramatic, but so are the challenges to such a ministry.

- This type of ministry does not mean listing our sins for everybody in order to *prove* our transparency, for we need God's wisdom to know what to share and in which settings. Yet Christian leaders are called to function at a level beyond that of just measured words and a good image and we must find the balance to this style of leadership.

- It takes great courage and humility to be such a leader, for it makes us vulnerable for others to question our motives and even misunderstand us. Others may question our leadership, have less respect, or even try to use our weaknesses against us.

- However, the cost of trying to present a *perfect* image has even greater consequences. Allowing others to put us on a pedestal, only ensures that our fall one day will be even greater, for no matter how spiritual we may be, we will make our fair share of mistakes and failures.

- If we are truly dead to self, however, there is no option but this style of leadership. Being dead in Christ, and being a servant-leader means that we are not motivated to attain or keep a position, or try to correctly position ourselves to climb up the ladder of success. Our mandate is to serve others, not self.

- A very real danger is to *seem* like we are serving others, but to be doing so with impure motives, merely as another means to manipulate them. These leaders have not only lost their own integrity, but will inevitably been seen for what they really are.

How "close" do you think you can get to those you are serving (or in leadership with). In your opinion, are there limits to this transparency? What are they?

To Please God

- The crucial question leaders must ask themselves has to do with who they really want to please, man or God. This is not a one-time event but, if we are honest, an ongoing struggle for all of us.

- Paul's ultimate desire above all else was to please his master, Jesus Christ (2 Tim 2:3-4). Throughout his eventful ministry, we see him graciously accepting the consequences of this decision. He was repeatedly beaten and left for dead, rather than compromise the message of the Gospel which he was called to take to the world. Yet he was not only misunderstood by those in the world, but also by those in the Church.

- Having the singleness of motive to please God also keeps the leader from embarking on projects or ministries just to be seen by others, rather than doing that to which God has called them. Motivated by a desire to please God, also assists the leader from being swayed by every ministry *fad* or *trend*. Following fads in Christian ministry creates an instability in the leader, as time and energy is wasted by following after things which are not God's best for them or their ministry.

- A motivation to please God also keeps the leader true to their ministry and calling. Even if there seems to be not much fruit or success at the time; they will look to God for affirmation, not the size or prestige of their ministry.

- In order to have integrity and remain effective, we must continually allow the Lord to test our ambition: *Are we committed to pleasing him above all else?*

Are there areas in your life in which you are more focussed on pleasing others rather than God?

THE CHALLENGES

- Along the leader's journey, there are many obstacles that have the potential to poison our heart.

- Some of these pitfalls are of our own making and others seem to materialize from nowhere. Some can be prepared for and others arrive when least expected.

- Yet whatever their source, or the degree of their intensity, they have the potential to harden our heart and invalidate our contribution for the Kingdom. The end result is that we never reach our full potential.

Identify and discuss with your mentor some of the challenges in your life which have affected your heart condition. Together with your mentor commit together to see God bring clarity and healing in those areas where it is needed.

Loss of Hope

- Along the leadership journey there are those inevitable times of apparent hopelessness, which often result in the questioning of our call.

- While it is inevitable that the leader will experience some measure of this, an effective leader learns to not lose faith and trust, in the midst of apparent despair. The importance of developing the spiritual disciplines as habits, is so that when these times occur, the leader can build themselves up by going to God as their source.

- Practising the spiritual disciplines places leaders in a position to be able to recover their trust in God and his character, in spite of the circumstances. While we may recognize him as our source, at times the pressures of leadership make it difficult to even receive from him, which is why the *habits* of a relationship can be helpful to draw us back to him.

- This loss of hope and perspective can often lead to burnout. As in Elijah's case (1 Kings 19), this often occurs after great victories. If serious enough and long enough, it can lead to a loss of right motivation and healthy attitude towards others. Leaders can become isolated and even develop a bitterness to the very ones they are called to serve.

- The danger is that if steps are not taken, over a longer period of time the leader's heart can become hard towards God and even difficult for him to reach. While we often do not have control over our circumstances, regardless of what happens, we can guard our heart and keep it soft towards God.

- While this loss of hope and even burnout may occur for a time, it is very difficult to minister effectively for a long period of time in this condition. But God in his grace does not leave us and regardless of how difficult the circumstance, if we keep our heart open to him, he will restore us.

Trials and obstacles

- Often the challenges of living life, with all its heartaches, setbacks and severe disappointments, can also cause the leader's heart to become hardened.

- It is important to realize that God understands our disappointment and disillusionments and does not condemn us for experiencing these emotions, regardless of how deep they may be or how long they may last. This is important to remember, particularly as Job's counsellors always seem to have quick advise for the leader during these times!

- The challenge is to continue to serve others with the same openness and vulnerability while struggling with the effects caused by deep disappointment. Being willing to go through these as a leader will deepen our ministry and effectiveness, for we will be able to identify with others. As mentioned previously, however, without living a transparent life with others, the full benefit of these lessons can be lost.

- As the children of Israel gathered up stones from the middle of the Jordan as a remembrance for others (Joshua 4), so should we use whatever we have gone through as an opportunity to express God's character.

- While leaders do not need to pretend that they do not go through deep valleys, they usually cannot afford to stay in that state for too long – leading means being able to move through the valley so that we can encourage and minister to others.

- Depending on the depth of the personal crisis, this is often a great challenge for the leader and at times may even necessitate a relinquishment of service for a period of time until new perspective is gained. We all need to exercise God's grace towards those in these deep crises, knowing that the next time we may be in need of the understanding and grace of others. Patience and endurance are required to walk out of these dark nights of the soul.

- In spite of the trials and obstacles, we must learn to rebuild our faith and hope in God, so that our hearts remain soft and we can continue to serve others out of a pure heart. The challenge for the Christian leader is to keep one's heart soft and pure even when circumstances occur which we do not understand or even fully appreciate at the time!

Wrong priorities

- Developing wrong priorities is usually a matter of many small wrong choices over a period of time. The result is that we no longer have God's priorities, but our own.

- Even though most ministers begin serving with pure motives, the temptation to begin to build one's *own* kingdom can develop as we begin to become more comfortable with our gifts and callings and see our influence and ministry grow.

- However, as our ministry grows, our priorities need to remain consistent. The top priority of the Christian leader needs to be to continually seek God's Kingdom first (Matt. 6:33). With outward success and influence this may become even more difficult, which is why leaders must guard their hearts and keep them open to God's evaluation.

- Also, as the leader sees God work through their efforts, they can begin to wrongly assume that the success is a result of their own abilities or commitment. This can lead to a shift in priorities, away from those priorities that were once the center of their ministry. However, the focus on "things above" must be the number one priority of our life and ministry (Col 3:1-2).

- As mentioned in the previous section on Leadership, there are many things that can distract the leader and cause a change of priorities. Yet Christian leaders, who grow in effectiveness and influence, learn the discipline of guarding their hearts, so that he may continue to have God's priorities.

- As we pray for God to reveal our hearts to us, he will begin to show us those areas where we have become more preoccupied with *our* ministry, rather than his agenda – building our kingdom and not his Kingdom.

- Our response to the success of others will also indicate our heart condition. *How do we respond to our peers whose ministry and influence has grown faster than our own? Do we continue to have a Kingdom focus or feel threatened and envious?* Desiring the success of others indicates that we want to build God's Kingdom, not our own.

- If our priorities are right, we are also always willing to surrender our very calling and ministry back to God, should he so desire. Our source of identity and value does not come from our role or ministry position, but from our relationship with

Together with your mentor, evaluate your priorities in all main areas of your life and ministry. What steps do you need to take in order to realign your priorities?

God. Maintaining a servant attitude, instead of seeking after prestige and power must be our top priority if we are going to continue to be effective for the Kingdom.

- In all the "doing," maintaining a balance in life is a priority for the servant-leader. This begins with our families, but also includes our own personal needs, such as our physical and emotional well-being.

Impurity

- Rather obvious, but worth repeating, is the negative affect unconfessed sin has on Christian leaders and their ministry. While we all have failures and even transgressions, the choice to keep our heart soft by continually seeking God's forgiveness, will determines our effectiveness (ie. King David).

- Leaders need to pay particular attention to what they allow in their senses, such as their eyes. This is often where the battle is won or lost and is where the first thoughts are produced that can lead to sin.

- It is also important for the leader to examine if they have any unforgiveness towards others. Unforgiveness hinders not only our relationship with others, but also our relationship with God.

- If we allow impurity to remain in our hearts it will begin to affect our personal life and ministry. We will begin to shift our focus from people and meeting their needs to personal success and even vanity. We can even find ourselves beginning to covet the ministry, gifts and callings of others.

- To be the servant-leader that God desires, spiritual surgery is needed so that these impurities cannot destroy our effectiveness and spiritual life. We need to regularly pray the prayer of repentance that David prayed in Psalm 51 and allow God to cleanse us again. God bought David back from the brink of self-destruction, as he has done with many leaders since then and if we have impurity in our hearts he can do the same for us.

Stagnation

- As in many arenas of life, over time it becomes easier to rely on our experience and familiarity to achieve our goals. This can also occur in Christian leadership. Continued spiritual and mental preparation is vital if we are to fulfill our calling and leave a legacy.

- In our service with others we also can begin to rely on our own experiences and ability, instead of continually developing ourselves, both naturally and spiritually. We can detect this stagnation by a growing lack of preparation and "freshness." More and more we depend on *old manna*, instead of making the effort to receive something fresh from God.

- Weariness can also lead to stagnation, as we no longer take the time necessary to grow and develop. Continual weariness causes us to lose our focus and can eventually lead to a hardened heart. Time with God is important, but it is also important to have personal time off as well as time with the family, away from the ministry, in order to remain mentally and physically strong.

- Pressures and obligations can even lead us to no longer want to (or feel we can) fulfill our calling. However, this challenge of leadership is usually a result of wrong priorities and with effort can be changed. Instead of focussing on tasks or *doing*, it is the responsibility of Christian leaders to maintain the spiritual disciplines that foster an active relationship with God. It is as we keep our relationship fresh with God that we find that our spirituality and service for others does not stagnate.

Commit to having a readiness to accept responsibility for sin and asking for forgiveness.

Have you become stagnant in any area of your life?
What steps are you taking to continue to grow spiritually, intellectually, personally?

THE GREATEST IS LOVE

For the Body

- The ultimate purpose of every Christian is to make disciples of all peoples (Matt 28:19-20).

- God has placed gifts in the Body in order to prepare the saints to do the work of the ministry (Matt. 28:19), a topic we will discuss more in our last two chapters.

- Yet those who have influence in the Body of Christ, need to regularly evaluate their heart condition towards those they are called to serve. *Is it still out of love or have other motives taken root?*

- Due to hurts, criticisms, and painful misunderstandings, our heart can become cold and hard towards the very ones that we have been called to serve. Yet, through his power, it is possible to follow Christ's example of continuing to serve and sacrifice, even when misunderstood and rejected by the very ones he was called to serve.

- To be able to serve others with this attitude of love, it is crucial to be aware of the condition and needs of those to whom we are called to serve. As we see their needs, it will become more difficult for our hearts to become hardened towards them. The leader's prayer life is often an indicator of their heart attitude towards others. *Are we critical and removed, or do we remain personally broken for the needs of others?*

- In 2 Corinthians 7:2-3, we see the Apostle Paul willingly sacrificing for the Corinthian Church. He was willing to even lay down his life for them. This is an example for all those who serve in the Body of Christ.

- As previously mentioned, this heart attitude is also reflected in an open heart towards those we minister, which is expressed through our words and actions. *Are we aloof or approachable and real?*

- This does not mean that ministers do not need to have healthy boundaries in their dealings with others. Being open, sacrificial, and vulnerable, does not mean that the leader does not need to be wise in the setting of priorities as to the amount of time they spend with others (see *Leadership* Section for a discussion regarding these areas). Yet *boundaries* should not be an excuse to avoid those to whom God has called us.

For the World

- To keep a right heart motivation in serving the Church, we must also have the right heart attitude towards the *World*. Defining *World* as those people who have not yet responded to the gracious invitation of their Father.

- Leaders must evaluate the real attitude of their heart towards the lost: *Has our heart become cold towards the most needy around us? Have we even used the Church to insulate us from ministry in the "real" world?*

- Our attitude towards a needy world, will be reproduced in those we influence. If we do not have a heart for the world, neither will those we minister to.

- It is through prayer that we sense God's heart for all peoples and become moved by what moves him (see Chapter 4.2). Only through this divine work in our hearts will we be able to communicate this to others.

- Examining our hearts in terms of our attitudes towards the world, means evaluating what propels us in ministry. Do we only desire to get ahead and be *successful*, gaining the approval of others, or is our passion to reach a lost world, sharing God's burden for *all people*?

How would you characterize your heart motivation towards the Body of Christ?
Have your motivations changed since you first began serving others? How?

Evaluate your heart motivation towards those who do not personally know Christ yet.
Compared to Jesus' attitude, how would you characterize your own? What adjustments do you need to make in order to have his heart for the world?

Be accountable with your mentor in those areas of necessary change that the Lord has showed you from this chapter.

Keep these action steps in mind as you study the last two chapters regarding our mission in the world and your responsibility as a leader in that mission.

• Only then will we be able to reflect the ministry of Jesus, being moved with compassion for the many he saw without someone to lead them (Matt 9:36). At the root of what moves the leader's heart for the church and the world is Love. Without this as motivation, all that we do will merely be empty self-glory which will not produce real life in others (1 Cor 13).

SUMMARY

• As we began our discussion in this last section, our focus is towards our *Ministry* – our service with others. In previous sections we have laid a foundation of *who* we are as a *Person*, have then applied the foundational truths of being a *Disciple*, as well as discovered some principles of being a *Servant-Leader*.

• In this chapter we have discussed the necessity of a pure heart with pure motives in order to be effective in our service as a minister.

• While this is a divine work of grace, we do have a responsibility to guard our hearts and give him permission to examine our heart. For it is only with the right motivation that we will be effective in producing fruit that will remain and leave a legacy for other generations.

• As we turn our attention to the next chapter, we will begin to get a clearer picture of God's heart and priorities and begin to grasp the scope of the mission to which he has called us to as partners.

Minister

Mentoring
thru
Intentional Relationships

Chapter
4.2

Your Mission:
Having God's Heart

INTRODUCTION

- The purpose of discovering our gifts and calling (Section 1.0) and developing spiritually through the spiritual disciplines (Section 2.0) is so that we can more effectively be about God's business. The purpose and focus for being people of influence (Section 3.0), is so that we may be about the Mission of the Kingdom.

- Our purpose in these last two chapters is to discover what God's mission is and how we can partner with him. In this chapter we will see God's heart and what his purpose is for mankind. Knowing this is crucial if we are going to be about his business. We will focus our attention on God's mission throughout the ages and how he desires that we partner together with him.

- The ultimate purpose of this program, and mentoring in general, is not just for personal growth, rather it is so that we are better prepared and equipped for God's purposes throughout our lives. God has a purpose for each one of us specifically in redeeming *all peoples* to himself.

- In this chapter we will overview only a few key missions concepts. Much more can be found in the reader and manual, *Perspectives on the World Christian Movement,* by the US Center for World Missions, and is recommended highly as additional reading (course available online through icm-international.org).

THE MISSION

Mission Lost

- For our purposes, the term "mission" will being used to mean God's overall plan for the redemption of humankind (Rom 8:18-25) and "missions" as the various human initiatives which are used to further God's mission.

- In pluralistic societies, in efforts to not offend anyone and seem *open minded*, it has become trendy to champion the idea that there are no real absolutes and all well-meaning paths lead us to God.

- Consequently, it can even be seen as arrogant and exclusive in such societies to be involved in missions – in attempting to further God's mission of redemption.

- So while it is recognized that these principles will not be valued in the society at large, this attitude has also infiltrated some church circles, to the extent that, even in some churches, the idea of intentionally spreading the "Good News" is seen as being too proactive.

- In churches that are more evangelical in perspective, there has also developed another challenge to this Mission. Some have begun to question even the validity of sending missionaries when the spiritual needs at home seem to be as great as anywhere else. Some believers are beginning to question the rational of sending missionaries to other countries, in light of the current spiritual state of affairs in their own country.

- These issues are representative of some of the challenges facing the Mission in the 21st Century.

Is the idea of missions irrelevant?
Why do you think it is still valid to send missionaries?

Study Isaiah 53 and 54. What insights do you gain about Jesus redemptive work and the task of reaching the harvest?

Mission Found

- Throughout Church history an artificial separation between the "Church" and "Missions" began to develop. Often a direct connection was not made between those redeemed and their responsibility of world evangelism and the biblical perspective was lost.

- However, in Gal 4:25-27 Paul quotes Is 54:1("...more are the children of the desolate woman than of her who has a husband.") and applies this to the New Testament Church; for just as the complete meaning of the *Suffering Servant* of Isaiah 53 could only be really seen in the resurrection of Jesus, so could the full harvest of Isaiah 54 only be realized after the birth of the Church on Pentecost.

- David Bosch quoting Aargaard says, "Mission...is seen as a movement from God to the world; the Church is viewed as an instrument of that mission. There is a Church because there is a mission, not vice versa." So the two are inseparably linked. It is not so much a question of *IF* we should be involved in missions, but rather *HOW* God wants us to be involved.

- Jesus' life, death, and resurrection was focussed on the whole world. God's love for the whole world motivated him to send his Son. Jesus then commissioned his Church to fulfill this mission.

- God's mission is fundamental to who we are as Christians. Better understanding our personality, interests, abilities, gifts, and callings, assists us to better partner with God in his mission in the world.

Respond to the statement, "There is a church because there is a mission, not vice versa."

A BIBLICAL PERSPECTIVE

A Missionary God

- Missions is a divine activity; it represents God's heart is for *all peoples.*

- This theme is evident throughout both the Old and New Testaments, with the clearest representation of God's heart being in the person of Jesus Christ.

- God's heart has always been to bless *all peoples* and throughout Scripture we see how he has desired to accomplish this. In the Old Testament there was a partial fulfilment through Abraham and Israel, which Jesus then more fully fulfilled during his earthly ministry. Ultimately, however, this will be accomplished at the *end of the age* through the partnership of Christ and his Church.

Discuss the statement, "Missions is a divine activity; we only find the meaning for our faith as we identify with God's purpose."

- Though progressively revealed, each progressive revelation speaks of a partnership God desires to have with man to fulfill His mission. We can only really find the meaning for our faith as we identify with God's purpose, for to have God's heart means that we are interested in what interests him

- But he sees us more than unwilling, obligated employees, but as co-workers and partners together with him. To grasp this is to realize the awesome opportunity we have to be about something so much greater than ourselves, which has the potential to eventually extend beyond even our own generation.

Old Testament Foundation

- In Genesis 12:1-3 we see the foundation of God's intention: "I will make you into a great nation and I will bless you; I will make your name great, and you will be a blessing. I will bless those who bless you, and whoever curses you I will curse: and all peoples on earth will be blessed through you."

- Abraham was not only to be blessed for his own benefit, but was blessed in order to be a blessing for others ("in you all the families of the earth will be blessed."). Further, it was not a task to be done in self-strength, but a promise to him of what

God wanted to do through him.

- Paul continues this theme in the New Testament, "The Scripture foresaw that God would justify the Gentiles by faith, and announced the gospel in advance to Abraham: 'All nations will be blessed through you.' So those who have faith are blessed along with Abraham, the man of faith." (Gal 3:8).

- The original promise began with the gospel coming to Abraham; the promise of which can be traced throughout Scriptures and human history. But it did not end there. It was meant for all those who would believe as Abraham did, for though one man was chosen, the blessing was for all peoples.

- One people group (Israel) were to show the nations the character of Jehovah, but the blessing was for all nations. It was always God's purpose that Israel would play a more active role than just attracting the nations to their God, for there was always a "go" component (illustrations being the lives of Jonah, Naomi, Daniel, Esther and many others).

- We see this loving heart of the Father revealed in Isaiah 52:10 - 54:17. The Messiah is the *Suffering Servant* who will bring man back into fellowship with him.

- Yet the Children of Israel failed in their role of *blessing all families of the earth* and, and yet even with greater revelation, the New Testament disciples also had trouble grasping this concept. It was difficult for them to understand why Jesus was interested in the Samaritans, the Greeks, and even the hated Romans, all of who were outside of the Jewish faith.

- It was not until after Pentecost and Paul's eventual confrontation of Peter, that he and the rest of the disciples began to see that the Abrahamic Covenant included *all peoples*.

New Testament Fulfilment

- This biblical theme is most clearly revealed in the coming of the Messiah – he came to *seek and to save all that were lost.* Jesus was actually the first *missionary* and became the model for all believers.

- Missions is a natural outflow of a relationship with Jesus, they cannot be separated. This *Great Commission* ("Therefore go and make disciples of all nations, baptizing them in the name of the Father, of the Son & the Holy Spirit and teaching them to obey everything I have commanded you." Matt 28:19-20) is only written in this form once, but it is assumed throughout the New Testament (from the Gospels, Acts and the Epistles).

- It was this that was at the root of the early disciples' passion to evangelize the whole world. They understood man's condition without God and his great sacrifice to restore man to fellowship with him. But they then realized that this was only the beginning, for God desired them to join him as partners in reaching those who had never heard of him.

- The members of the Body of Christ are joint-heirs and a royal priesthood; holy and distinct from the world, and yet to show God's heart to the world. The ultimate purpose being that God would receive glory from all the nations. While it is God's mission, he has purposed to fulfill his mission in the world through his Church.

- Motivation for this mission is more than just compassion, it is motivated by a love for God; it is more than just benefiting people, it is for God's glory.

What have you seen from the Old Testament regarding God's purposes that you had not seen before?

Discuss the statement, "To meet Christ means to become caught up in a mission to the world." How has your view of the Great Commission and its priority in your life changed?

The Mission and the Kingdom

- There is a connection between Jesus' teaching regarding the Kingdom and God's Mission.

- Jesus came announcing the arrival of the Kingdom, a Kingdom that referred to his rulership in people's hearts. Then between his first and second coming was a period during which time the Gentiles have the potential to be heirs with Israel; partakers in the same promise (Eph 3:6, Rom 15:8-9). The mystery of the Kingdom was that they were somehow partakers of this same blessing and mission.

- At his first coming, the Messiah was revealed as the *Suffering Servant of God* (Isaiah 42, 49, 53), delivering people from evil's power and offering them the blessing of God's rule in their hearts. During this period, the Kingdom was "hidden," but at his second coming he will come visibly in power, eliminating all evil and sin from the earth, culminating in a celebration around the throne with those *"from every tribe, language and people and nations"* (Rev 5:9-10, 7:9 10:11).

- Yet before this future coming, the Gospel of the Kingdom must be proclaimed in all the world, among all peoples, and only then would the end come (Matt 24:14). This was Jesus' main theme with his disciples after his resurrection. His desire was to explain this divine-human partnership and the relationship between his second coming and God's mission for the Church. The culmination of God's Kingdom is connected with the fulfilment of his *Mission* through his *Church*.

The Commission of the Church

- The theme of the *Great Commission* is extensive throughout the Scriptures. Matthew 28:18-20 has been referred to as *The Great Commission*, yet its focus is not only the spreading the message, but making disciples from among all peoples. It includes both *going* and *growing*, the twin mandate of the Church.

- Various other passages specifically confirm the Church's commission. In Mark 16:15-16 the focus is to communicate to every individual on earth, so that all men may have the opportunity for a personal faith in the Christ. Elsewhere, using many Old Testament passages, Jesus confirms his atoning work, and its proclamation to "all peoples." (Luke 24:46-49).

- As Jesus was sent from the Father, likewise he sent his disciples (and every disciple that would follow in the centuries to come) with his same authority to accomplish this task (John 20:21-23). Yet another version of this Commission is in Acts.1:8. This Commission includes not just those far away, but also the near and mundane. The concern of the Church must be for the whole world, just as the Father's heart is moved for all peoples.

Discuss the concept that the Great Commission of Matthew 28 has more to do with making disciples than mere evangelism. What is the difference?

The Imperative

- During Jesus earthly ministry he chose a few in order to reproduce his character in them. In Matt 28:19-20, he then gave the command to them to go and "make disciples." A reproducing structure – the Church – was then launched to facilitate this discipling of *all peoples*. This imperative includes both the *act* and *process* of regeneration; referring to both becoming a disciple of Jesus and then being discipled in obedience to him.

- "All peoples" is derived from the Greek phrase, *panta ta ethne,* which is often translated as "all nations." Using the term *all nations* is somewhat misleading, for the original meaning is better understood as *all peoples*, not political entities (nations) or just the general term, "the Gentiles."

- While the salvation of *every individual* of every people group is not the criteria for the return of Christ (Matt. 24:14), "reached" does mean that there will be a *reproducing witness* within each *people group* (People group defined by language, lineage, or socio-cultural factors).

- The Father was motivated by love as he sent his Son to redeem fallen man. He has then commissioned his Church to be partners together with him. The Church is not to be motivated out of guilt or coercion to participate in this task, but out of a pure love for the lost. It is an expression of our very relationship with him. We are co-laborers *WITH* Christ, not just working *FOR* Christ.

How has your understanding of "all nations" changed? How will this affect your life and ministry?

God's Plan: The Church

- After Jesus returned to the Father, the disciples waited in Jerusalem for the coming of the promised Holy Spirit, who was to empower and establish the early band of believers, later to be called the *Church*, or *called out ones*.

- From the very beginning on Pentecost, it was international in scope, with those witnessing the events representative of all nations. From Jerusalem this movement was to then affect all nations and *all peoples*.

- Yet even with this dramatic beginning, there was some human resistance to the divine universality of the Gospel. The real turning point occurred in Acts chapter fifteen, where the fundamental issue of the intended scope of the Gospel was dealt with. The real issue was if this new initiative would remain a small sect of Judaism or would it encompass every language, culture and race of the world? It was this early Council that affirmed God's intention that the Good News proclaimed by Jesus was indeed for all peoples.

- From its early beginnings, it was also clear that God's intent was not just individual conversions, but actually the planting of *churches* – communities of local believers. It was only through this structure, or form (initial discussion on form and function in Chapter 3.1), that the *Great Commission* could be fulfilled.

- Initially, even among the Gentile believers, the initial pattern seemed to be similar to the synagogue model. The simple house churches quickly grew and evolved into a distinct structure, eventually becoming parish congregations. These were simple structures where believers were nourished, while providing the context for outreach.

- Also very early in the development of the Church, was the emergence of *apostolic band*. This was a distinctive *structure* of the church, whose purpose was outreach into areas where there was yet no Gospel witness.

- As a structure, it seems that these were patterned after the travelling Jewish proselytizers, the first of which was sent out from Antioch. However, it is clear from Paul's writings, that he did not expect these apostolic bands to fulfill God's work on their own, he expected God to work through the Church as a whole.

Discuss the "nurturing" and "sending" aspects of the Church. Do you see this dual priority in your ministry? How does this relate to your personal ministry gifts?

POST NEW TESTAMENT

Some Misunderstandings

- After the First Century, various factors contributed to a misunderstanding and resulting lack of participation in world evangelism and world missions. While there was always a remnant witness of the Gospel during this period, the mission that God had given his Church often became dim and nearly non-existent.

- The following are a sampling of some of the key misunderstandings and factors which developed and hindered the spread of the Gospel subsequent to the First Century.

■ Apostle or Missionary

- Historically, there has been differing views regarding the role of the apostle. In 1 Corinthians 12:28 Paul writes, "God has appointed *first* apostles...," which has been usually interpreted as "first in order of importance," in the sense of a hierarchy. However, perhaps a better meaning would be to relate "first" in terms of timing; the order in which the gifting and ministry is actually needed. For example, since the gifting of the apostle is needed to actually plant the church, they would be considered *first*.

- This seems to be confirmed by Paul's life for though he used the term *apostle* to describe himself, he did not exercise ultimate control as *Apostle* over all the churches he planted (as we generally think of the term *bishop* today). Rather, he seems to have seen the role of the *apostle* as the one who initiated or planted a new work, therefore having to do more with function than position.

- Our understanding of the role of the *equipping* gifts of Ephesians 4:11 (see discussion in Chapter 1.2 and 3.1 regarding), also influences our understanding of the term apostle, though not all who see these as *offices* or *positions* are consistent in their view of the equipping gifts.

- As in our other discussions regarding leadership, spiritual gifts (of which *apostle* is one) have to do more with *function* than *position* or title. Its New Testament usage seems to refer primarily to a spiritual gift that is to be used for the initial advancement of the Church. However, its usage has developed over the years to a meaning that has more to do with authority and structure, consequently being avoided by segments of the Church, in order to avoid this misunderstanding.

- To further complicate matters, the term *mission, missions* or *missionary* do not appear in the English Bible and so, among other segments of the Church, there is a reluctance to use these terms. Others have pointed out that the term *missionary* is derived from the Latin word which is the equivalent to the Greek (biblical) term for *apostle*, indicating that they are actually synonymous terms, both having to do with establishing and extending the Kingdom.

- The result of all these issues has been a misunderstanding of the Mission of the Church and *who* is responsible to fulfill this task (which is our purpose here, not to present the final definition of "apostle" or "missionary").

■ Creeds and Structures

- After the First Century several historic issues conspired to limit and cloud the believer's understanding regarding the true mission of the Church.

- Due to early heresies which began to infiltrate the Church, the early Church began to establish creeds to preserve the truth of God's Word. However, the purpose of these were to combat error which had begun to creep into the Church, not to articulate the responsibility of the Church to evangelize the world.

- Consequently, the theme of the Mission of the Church was not articulated and those who later relied on these as sacred documents saw the omission as purposeful and normative (applicable for all believers).

- The developing structure of the pre- Reformation societies and the amount of control exercised by the official Church began to greatly limit the participation of believers in the *Great Commission*. "Control and consolidation," not "releasing and going," were the emphasis of this period.

- Unfortunately, the Reformation fires did not kindle missionary zeal either. The early reformers (particularly the theologians) were rather silent on the issue, though groups such as the Anabaptists, Pietist and Moravians, continued carrying out missions work. Perhaps one of the greatest surprises of the Reformation was that it did not result in a resurgence of missionary activity.

- Some possible reasons for this lapse during the Reformation Period, may have been the opposition to the new Protestant movements by the official Roman Catholic Church (and its inherent parochial structures which inhibited missionary expansion), as well as the barrier of Islam, which by then had surrounded Europe.

- In this regard, the passivity of the creeds, the hierarchical structures, as well as the lack of biblical understanding of missions by the early Protestants, not only affected Christians then, but also the Christian view of missions to this very day.

■ The "Great Commission"

- The very term, *The Great Commission,* has also led to misunderstanding. This term, referring to Matthew 28:19-20, was not really used much until the *Modern Missions Movement* (the beginning of which is attributed to William Carey around A.D. 1800).

- Many key reformers had assumed that it (world evangelization) had, to a large extent, been achieved by the Apostolic Church of the first century, so only local witness was required. William Carey's key contribution was showing the fallacy of this position and the relevance of Jesus' command to the Church of all ages, which in turn impacted all of its members.

- Since Carey, there has been much emphasis of this term and concept by Evangelicals. So much so, that the emphasis on this one passage has led to a lack of understanding how missions encompasses the whole of Scripture. This has, at times, led to a faulty understanding of the mission of the Church today.

A Remnant Remains

- In spite of these challenges, and the subsequent failure of the Church in fulfill its calling and mission, God has been at work to sovereignly accomplish his purposes throughout history.

- Though muted, and at times seemingly non-existent, God's purpose has continued to be fulfilled throughout human history.

- Ralph Winter has outlined four ways in which missionary activity has continued throughout history: *Voluntary* and *Involuntary Going* and *Voluntary* and *Involuntary Coming.*

- *Voluntary Going* is illustrated in the Old Testament by Abraham to Canaan, and in the New Testament by Paul and Barnabas going on their first missionary trip. Later in history groups like the Moravians and William Carey voluntarily went to foreign lands.

- *Involuntary Going* is illustrated by Joseph being sold into slavery, and more recently during times of persecutions, such as Ugandan Christians dispersing throughout Africa, through no decision of their own.

- *Voluntary Coming*, for example, occurred in the Old Testament as Naaman (a Syrian) came to Elisha and Cornelius sent for Peter, in the New Testament. Other examples include the Vikings invading Christian Europe, and International visitors coming to the "Christian" West today.

- *Involuntary Coming* examples include the Gentiles settling in Israel under Cyrus the Great, the Roman military occupation in Israel, as well as slaves brought to America, boat people and other refugees in transit around the world.

- We can see that even in those times when there was no strategic or targeted Gospel witness, the Gospel has continued to spread in all four of these ways.

How can an understanding of history better help us understand missions today?
How does the history of our own denomination/ church/organization affect current effectiveness in missions?

While there have been many low periods in history, when the light of Christianity seemed at a very low ebb, there has always been a remnant.

- Ralph Winter further outlines this expansion (see *Perspectives* material) over the last 2000 years in five, four hundred year periods. Of course, there are huge generalizations made and it must be remembered that the focus here is mainly on the expansion of the Gospel.

■ A.D. 0 - 400

- During this initial period Paul and the early church "go" into the then known world, both voluntarily as well as by dispersion due to persecution. The Gospel then followed Roman expansion and spread across national boundaries. However, once Christianity became the official state religion, its expansion slowed.

■ A.D. 400 - 800

- Barbarian tribes who had begun invading areas of the Roman Empire, became evangelized in the process and eventually the tribes (Goths, Visigoths, Vandals and Anglo Saxons) that displaced the Roman Empire in Europe also received the Christian faith from those they invaded.

- During this time the development of the monastic orders served to preserve the Gospel, but some of these monastic orders were also committed to "going," particularly the Celtic evangelists. Other key personalities encouraged educational and economic development (Charlemagne) and this "mini-renaissance" helped to keep Christianity alive throughout Europe.

- Yet little was done to evangelize the Vikings who had begun attacking from the north. This fact was to negatively affect the expansion of the Gospel during next period of history.

■ A.D. 800 - 1200

- The Vikings came into contact with Christianity as they invaded Europe, though they had no appreciation of anything Christian and destroyed everything in their path. However, it was the monks and "forced wives" (Christian women taken by Vikings) who influenced the *Northmen* with the Gospel.

- Their descendants then became the first evangelists of the next era, eventually spreading the Gospel to Scandinavia and other northern European areas. Through the eventual Gregorian Reform, these northern areas were incorporated within Europe, though Europe had not actually reached outside of its borders with the Gospel message.

■ A.D. 1200 - 1600

- This era was dominated by the Crusades – a dark spot on Christianity. Ironically, every major Crusade was initiated by a Viking descendant. These campaigns conquered territory and people without the Gospel message being of any "blessing" or benefit for those of the Muslim world. This scar is still not healed and affects the evangelism of Muslim people today.

- During this period, the Friars were missionary in nature, but stayed within the borders of Europe. Roman Catholic missionary activity predated Protestant activity by two hundred years, but only with an emphasis on monastic structures alongside of colonial expansion.

- The decentralization of European Christianity began with the Renaissance and Reformation, however, again, the new Protestant movement had virtually no missionary activity.

How has the influence of western culture affected the values of those in your region or ministry?
How has the reversal of Western Powers affected missions and the expansion of the church in your region?

- **A.D. 1600 - 2000+**

  - During the first two hundred years of this period, Roman Catholic missions predominated. This began to shift as by A.D. 1800 Protestant missions began to predominant. After centuries of lethargy, Protestant missions began in earnest in A.D. 1800, which enabled democratic structures of government, schools, and hospitals to flourish in regions which they touched around the world (Though often not stated, in the 1700's the Moravians and Count Zinzendorf were sending missionaries around the world and had a remarkable influence on leaders such as the Wesleys).

  - At the beginning of this period, Europeans had only a minimal presence in the rest of the non-western world, but by 1945 politically controlled virtually all (95%) of the non-western world. Within 25 years after World War Two and the explosion of nationalism, western nations had lost "control" of all but 5% of the non-western world. During this period (1945-1969) there was an incredible explosion of missions around the world. Ironically, the lack of colonial political control opened the door for more legitimate evangelism, which was to bear even greater fruit.

  - Currently, Christianity is numerically at its strongest in the non-western world and God is beginning to raise up the Church from these regions to "go into all the world." Those that were once a *mission field* are now becoming a *mission force*.

MODELS OF EXPANSION

Nurture and Expansion

- As mentioned in our discussion regarding form and function (Chapter 3.1), *structure* or *form* is not neutral, but is an important vehicle to properly express truth and meaning. Further, our effectiveness is actually often dependent upon the implementation of the right form (ie. new wineskins for new wine).

- History confirms the importance of having right structures to achieve goals and this is particularly applicable in terms of the Mission of the Church.

- There are two general structures that apply to the Church and the expansion of the Gospel. One emphasizes *nurture* and the other *expansion*. Ralph Winter has used the words *modality* and *sodality* to describe these forms, where *modality* refers to nurture-oriented congregational church structures and *sodality* refers to task-oriented mission structures of expansion.

- While these structures and their implications are not unique to the Church, we will confine our discussion to how they apply to the expansion of the Gospel.

- Both of these structures are important and necessary. Modality structures are more nurture-orientated, which help the church to grow from within, while sodality structures help to encourage the "go" or mission function of the Church.

- Throughout Church history the relative strength or weakness of these structures affected the mission of the Church. Observing this paradigm throughout history can help us understand our current structures and how we can be more effective.

Discuss the differences between Modality and Sodality structures. Why are both important for the spread of the Gospel?

Historical Overview

- We see both of the models in the first century. The synagogue and early local groups of Christian believers were nurturing in nature (*modality*), while the early mission teams were focussed on expansion (*sodality*). Paul built upon the proselytizer structure of those who travelled throughout the Roman Empire to win converts. These early teams were sent out from, as well as somewhat independent, from the nurturing structure.

Within your church/denomination is there room for healthy sodality structures? How does your answer affect the mission outreach of your group/church?

- During the Medieval Period, the congregational structure continued to develop and though they began to join together into diocese, they were still more of an organism than organization. Simultaneously, the monastic order began to develop as a positive spiritual influence upon the Church. The local church structure (parish) survived in large part due to these monastic structures, which also resulted in some missionary endeavours.

- It was the Roman Catholic ability to function with both structures – local diocese and monastic orders – that is a positive legacy to this day. However, as some monastic orders became wealthy and lost purpose, there was spiritual decline and decay. Fortunately, renewal initiatives, such as the Anabaptists, remained as a foundation which was built upon during the Reformation.

- For all its good, a negative of the Reformation was its abandonment of the monastic structures which were really the only mission structures of the time. Consequently, for almost 200 years after the beginning of the Reformation, there was essentially no mission activity. The early Lutheran movement had virtually no mission patterns (sodality) and the Pietistic and Anabaptist movements reverted back to only a modality pattern of biological growth, which led to their ineffectiveness as a renewing or mission structure.

- The early Protestants rejecting the only sodality (expansion) structure of the time (the monastic movement), and so had no pattern or vehicle for missions for several hundred years. Though there were some exceptions (ie. the Moravians), it was not until William Carey (ca. A.D. 1800) that there was a rediscovery of a sodality structure as a vehicle which initiated the explosion of Protestant missions and missionaries.

Some Applications

If you are part of a church or group that was started by foreign missionaries, analyse your structures.
Are you only a modality structure or do you also have sending structures? Are you also now sending missionaries?

- Unfortunately these first sodality (expansion) structures of the Modern Mission Era were often independent of recognized church structures. Though they were eventually incorporated within the nurturing (or modality) structures, this often changed them to the degree that they were no longer as effective as "going," or apostolic structures.

- This tension between these *nurturing* and *sending* structures has affected the expansion of the gospel, in that the Church structures which developed on the mission field did not reflect both of these structures. As well, those who were sent out from a sodality structure (missions organization) often only envisioned planting a nurturing structure (local church congregations), rather than churches that had both modality and sodality aspects. Consequently, many missionaries coming from the developing nations have had little national church support, as they have sought to be sent out from their church.

- For a healthy local church, as well as healthy missions, we need to recognize and value both of these structures. One cannot replace the other, both are needed simultaneously (in the next chapter we will continue our discussion regarding structures and their effect on the Mission of the Church).

MISSION PRINCIPLES

Modern Missions Era

Which Era was your church or denomination birthed in? How does this affect your groups' understanding of the mission of the church and your role in this mission?

- Ralph Winter has identified three main eras of the *Modern Protestant Missions* (A.D. 1800 to present day). The *First Era* (1792-1910) was characterized by great sacrifice and early pioneers such as William Carey and the *Second Era* (1865-1980) was pioneered by Hudson Taylor and the *Student Volunteer Movement*, which was so successful in planting churches worldwide, that by 1940 some had thought the era of missions was over.

- The *Third Era*, according to Winter, was pioneered by Townsend and McGavran, with the emphasis being on "people groups," as opposed to just reaching into geographical regions. During this era many non-western mission agencies surpassing the influence of their western counterparts. Some see a final era where the gospel message truly goes "from all peoples to all peoples." This is a stage of new partnership where the once *receiving* nations also become *sending* nations.

- Mission endeavors typically have four stages of development. The *Pioneer* phase is when there is first contact with a people group. Next expatriates begin to train national leadership during the *Paternal* phase, which eventually should transition into the *Partnership* phase, as national leaders work as equals with expatriates. Finally, expatriates are lesser partners and only participate by invitation during the *Participation* phase of the mission process.

- The overlap of these stages of mission work throughout the last three *Mission Eras* has led to confusion and even conflict. Being aware of these phases can help us understand why churches and agencies sometimes pursue different mission priorities and why it is not always easy to correctly identify what the current priority should be on any given field. Balance is required between the needs of the local church and the need of evangelizing the unreached (modality and sodality).

What priorities are needed in your location, in relation to the stage of your mission field?
What are some of the practical implications for your own ministry?

Types of Evangelism

- In the missions endeavor we must also take several other key factors into considerations. Ralph Winter has developed a *E-scale* (*Evangelism*) and *P-scale* (*Proximity*) to assist in describing this process. To be targeted and effective we must consider the cultural distance between the one sharing the Gospel and the intended hearers *(E-scale)* and how close the unevangelized in the society are to any existing churches (*P-scale*).

■ E (Evangelism) -Scale

- The E-scale ranges from E-0 to E-3 evangelism. E-0 describes evangelism to those of Christian families and people where no real cultural barrier is crossed. E-1 is evangelism that is directed to those outside one's church, but still within one's own culture. It is often very effective for the hearers are most likely to understand the communicator.

- Evangelism that is somewhat more difficult is described by E-2 and E-3 on his scale. E-2 is the evangelization of those from different, yet similar cultures, while E-3 evangelism is to those from very different cultures. This latter one is most difficult for the communicator may have to cross three barriers: a church to non-church barrier, a language barrier, and a major lifestyle barrier.

- This scale does not so much reflect geographic issues, but cultural differences. As a strong national church is established through E-2 and E-3 evangelism, local churches can usually then continue with E-1 evangelism.

- The mission effort must not be blind to the reality of the differing cultures within a country, for this blindness can lead to the ineffectiveness of the mission effort in that country; the focus must be *people groups*, not just geographical areas.

■ P (Proximity) -Scale

- Within a culture, it is also helpful to determine how close the unevangelized are to the existing churches. The P-scale developed by Winter also ranges from P-0 to P-3.

- P-0 refers to those who are already church members in need of renewal and revival. In this case there is no cultural distance between them and following Christ (E-0 required). Similarly, P-1 describes the situation where people are in

What is the difference between the work of an evangelist and a missionary?
How does the cultural distance affect the message?
How should this affect evangelists in cross-cultural settings?

What have you learned about different types of evangelism? What has been the primary focus of your ministry? Does this accurately affect your ministry gifts and calling? What changes would you have to make in order to be more effective?

close proximity to culturally-relevant local churches, who are able to share Christ with them (E-1 required).

- As E-2 and E-3 evangelism is more difficult, so the P-2 and P-3 scale indicate a more difficult scenario. In a P-2 setting, people have no church within their own culture, but there is a witnessing church in a culture which is near to them, however, the potential follower of Christ must cross over a cultural barrier, as well as the social and cultural values of members of a local church which are different than their own (E-2 required).

- In the most difficult case, P-3, individuals are from a culture that has no relevant church and where there is no relevant church in a culture near to them; they have significant barriers to cross in order to follow Christ (E-3 required).

BLESSING ALL PEOPLE

Some Applications

- Over the last several decades, it has become more common to speak of *people groups* (generally defined as the largest homogeneous group of people within which the gospel can spread without encountering major acceptance barriers) and *unreached people groups* (a group of people within which there is no indigenous community of believing Christians able to evangelize them).

- The Gospel often spreads within homogeneous cultural groups within a region where a church has been established, however, prejudices between people groups can limit its expansion between peoples who have large cultural differences.

According to this "P" scale, how close are those around your church (or within the sphere of influence of your ministry) to the Gospel? What inherent barriers have to be removed in order for your ministry to be effective to those around you.

- The E-scale views the process from the perspective of the communicators – it is the distance between them and the potential respondents, while the P-scale views the process from the perspective of the potential converts and the churches that are planted within their culture.

- Some have defined the term, *missionary,* as referring to those engaged in E-2 or E-3 communication of the gospel, while those engaged in E-0 or E-1 evangelism as *evangelists*. While all believers are to be witnesses of Christ with those they know, the reality is that not all believers have been gifted or given the sphere of influence of an evangelist. Similarly, not all evangelists may have the gifting or sphere of ministry to cross the largest of cultural barriers that a missionary is uniquely gifted and called to do.

- From the P-scale, Winter further divides missionary work into either *Regular* or *Frontier* missions. *Regular* missions occurs when cross-cultural Christian work is spread within a culture where churches have already been established (P-0, P-1), while *Frontier* missions is cross-cultural Christian work that seeks to establish churches within people groups where one does not yet exist (P-2 or P-3).

Define the people groups within your sphere of ministry/influence. Evaluate those in your region according to the "E" and "P" scale.

- Obviously, differing strategies are needed in order to be effective in each of these stages, particularly in difficult *Frontier* missions, yet it is important to not define these types of missions just according to geography. For example, someone may be in a far away location training Christians (P-0) while someone could be in their "passport" country (closer geographically), yet be working to evangelize a minority that has no church yet established (P-2 or P-3).

- Various definitions have been developed to describe people groups according to major cultural blocs (which are defined by their culture, traditions, language, and values) and social groups. Differing cultural blocs usually need individual churchplanting efforts, while differing social groups usually need specific evangelistic tactics. (More regarding this will be discussed in the next chapter though only some of the basic introductory mission concepts will be presented).

The Remaining Task

- Barrett, a leading Christian researcher, divides the world into three regions: *World A, B,* and *C. World C* as all those who identify themselves as Christians (E-0), *World B* as all non-Christians who live in cultures where they are likely to hear the gospel during their lifetime (E-1), and *World A* as all non-Christians who have not yet adequately been exposed to the gospel, and will likely not be exposed without pioneering efforts of those crossing barriers to bring them the gospel (E-2, E-3).

- Generally held statistics indicate that one-third of the world's population claims to be Christian *(World C)*, one-third are non-Christians living within reached peoples *(World B)*, and one-third live within unreached people groups *(World A)*. This, of course, is using the broadest definition of "Christian."

- As we look to future there are particular challenges facing the Church. The greatest of which will include reaching into an increasingly urban context, as well as making inroads into resistant blocs of people clusters, particularly Islam.

Are your ministry strategies applicable for the needs of the community?
Do the strategies that you use accurately apply to the evangelism stage of your target field?

Mission Accomplished

- There is some discussion in mission circles as to when, or if, this task of world evangelization will ever be completed. Over the years some have already prematurely announced completion of the mission, yet is this even possible? Will the task of world evangelism only be complete when every *individual* on the planet is a believer? God's heart is that the whole world may hear the Good News, yet is this even an attainable goal?

- As previously alluded, the evangelization of the world does not mean that every individual will be personally reached, or that every individual in every people group will have personally heard the Gospel. However, it does mean that every group of people represented on the earth will have easy access to a reproducing church within their own culture (for more discussion, refer to mission resources listed).

- As Christians continue to take the message around the globe this can one day be a reality. There can be a time in the foreseeable future where there will be no more P-2 or P-3 non-Christians, those who have no access to a gospel witness. In simplest terms this is what *world evangelization* means.

SUMMARY

- In this chapter, we have seen that God's heart is to bless all nations and to use his Church to accomplish this mandate. We then traced God's hand at work throughout history, as we looked at those who never abandoned the *Great Commission*.

Discuss with your mentor how this chapter has influenced you in seeing how the mission of the Church relates to your personal life mission. Reflecting on what you have learned about your personality, gifts and calling, how can you envision being more involved in the Great Commission?

- Through a discussion of various mission principles, we also began to grasp some of the issues of world evangelization and the challenge remaining. Though the missionary task is still not complete there have been incredible breakthroughs and strides forward.

- We are called to participate with God's purpose, being expressions of his heart of love for all peoples. Regardless of our role, gifting or sphere of influence, this is our ultimate purpose. Not all may be called to cross-cultural service, but all believers are called to participate in fulfilling the mandate.

- As we come to our last chapter, we will discuss various strategies of ministry and how this Mission can practically be expressed through us, the Church – the Body of Christ in this world.

Minister

Your Ministry: Following God's Strategy

Mentoring
thru
Intentional Relationships

Chapter
4.3

Your Ministry: Following God's Strategy

INTRODUCTION

- We have learned that God has a mission to reach all people and has commissioned his Body to partner together with him to see this accomplished.

- Building upon what we have learned, in this our last chapter we will look at various models or patterns of ministry from the Bible and Church history, seeking to learn the lessons to bring balance and focus in our own ministries. Seeing how we can reach our full potential within our own sphere of ministry and become all that we can be as his *minister*.

- Our purpose will be to see how to accomplish the mandate in practical ways. This will not be a discussion of specific methodologies, but rather a broad view of some of the issues which relate to the implementation of the global Commission, at the local ministry level.

PATTERNS OF MINISTRY

- As we have seen thus far, structures are important in that they can be vehicles to help us accomplish our goal, or they can hinder that goal from being accomplished. As we saw with the illustration of the new wine and old wineskins (Chapter 3.1), our forms need to be appropriate in order to effectively fulfil our purposes.

- In the last chapter we saw the big picture of God's intention to reach *all people* and that he desires to use his Church to do this. We also saw that to accomplish this, there is a need for both nurturing (*modality*) and expansion (*sodality*) forms; that there must be a design for nurture/preparation as well as for mobilization/expansion.

- Yet, more specifically, how can we accomplish this within our own expressions of ministry? How does this big picture affect our particular *sphere of influence* or *role in the Body*? We will view biblical ministry patterns and their subsequent historical expressions, in order to understand how our effectiveness in the ministry is dependant upon implementing appropriate strategies through appropriate structures.

- Many have found Patrick Johnson's introduction and discussion of the concepts of these structures very helpful in their understanding of the Mission of the Church (*The Church is Bigger Than You Think,* Patrick Johnstone). Though not without some controversy, the initial concepts are included here to encourage more discussion in our understanding of the Great Commission and the challenges in its fulfilment.

A Biblical Foundation

- Though the terminology of *forms* or *structures* is not used in the Scripture, we can see these principles at work in the expression of God's Spirit within the human experience.

- Before the Exile in the Old Testament, there was a foreshadow of the three

What insights have you gained from looking at the nurturing and expansion models of the Church?

patterns or structures within the human experience to express God's divine purposes.

- For example there was the "gathering" or "worship" structure with the *priests*, the *prophet*s, who operated somewhat outside the normal worship system, but still identified with and ministering to God's people, and a limited *discipling* structure through a "school of prophets," as well as those like Gamaliel who gathered disciples to teach.

- In Jesus' ministry we see an expression of each of these three structures and the need for each. There was the *Synagogue,* which continued to be the nurturing structure for God's people, the *Seventy* (the apostolic or sending structure for expansion), and the *Twelve* (discipling or training structure).

- Then in the early church we again see these three structures: The *Local Church* (gathering), *Apostolic teams* (sending) and *Discipleship* (training). In Acts thirteen, the local church is the fundamental structure for missions, but soon thereafter an apostolic or "sending" structure also begins to development, as the local church recognized the Holy Spirit's call on Paul and Barnabas and set them apart to *Go.*

- By "sending" them the church was recognizing God's call on them and their responsibility to release them for this new work. While this early *apostolic* or *mission* structure remained accountable to the local church, it seemed to also be responsible for some of its own operational control.

- Finally, as in Jesus' ministry, by Paul's second missionary trip there was the development of a third structure, the focus of which was to *disciple* and *train* others.

- It should also be noted that this concept in no way diminishes the role or calling of the local church, as it is indeed foundational in God's plan. Yet, by design, the current structure of many local churches makes the expansion phase of the Mission difficult, if not impossible. If the local church is only a "nurturing" structure, then it will not be able to adequately fulfill the Great Commission, there must be a "go" component and strategy.

Gifts and Callings

- Each of these three forms, or structures, need to be balanced in the Body of Christ in order for the goal of world evangelism to take place. When they were out of balance with each other during periods of history, the purpose of the Church was not accomplished.

- As we discussed in the chapter regarding gifts (Chapter 1.2), everyone in the Body of Christ are ministers, for in the new Covenant there is no division between the clergy/laity (Eph. 4:11-12). Yet each believer, as a member of the Body, has a calling and gifts that give them an unique role.

- These three structures affect our understanding of the application of the gifts of Ephesians 4:11. While each gift here is not exclusive to just one structure (there is much overlap), in very general terms, particular gifts are most naturally expressed within certain ministry forms.

- For example, the pastor and prophet gifts are often used to encourage and equip the saints (local church structure), while the evangelist and apostle gifts are needed in the mission or expansion structure, and the teaching gift functions best within training structures. Obviously, there is overlap between the gifts and the forms within which they are expressed and so this is an oversimplification, but in very general terms we can see there is a correlation.

- Failing to understand the balance between these three main forms can lead us to try to fit all the gifts (1 Cor. 12:28 and others) into just one structure, such as

---

What can we learn from the patterns of Jesus' ministry?

What is your view the interrelation between the early church and the newly formed apostolic bands?

Is your ministry structured is such a way that all members are released as ministers, or are there two classes of believers in your church?

Discuss how the application of our gifts is affected by our sphere or role of ministry.

a local nurturing church. Yet other gifts like the apostle, evangelists or even travelling teachers, need more flexible structures at times in order to function effectively and accomplish their role in world evangelism (without diminishing the role of the local church or God's mission to the Church as a whole).

- The danger is that when a gift that does not "seem" to fit easily within a local church structure and is not given legitimate avenues of expression, those with this gift may feel like they do not fit and the local church, as well as the Body of Christ does not benefit from their gifts.

- Within these three general areas, relevant structures need to be developed every generation that are flexible (new wineskins) enough to fulfill God's mission. For example, western models of missions may not be as effective for the missions/missionaries coming from the new emerging sending nations of Africa, South America, or Asia. Training models, as well, may have to change to reflect current needs of emerging leadership.

An Historical Perspective

- Unfortunately, the historical record of maintaining a proper balance between these three (nurture, sending, training) is not very good. Throughout Church history, to greater or lesser degrees, this lack of balance has even contributed to the Church's ineffectiveness in fulfilling the Great Commission,.

- In the centuries after the birth of the Church, it began to become more and more institutionalized. For nearly 1,500 years, the only missions endeavour that was initiated by the official Church was that of the monastic orders. While each of the three structures still existed, they had become institutionalized and were not functioning as effectively as they were during the New Testament Age.

- Instead of the Great Commission and God's mission being the central focus of these forms (nurture, sending, training), the focus became the Pope and the need to maintain power and control.

- Even after the Reformation of A.D. 1500, there was virtually no reform of the dominance of hierarchal structures for several hundred years. Instead of each member being equipped and released to fulfill the role God had designed for them, local congregations remained divided along a clergy/laity model. Even the monastic orders, virtually the only structure left for outreach, disappeared.

- The training structure (universities) became increasingly independent of the Church, consequently becoming more secular and influenced by the unbiblical concepts of the Enlightenment. So as the main structure that would facilitate world evangelism was lost by the Church, so the key structure of training another generation of leaders was also essentially lost by the Body of Christ.

- By A.D. 1800 a return to biblical teaching within the Protestant movement, began to reform these structures. With this reform, world evangelism began moving back into alignment, as the central point and purpose of all three of these forms – the local church, training institutions and sending agencies.

- In addition to the local church, many agencies were established to meet a variety of needs, and training institutions were established to combat liberalism and spiritual deadness. Yet each of these structures still remained independent, as they were not functioning together in order to fulfill the common mandate of the *Great Commission.*

Negative Consequences

- Three autonomous structures developed (local churches, training institutions, and mission agencies), each with their own goals. World evangelism was left as the primary responsibility of the new mission agencies, however this separation

What specific negative consequences do you see in your ministry originating from this lack of unity between the varied emphasis of each structure? What steps can you take to improve this in your life and ministry?

Do you see this concept of the necessity of three structures in contradictions with God's promise to work through his Church? Why or why not?

caused frustrations and often resulted in a minimal emphasis on world evangelization by the church.

- Some mission agencies, frustrated by the lack of vision of local churches, began acting independently of the Church (and local churches). Some Church leaders have also been frustrated by the proliferation of agencies, that seem to be competing for the limited personnel and financial resources of the local church.

- The fact is that some agencies have merely *used* the local church for their ends, at the same time that some local churches have lost sight of the big picture of world evangelization.

- Yet just as each local church needs a variety of gifts expressed within the Body in order to be healthy, so must each of these three structures be functioning in balance in order for the Body of Christ to retain its focus on the Great Commission.

- History has proven that an emphasis on only one of these, leads to ineffectiveness and the Church not fulfilling the task for which God has commissioned it.

Structures in Balance

- When each of these function together in mutually accountable partnerships, however, the result is that the Gospel is most effectively taken to the ends of the earth.

- *Training* needs to have the Great Commission as its top priority and not become an end in itself; it must serve the needs of the Church for equipped leadership in order to fulfill the task. This must be reflected in an even greater flexibility in program design and curriculum, so that another generation can be equipped to *go into all the world*.

- *Mission agencies* need to be seen as part of the Church and not viewed with suspicion, but rather as fulfilling a vital role in the Body of Christ, for which they are uniquely gifted for. They need a certain freedom from ecclesiastical structures (as Paul and Barnabas), so that their apostolic nature of reaching into frontier areas is not stifled or hindered, however, while still remaining accountable to the Church.

- For their part, agencies (both non-denominational or denominational) need to remain flexible so that they themselves do not become irrelevant for the mission task. New models are needed where agencies can work together with local churches, recognizing their needs while helping them see the big picture of the Great Commission. To the degree that agencies become separated from the other structures will be the degree that they will become ineffective.

- *Local churches* must also experience a realignment to function as a structure that facilitates the Great Commission. Johnstone has estimated that ninety percent of all Protestant churches in the West, have no direct commitment, as a congregation, to a real missionary.

- The Mission of the Church, most often labelled as *missions*, has become such a general concept that it has lost its real meaning – coming to mean any humanitarian effort, or periodic financial donation. Instead, it must be seen again as central to God's purposes here on this earth.

- Fulfilling the Great Commission is the responsibility of all three structures. The Mission of the Church is a partnership of the whole Body of Christ, so it must include all three structures. Each of these has strengths to contribute to the whole, but cannot fulfill the Great Commission without the partnership of the others.

Has your particular emphasis in ministry brought the Great Commission in focus or out of focus? What adjustments need to be made?

In your opinion, what part does the local church play in fulfilling the Great Commission?
How is this the same or different than the treatment of the subject here?

THE LOCAL CHURCH

- None of the above is intended to detract from God's promise to raise up his Church and his commission to her, "to make disciples of all nations." God has commissioned to work through his Church, expressed through many local churches.

- Yet since the nurture of the believer occurs within a local church, this is where participating in God's Mission usually begins. Each believer's membership in the Body needs to have an expression within the family of a local community of believers – a local church. Only as the local church sees its true purpose being to fulfil God's Missions (local or foreign), will it really function as God intended.

- To better understand God's Mission and our role in his purposes, it is necessary to understand some key concepts related to the growth of the Church. Usually principles of missions and church growth are dealt with separately, yet the traditional division between them is artificial and less than helpful in fulfilling God's Mission and so we will discuss them here together.

Discuss the statement, "Only as the local church sees its purpose as missions can it really be a biblical church." Do you agree or disagree? Why or why not?

Types of Growth

- George Patterson has outlined several ways in which all churches grow. They are *internal, expansion, extension,* and *bridging.* (see *Perspectives* material for further reading).

- *Internal* growth refers to maturity and internal strength. It can include structural growth (such as youth groups, schools, etc.), spiritual growth as member grow in spiritual maturity and conversion growth as nominal members come to a genuine faith in Christ (E-0).

- *Expansion* growth is the addition of new believers from the immediate community. It can include biological growth as children become church members, transfer growth as members join from other churches, or conversion growth as people are won to the Lord from the surrounding non-believing community (E-1).

"Beyond Ourselves"

- *Extension* growth refers to the multiplying of the local church through reproducing and planting daughter churches. This includes the gifting and skills necessary for both internal and expansion growth, but also requires other skills. Patterson points out that relying on only *Internal* and *Expansion* growth and not planting new congregations (*Extension*) will cause a church movement to eventually stagnate.

- *Bridging* growth is the extending of a church's efforts beyond its own culture. It relies on E-2 and E-3 evangelism (see Chapter 4.2), planting churches cross-culturally among a people who may or may not be "reached." (See Chapter 4.2 for meaning of word, "reached.")

- There is a progression to these types of growth, for if a church is not mature enough, it will be difficult for it to *extend* itself. Consequently, if members are not encouraged to evangelize, then stagnation will also soon occur. However, churches must not necessary be numerically large, or exceptionally mature, in order to be involved in planting daughter churches.

Begin to formulate ministry priorities as you view where your church/ministry is and where you feel it needs to be.

- From his experience, Patterson emphasizes that the two principles necessary in order to see a church multiply is that its members are growing disciples and there is ongoing leadership development and training.

The Initial Church Plant

- In order to plant churches that are multiplying, there must be intentionality.

- Particularly during the first generation growth of a church, a target group must be identified and focus for the vision given. Usually it is helpful to know the specific people group that you can be most effective with (with your gifts and resources) and be creative in determining how to best present the Message in that community.

- At this initial stage the focus needs to be on making disciples, not developing programs. It is crucial to immediately begin to train these initial disciples and release them for ministry. This necessitates a pastor who learns to nurture the flock relationally, helping to develop these ties between members, not trying to dominate the church from the platform. These discipling ties among members provide not only a relationship strength for the church, but also encourage further multiplication.

- The use of "preaching points" (ie. an outdoor event), as a method to begin a church is not usually that effective of a long term strategy. Preaching points often take on a characteristic all their own and are difficult to transform into growing, vibrant communities of believers who will plant other churches.

- The early church must become a relational growing group of believers who see the beginning church as their own. Local initiative can easily be discouraged if most of the help is from the outside, so it is often better to utilize the *lesser* local resources, than utilizing possibly *greater* resources from the outside.

The Indigenous Church

- An indigenous church is made up of growing believers who are embedded in a community. They have characteristics of that community, yet are looking to transform the community from within.

- This actually means that the more indigenous a church plant, the more culturally distant it will be from the external church planter (missionary), to the point that he or she may even feel culturally uncomfortable.

- The missionary's role is really that of a catalyst and at best can really just create the conditions for the planting of an indigenous church. An indigenous church is something that develops and takes on a life and characteristic of its own from within the community in which it is planted, not just the transference of an outside model.

- Traditionally in missions, an indigenous church is one that is *self-governing*, *self-supporting*, and *self-propagating*. Yet it needs to be emphasized that *self-governing* does not mean a western approach to church government, but may incorporate what self-governance means locally.

- Also *self-supporting* does not mean that there cannot be any funds coming from external sources, but has more to do with how these funds are handled and disbursed. The important issue is who is in control, managing these funds and determining the priorities.

- Finally, *self-propagating* does not necessarily mean that there is no longer a foreign component to the church, this component may be the very reason it is growing. Alternatively, a church is not necessarily indigenous just because it is growing with no external help.

- The reasons behind these issues need to be understood and analysed in order to ensure that it is truly an indigenous church, not just a transplant from another culture and place, for if this is the case it will not multiply and reproduce. It will only survive as long as it is propped up and supported from an external (in relation to that community) source.

- An indigenous church, that is a fit with the surrounding culture, will be able to speak to that culture and society. Jesus' commands are supra-cultural (above culture), they never change and apply in every culture. Yet it is possible (and

Sidebar notes (left margin)

How important do you think it is to have a target for your mission efforts. Explain.

Discuss your view of the role of the missionary in planting an indigenous church.

Is your church truly indigenous? Why is this important?
What steps do you need to take to move in this direction?

desirable) to have varied cultural expressions from within the local community which those from within the community identify with (though the external church planter may not).

- This adaptation must not necessarily lead to a compromise of the gospel message. Two extremes need to be avoided. _Legalism_, where all aspects of the culture are viewed as negative or anti-Christian and _syncreticism_, where all aspects of the culture are seen as good or Christian.

- The goal is to help others follow Christ and obey the Scriptures, within their cultural context. The challenge is to encourage obedience to Christ without imposing one's own cultural norms or ideals; working together with the Holy Spirit to see strong reproducing churches planted within cultural contexts.

- For those who are called and gifted to plant churches, practical steps need to be taken to increase your effectiveness as well as seeking the right time and place to be released into this ministry. Time should be taken with your mentor, team, or church leader to determine the next steps you can take in this direction.

Church Planters have emphasized that a church does not need to be large in order to plant new churches. Do you agree or disagree?

FULFILLING THE MISSION

The Purpose

- We have discovered that God's heart is to reach _all peoples_ and, in very general terms, we have discussed the structures needed to facilitate this, particularly in relation to planting reproducing churches. Yet the challenge for local churches is to keep on focus with God's Mission and not become ineffective in fulfilling this mandate.

- Rick Warren in his book, _The Purpose Driven Church,_ outlines the five purposes of the local church as he sees them from Scripture: Love the Lord with all our heart (Worship), Love our neighbour as ourselves (Ministry), Make disciples (Evangelism) and Baptizing them (Fellowship), and then Teaching them to be obedient to Christ and his Word (Discipleship).

Together with your mentor, evaluate your gifts in relation to church planting. Discuss issues such as your calling, timing, gifts, motivation, abilities and interest.

- While most churches do all or some of these, few do all equally well. Each is important and in order to balance all five of these, there must be intentionality and the right forms (new wineskins). The necessity of such a balance was highlighted in our discussion in Chapter 1.2 as we looked at Schwarz's Three-Color ministry paradigm.

- To focus on just one area will put the local church (and leadership) out of balance and therefore ineffective in fulfilling the Great Commission. While movements may be raised up to specialize in one area or another, the local church must maintain a healthy balance of all of these.

Do you agree or disagree that these are the five purposes of the church? Explain why or why not.

The People

- In order to fulfill the Mission of the Church, a local church must understand its varied ministry to the groups of people with which it is in contact.

- Warren has developed a model in the from of concentric circles (which has been adapted by others) which describes the balance a local church needs in relation to those it ministers to. From a small central circle each circle forms an increasing larger circumference.

- Beginning with an inner circle, each larger concentric ring of the circle represents a group of people whom the church has less direct contact and influence over.From the center to the edges Warren labels these as: _Core, Committed, Congregation, Crowd, and Community._

- The *Core* is those who are committed to ministering to others, the next group, the *Committed*, are those who are serious about their faith and growing, but not yet serving in a ministry. The *Congregation* are official members of the church who are committed to fellowship, but nothing more. The next circle away from the center is the *Crowd*, those who attend somewhat regularly, and finally the *Community*, which represents those who are unchurched or only occasional attenders.

- The point of the illustration is to realize that not everyone that is touched by the local church is at the same level of interest, involvement or commitment, nor have all the same needs or can be related to in the same way. However, the goal is to move people from the *community* (outside circle) to the *core* (inner circle).

- Through evangelism, discipleship, equipping and training, the local church should be helping people move from the outer circle of low commitment and maturity to the inner circle of high commitment and maturity.

- Yet to be intentional about this, leaders need to know where their attenders fit into one of these groups. This necessitates keeping records and an attention to details. Our people must be identified and then helped in their progression of commitment and maturity.

- The purpose, of course, is not impressive record keeping, but that individuals and the whole church grows in its effectiveness to be about God's Mission, which is to reach the world through the planting of indigenous churches.

The Application

- Moving people that we are in contact with, as a church, from the edges to the core, does not just happen by chance or coincidence. It must be intentional, or to use Warren's words, *Purpose-Driven*. But whatever words are used, without this intentionality, the church will lack focus and will not fulfill the purpose God has for it.

- In what almost seems like a contradiction, Warren emphasized that in order to grow, the focus must be on assimilating and discipling those coming from the outer circles. If the only focus is the core, by the time they are discipled they will have lost their natural contacts with others in the community, thereby stunting further church growth. He believes that it is important to start with the *crowd* and move them towards further levels of commitment/maturity.

- It takes a variety of programs, or forms, in order to minister to the varied needs of those in every level. According to what we have seen regarding form and function, the right form is needed in order to achieve the right goal at every level. For example, if those in the core are not challenged to commitment and ministry, they will become stagnant and not grow. Alternatively, if those in the crowd or community are overly challenged they may leave prematurely. Mature leadership recognizes the different needs of the varied groups of people and prepares appropriate ministries.

- Rick Warren has impacted the Body of Christ by showing that for a church to grow and fulfil its purpose, each area of the church must be evaluated through a *purpose-driven* paradigm. This means the teaching/preaching, each small group, every staff member and worker, the budget and calender – all need to be aligned according to their conformity to the purpose of the church, which he has outlined as evangelism, worship, fellowship, discipleship, ministry (for greater detail read, *The Purpose Driven Church* by Rick Warren).

- Often church growth lacks this intentionality and consequently the church remains weak and has a limited witness in the community.

What do you think is meant by the statement, "There must be a correct structure to ensure that the church keeps these five purposes in balance?"

What steps can you take as a church/ministry in order to assimilate new members? What first impression does your church leave with the first time visitor (ask some)?

Are your programs designed according to your purposes? Are there programs currently in the church that do not line up with the purpose of your church?

What is your plan for equipping and training your members? Do you have a plan to release them into ministry?

Looking Within

- As we discussed last chapter, God's heart is that his Church would reach *all peoples*. This is the macro, or large view, but we will also view it now from the perspective of a local church. While the goal of the Great Commission is the whole world, can every local church really reach *all people*?

- While strategies are many and varied, the simple fact is that the Gospel spreads through relationships. We must understand this on an individual level and evaluate who we are and what God has given us (Section 1.0), in order to be as effective as we can be in our witness with others. However, local churches must also be realistic as to who they can best reach given their gifts and resources.

- The first step is to determine the people-mix of those already attending, for it is unlikely that a church will attract (and keep) those who are very different culturally from existing attenders. This also can be related to the predominate gift-mix of a congregation or what gifts are most valued (see Chapter 1.2). While we are welcoming to everyone, it is important to understand this fundamental truth of human nature which is based in relationship.

- When people first attend they are looking to see if they will fit in with the other people who attend and this fact is usually more important than most other criteria, including the sermon. This is sometimes a difficult reality to accept.

- In addition to an evaluation of who God has placed in the Body, it is also important to determine what is the cultural background of our leadership team. While leadership itself may not attract first time visitors, the style and personality of the leadership will determine if they come back and become members. Thinking throughout questions such as, *What kind of leader am I?* and *What kind of people do I naturally relate to?* can be helpful in reaching our potential and being effective as leaders.

- We have come full circle since Section 1.0, for we are again seeing the need to take into account who and how God designed us. This course has given us the opportunity to reflect on our personality, gifts and callings, all of which can help us in our evaluation of who is naturally attracted to us and our ministry.

- Instead of seeing this as a negative, it can be positive and quite freeing to realize that we cannot be all things to all people. That being said, this does not exclude those with cross-cultural or missionary gift from being able to initiate a church, which is quite different from their own culture. However, ongoing expansive growth will only continue as others in the community continue to relate culturally to those within the existing church.

Reaching Out

- Understanding who we are and who God has specifically called us to (individually and corporately), will give greater purpose and direction to our particular role in reaching *all peoples*.

- While the message of the Gospel does not change (function), who we are best suited to reach as a church will determine how we present the Gospel for greatest impact (form). For example, the greatest church planter of all time, Paul, had a completely different approach depending upon whether the community was primarily Greek or Jewish. This had to do with who he was and who his audience was.

- The question we must ask ourselves is, Who are we (as leadership team and congregation) best suited to reach? What is the specific reason for our church to exist; who are we best targeted to reach? Answering these questions will help us determine what styles of evangelism will work and how to best use what we have for the Kingdom.

Do you think it is possible for any local church to reach "anybody?" Why or why not?

Evaluate your existing attenders and leadership team. What have you learned about who you are as a group and who you may be best suited to reach?

Does adapting how we present the message mean that we are compromising that message? Why or why not?

- This does not mean that we compromise the Gospel message, but as Paul adapted himself (not the message) in order to be able to reach others, so must we if we are to be effective as a local church.

- Jesus himself recognized that he had been sent to the lost sheep of the house of Israel (Matt 15:24); he had a focus and a target. In the early church, Paul recognized that he had been entrusted with the task of taking the Gospel to the Gentiles (Gal. 2:7), while Peter knew his primary commission was to the Jews.

- Knowing our target is crucial if we are going to be effective and fulfill our specific mandate. Likewise, it is impossible for a local church to appeal equally well to all people. This is especially true of small churches, for while large churches have the resources (facility and people) to address a greater scope of needs and can target varied audiences, smaller churches often do not have this option.

- While the whole Body, world-wide, is commissioned to reach the whole world, it is freeing to know that each of us, and every local church, does not (and can not) do it all. We all just have a part to play.

- There are various ways to view those who we are particularly called to. Warren (among others) has outlined these in four main categories: *geographic, demographic, cultural,* and *spiritual.*

■ Geographically

- In a local church setting these are those that are a reasonable distance from the facility. In a mission setting, this means determining the area which we can realistically reach. In a rural area, we must decide if it is one valley, or one group of villages we can reach. If in a city, what particular part of the city?

- However, it is important to note that in mobile cultures and urban centers, geographic location is not always the most important homogenous factor. Due to cultural barriers, we may not be able to reach even those physically closest to us.

- Another reality is that the size of the geographic target group will determine the size and scope of the local church. If the church is in a small rural community, it is likely that it will never become a mega-church (and that is okay). Accurately assessing "success," means matching our expectation level with the reality of our situation.

■ Demographically

- Church growth is not solely dependent upon a highly detailed demographic analysis of those in the surrounding community. While demographic studies can be helpful, they can also become a distraction if taken to an extreme. Much beyond the ages, marital status, income levels, educational level, and main types of occupation of our target, is not needed.

- Each of these factors (age, marital status, education, etc) creates different needs and affects how the Gospel must be most effectively presented. Understanding this will help determine the similarities between the community and the church's membership and leadership.

Evaluate the cultural makeup of your community or target group? What are their values and worldview?

- It is critical that we understand the community to which we have been called to reach. We must be like the men of Issachar in the Old Testament who knew the days in which they were living and what they needed to do (1 Chr. 12:32).

■ Culturally

- While there may be a variety of "subcultures" within the geographic and even demographic boundaries, there are some cultural similarities of those who we are called to reach that are important to understand. These are the factors such as their mindset, values, and worldview, which they hold in common and which tie them together as a community of people.

- As those going to minister in a cross-cultural setting need to be aware of the values, worldview and practices (and what they mean) of a culture, so within a particular society a local church must also be aware of the cultural makeup of the community which they feel particularly gifted and called to reach with the Gospel.

- Making the effort to understand and identifying with the culture does not mean that we agree or condone its values; but we will only be as effective as we can incarnate the message of the Gospel into their cultural language. Most of the cultural subtleties are not easily perceived by a quick glance at outward appearances. Time must be invested and relationships developed in order to truly understand the needs of these varied groups.

- ■ Spiritually

  - Knowing the spiritual background and presuppositions of our community is also necessary in order to know how to best witness to them. *Do they believe in God? In a universal being? In life after death?* and so on. Knowing the spiritual condition of our target community is the first step in being able to build bridges; we must begin with any beliefs or values which we already may have in common with them.

  - When we are new to a community, the best resource to determine the current spiritual climate of the community is other local spiritual leaders. While it takes time and effort to determine the spiritual needs of those we are targeting, without this understanding the "how" of evangelism becomes undefinable.

  - Our methods need to be born out of our understanding of the needs (evangelistic and other) of our target community. Without this, much time, effort and finances can be spent with little results for the kingdom.

  - We need to be wise so as to spread the seed of the Gospel in receptive soil. We need to ask ourselves what the particular spiritual condition of the soil is that we find ourselves in. In addition, we must be aware of the different season that we are in as a church, as a leadership, and the spiritual season of those in the greater community around us. We cannot ignore the cyclical seasons of planting and harvest or our efforts will not be as effective. This is applicable for both individuals and communities.

Existing Churches

- The reality is that most local churches are in a community in which they have been for many years. Perhaps when the church was first planted, it was effectively meeting the needs of those around it, and consequently it grew. However, over time, a local church may find itself in a community with which it no longer identifies, or in a community that no longer identifies with it.

- Church growth experts agree that it is virtually impossible for a church to completely change its culture and who it is. The likelihood of a church being able to re-invent itself is very low. If leadership does try to implement such a change (especially if attempted too quickly), either the congregation will leave (slowly or in large masses), or the leadership will be forced to leave. Neither of which are particularly effective church growth strategies!

- A better approach is for the church and leadership to take some time for honest evaluation and determine what it is called to do and what gifts it has that particularly will meet the needs of the community it is in. Some options would be to begin another service and develop another congregation simultaneously, while continuing to meet the needs of those who have stayed with the church, or start

What characteristics of your church are cultural and cause a barrier in your ability to reach those in your community?
What steps do you need to take in order to remove these barriers and at the same time not alienate your existing attenders?

Evaluate the spiritual condition and needs of your community or target group. What is your definition of success in reaching this group? What bridges of understanding are you building towards them?

a daughter church as a mission endeavour of the mother church.

Some Applications

- To be effective in reaching others for Christ we must have a strategy of how to apply the Gospel to the needs of those we are specifically called to.

- This demands that we are intentional about who we are called to reach (taking our gifts, abilities, culture, etc. into account) and then have a strategy to interact with them. We must make the effort to understand our target group and identify with them in order that we may understand them – as they are, not as we want them to be.

- While the Gospel message is eternal, we must adapt our own culture or comfort level in order to make it relevant to those God has called us to. Without compromising the Gospel, or erecting unnecessary barriers, we need to learn to adapt our preferences in order to reach those we love and want to win for Christ.

- This was the central issue in Acts chapter fifteen. The Early Church was wrestling with what were the necessary cultural practices that were necessary for the new Christians to adopt. To some degree we also deal with this today, for we must also differentiate between what is inherently *Christian* and what is mere *culture,* and learn to differentiate between the two (see Chapter 4.2).

- The Gospel is always expressed within a culture, for culture has to do with the human experience. To be effective to reach *all peoples* we must also be willing to adapt culturally if we are going to reach the unsaved with the Gospel.

- Jesus condemned the religious leaders of his day, who put burdens on people that they could not bear. In contrast, Jesus' ministry was about removing any artificial barriers, in order that needy people could come to the Father. We must be careful not to erect barriers that the Gospel does not erect. The only criteria for accepting Christ was accepting his work on the cross.

- Paul in his ministry learned this principle of adaptation from Jesus. He too tried to find common ground from which he could share the Gospel (1 Cor. 9:19-22). As Jesus and Paul, we are called to display this kind of unconditional love, accepting and loving others into the Kingdom.

SUMMARY

- This chapter began with our discussion of the three structures, or forms, which need to function in balance in order for world evangelization to be effective. There must be nurture, training and sending structures to facilitate the whole Body of Christ fulfilling the mandate that Jesus gave us.

- As we traced the biblical and historical record, we saw the need of these forms to be in balance in our own ministries, as we seek to be effective with the gifts and calling that God has given to us.

- We have also realized that God has a purpose and role for each of our lives and we have discovered that he has placed us in the Body to make a unique contribution. We have the privilege to be partners together with him on his Mission to reach *all peoples*.

Discuss with your mentor what you have discovered about yourself, your calling and your ministry through this program. What practical steps have you already taken in order to reach your full potential?
What steps do you still need to take?

Are you reproducing others, who are then able to do the same? Do you also have key leaders that you are mentoring?

FINAL WORD

- You have been on a journey discovery things about yourself and your ministry. We have discussed relevant issues regarding who we are as a Person, as well as a Disciple of Jesus. We have also learned some keys about being a servant-leader and the purpose of our preparation: To be on Mission with God.

- This manual has provided you with the opportunity to discuss and grow in each of these areas, however, hopefully you have been able to do this within the context of a mentoring relationship. Having someone who you respect help you along this journey and having this become a life-long practice is the real goal of *Mentoring thru Intentional* Relationships.

- A review and summary:

As a Person

- In this mentoring course we began by looking at who we are as a person of God's creation.

- This included discovering our personality type and how that affects so much of who we are, then to discover the gifts that God has given us, some of which are still waiting to be used.

- Our final focus in the section was to discover what we have been called to, both generally and specifically. We discovered that we all have been *called* and that this concept is perhaps not as mystical as we once thought. As we reviewed our *Time-line* we began to see how God had already been preparing us for our calling even when we were not aware of his hand in our lives.

As a Disciple

- Yet to be effective we must develop spiritual disciplines in order that we may grow as a spiritual person. All service for God grows out of a relationship with God, and this we discovered was foundational to our whole lives.

- But along life's path there are some very real challenges which can hinder us from reaching our full potential. We looked at three big issues, namely, how we deal with money, how to deal with our sexuality with integrity, as well as the temptation to use power to influence others.

- Finally in this section we looked at what it means to be led of God and how important this is for the disciple of Jesus. Practical aspects of God's leading were discussed, which are crucial if we are going to be effective in the next step as a leader.

As a Leader

- Servanthood is the foundation of Christian leadership and we saw that service from any other motivation will ultimately prove ineffective for the Kingdom.

- Leadership is not about position, but about learning to be a positive influence on others, so that they may reach their full potential.

- Our final step in this section was to discover that the real purpose of leadership is to develop others and leave a legacy. This is not just for a chosen few, but for all those who desire to make the effort to develop these disciplines and skills.

Discuss with your mentor how you have grown as a Person, Disciple, Leader and Minister.
In what areas do you still need growth, what intentional steps are you taking to reach these goals?

Our Journey thus far

The Journey Continues... Leaving a Legacy

As a Minister

- The very purpose of discovering who God made us, making the effort to develop spiritual disciplines, and then acquiring leadership qualities is that we may serve others by joining God on his Mission.
- We began by evaluating our hearts and motives for ministry and discovering that God's purpose is that all nations would be blessed through his people.
- Finally, we discussed some of the applications for our own ministry, as we are about the Kingdom business sharing the Good News with *all peoples*.

Leaving a Legacy. . .

- While this brings us to an end of this material the journey is just beginning. We are only at the beginning of seeing God accomplish what he desires through our lives as we join him on his Mission. God desires to partner together with us so that we may reach our full potential and be effective in fulfilling his purpose for our lives.
- It is now up to us to run our section of the race and then successfully pass the baton on to others.

Determine with your mentor the future level of your relationship together.
The end of the program does not need to be the end of your relationship, though there may be a need for changes.
Discuss the ongoing needs and expectations that each of you have.

Resource

Mentoring Model: Resource Material

Mentoring
thru
Intentional Relationships

Resource Material

For the Facilitator

The following resource material is designed to help you facilitate *Mentoring thru Intentional Relationships*. Permission is only given to photocopy the sample forms for personal use of those in a *Mentoring thru Intentional Relationships* program.

<u>LESSON PLANS</u>

- One lesson plan for every chapter is provided as a resource for the facilitator in leading a synergistic discussion group of mentorees. A lesson plan will most often cover several sessions, as it is usually difficult to cover a chapter in only one group session.

- The questions can be used as a tool to get participants to interact and learn from each other. The small group should not just be a review of the manual, as mentorees should be reading this and coming to the discussion group prepared to contribute. It is also not just a time for giving "advice" to others, though participants will learn from each other through the discussion and interaction.

- Synergistic learning differs from lecture or typical teaching in that the leader is a facilitator, not "resident expert." This is an extremely important role, for it demands that the facilitator be aware of the needs of the participants and understand where they are at and address their issues. Instead of being the "answer source," the facilitator needs to be a good listener and lead others to discover answers for themselves through the interaction with the material and each other.

- The goal of the facilitator is to have members of the groups share with each other from their life experiences – both the joys and struggles – so that they may learn from each other and carry one another's burdens. It is within this accepting environment that personal growth and life-change occurs.

- These lesson plans are merely a guideline and a help for the facilitator. They list the intended objectives of each chapter, as well as reading resources that are recommended for both the facilitator and mentorees as additional references.

- A sampling of questions are also included in each lesson plan for ease of reference. The questions are separated according to *Insight, Discussion, Application*, and *Mentoring Matters*, just as they are in the text. The facilitator can use these in the small group to initiate interaction and application. Of course, they will have to be adapted according to the specific needs of the participants and the particular dynamics of the group.

- Additionally, several *Group Learning Options* are provided as discussion activities, though the facilitator can incorporate any of the other insight, discussion or application questions as appropriate.

FORMS AND SAMPLES

Commitment Form

- A sample commitment form is provided as a resource to provide intentionality for the mentoring relationship. It is not an instrument to be used to "control" others, but rather a mutual agreement that can assist in the ongoing communication required between mentor and mentoree in order to regularly clarify expectations.

- It should either be presented to the mentor/mentoree at the beginning the program and then be reevaluated periodically throughout the program, according to the needs of both the mentor and the mentoree.

Timeline

- In Chapter 1.3 the concept of a *Timeline* was introduced. Included here is a form for the mentoree to develop their own *Timeline*.

- The value of doing a *Timeline* is in the process itself, not in merely completing it as a task. It is a tool that provides an opportunity for the mentoree to reflect upon their past and how God has led them. It is this process that can give them a context for the future.

- The *Timeline* is not a once in a lifetime activity, but is something that is helpful to do periodically as God continues to lead and guide.

ADDITIONAL REFERENCES

- In the Introductory Chapter, one book was listed that could be read with every chapter. In this section, additional reference materials are listed, that cover some of these topics from a range of perspectives.

- This list is not meant to be exhaustive, as there many other valuable books on the topic, but it will serve as a good starting point for both the mentor and mentoree. To obtain these resources contact the author, publisher, or a local book distributer.

An Introduction

Main Theme and Objectives

- The main objective of the *Introduction Chapter* is to give a brief overview of the mentoring process as used in this manual.

- Through this *Introduction*, each participant should not only see the need for mentoring, but be committed to becoming more intentional in their mentoring relationships.

- The ultimate purpose of this material is to enable participants to approach someone who could be one of their mentors and give leaders a framework within which to mentor others.

Preparation and Resources

■ <u>To Begin</u>

- Carefully read the *Introductory Chapter* to gain an overview of the mentoring process and gain an understanding as to how to best use this material.

- Overview the material and obtain both the DISC personality test for Chapter 1.1 (in Walk Thru the Bible's *Solving the People Puzzle* or other DISC Resource – see Additional Reference list) and Schwarz's book on the gifts for Chapter 1.2 (*The 3 Colors of Ministry* – NCD-international.org), or another resource that has a spiritual gift survey.

- If you a leader who wants to facilitate this mentoring program, take the initiative to gather several in your area for regular discussion sessions and organize the most convenient schedule for the discussion group, ie. every week, twice a month, etc.

■ <u>Supplementary Books</u>

- There are several helpful books on mentoring. Bob Biehl's book on Mentoring is the one listed in the Reference section and can be obtained (in English).

- Clinton's books, *Connecting*, or *The Making of a Leader* are other good resources.

■ <u>Additional Bible References to Study</u>

- Study Jesus' ministry with the Twelve and how he poured his life into them.

- Review Paul and Barnabas' ministry and reflect on the transition from Barnabas to Paul. Then reflect on Paul's dealings with Timothy in terms of mentoring.

Key Questions

■ <u>Insight</u>

- What is your understanding of Mentoring? How does this differ from what was outlined in the text?

- Who are the mentors in your life (you may have used another term to describe them) and what have you gained from them?

■ Discussion

- How much emphasis does mentoring have within your church setting? How does this affect your view of mentoring?

- What misconceptions have you had regarding mentoring before reading this material? How has this changed? In your view what is a good definition of Mentoring?

- Why do you think mentoring is so important in developing leaders and ministers?

■ Application

- In what areas do you need mentoring? What are you looking for in a mentoring relationship?

- What do you have to offer someone else as one of their mentors? Consider those in your life that you could already be a mentor to.

Group Learning Options

- Ensure that each participant has filled out a Commitment Form (located after Lesson Plans) with their mentor and that they have discussed their expectations and parameters for the relationship.

- Ensure that every mentoree has someone who they are regularly spending time with, one-on-one.

Mentoring Matters

■ Mentoree

- Approach someone who could be one of your mentors. Think through your expectations, needs and what you are looking for in a mentor and communicate this with your potential mentor.

- If you have not already done so, take part in a small group of mentorees in your area (If already not organized, you as a mentoree could also facilitate such a group).

■ Mentor

- What intentional steps can you take to mentor someone else?

- Plan a regular time every week or twice a month in order to meet with your mentoree.

- If already not organized, help to facilitate a small group of mentorees to go through this material.

Your Personality: Who You Are

Main Theme and Objectives

■ The participant will be encouraged to:

- gain an understanding and appreciation for their own personality strengths and weaknesses.

- understand the difference between personality styles and appreciate this diversity in the Body of Christ.

- begin to learn how to adapt their natural personality style in order to be more effective in their relating and ministering with others.

Preparation and Resources

■ Supplementary Books

- A helpful book to understand the different personality dynamics is Robert Rohm's book, *Positive Personality Profiles*.

- To enable participants gain an understanding of their natural personality style, a version of the *DISC Personality Profile* will be helpful. You may have the shortened version from Walk thru the Bible Ministries or you may obtain one of the DISC versions which are available in many languages.

■ Additional Bible References to Study

- Psalm 139 - We all have value as one of God's creation.

- 1 Cor. 12 - Though we are diverse, we are all part of the Body of Christ.

- Phil. 2 - Our goal should be to understand others better so that we can better meet their needs.

Key Questions

■ Insight

- Do you think it is "unbiblical" to study personalities? Why or why not?

- Do you think your personality is something you are born with or develops in our early years? How important are our experiences in forming our personality?

- What positive characteristics from other personality styles would bring more balance into your life?

■ Discussion

- After doing the DISC survey and reading through these qualities, what have you discovered about yourself? Were there any surprises in your discoveries?

- Consider your family members and those you work/minister with: What personality mix are they and how has this affected your relationship with them?

- What personality do you think Jesus was?

■ Application

- Using your two highest personality styles as a guide, read the suggested steps you can take to improve yourself and ministry.

- Take some time in your personal devotions to focus on your positive traits and thank God for who he made you. Begin to look at your potential weaknesses and identify what specific areas have caused you problems in your interpersonal relationships.

- Begin to look at your potential weaknesses and identify what specific areas have caused you problems in your interpersonal relationships.

- Reflect on your top two personality styles and which is stronger and which is weaker. How does this combination affect your actions and relationships?

Group Learning Options

- As a group or in smaller groups of 3-4 have participants discuss some of the Insight or Discussion questions. Begin with more general insight questions so trust is built between mentorees.

- Have participants complete a version of the DISC survey in class or on their own. Provide some time for them to share their "discoveries" with the group or in smaller groups.

- Direct discussion towards the key Application questions, which begin to focus on life change.

- Focus the mentorees on the mentoring questions and ensure that all participants have a mentor who they will be discussing matters with throughout the program.

Mentoring Matters

■ Mentoree

- Encourage participants to find a mentor (see Introductory Chapter) if they have not already done so. This is the real purpose and key to this mentoring model.

- Discuss with your mentor specific steps you can take according to your basic personality style. Be accountable with your mentor to begin to change in areas that you may have struggled with, perhaps for most of your life.

- Commit to your mentor the top three steps of action you want to take and give your mentor permission in the coming months to ask you how it is going in these areas of change you have determined as your priorities.

- Discuss with your mentor steps you can practically work on in adapting your particular personality mix with relationships that you have.

■ Mentor

- Help mentoree see their value as a person and who God made them.

- If you have not already done so, fill out the Commitment form and discuss expectations of the relationship with your mentoree (see Introductory Chapter).

- Share with your mentoree your personality style and discuss how both of your personality mixes will affect your mentoring relationship.

Your Gifts: What You Have

Main Theme and Objectives

■ The participant will be encouraged to:

- gain a greater understanding of the gifts and their particular gifting.

- increase in their awareness of the need to have a balanced approach and realize that there can be unity in the Body even among those with different emphasis.

- begin to consider their sphere of ministry in relation to their particular gifts.

Preparation and Resources

■ Supplementary Books

- *The 3 Colors of Ministry* by Christian Schwarz is a great resource that is available in many languages (www.NCD-international.org) and is highly recommended reading for this chapter.

- Peter Wagner book, *Your Spiritual Gifts*, has been widely read and has been appreciated by both non-charismatics and charismatics alike. Schwarz in his book bases his gift definitions on Wagner's, even though he comes from less of a charismatic approach. This manual has attempted to be as inclusive as possible, recognizing that there are differing views in the Body of Christ regarding the expression of the gifts.

■ Additional Bible References to Study

- The three key gift passages are: Romans 12; 1 Corinthians 12 and Ephesians 4:11-12.

- Other Scriptures include: Rom. 1:11, 11:29, 12:6; I Cor. 1:7, 7:7; 1 Tim. 4:14; 2 Tim. 1:6.

Key Questions

■ Insight

- Discuss your views regarding the differences between natural abilities, spiritual gifts, and offices or roles.

- Do you agree that the fruit of the Spirit is more important in the believer's life than the gifts? Why or why not?

■ Discussion

- Do you think these are all the gifts there are (the three Bible passages), or are they only illustrative? Do you think that would be possible for there to be divinely inspired spiritual gifts today not listed in the Bible?

- Is it possible for a local church to be balanced with regard to their gift-combination or is it inevitable that certain gifts will have greater prominence?

- Discuss the statement, "If you consistently do not get results when *trying* a certain gift, it probably is not your gift."

■ Application

- Are you ministering within a role for which you have corresponding gifts?

- Which area and with what gifts do you feel most comfortable?

- What steps have you taken to discover your gifts? What gifts bring you joy as you serve with them?

- What steps can you take so that your gifts function better within a body of believers?

Group Learning Options

- If participants have access to Schwarz's book, *The 3 Colors of Ministry*, have them take the "Compass" test on page 35. Divide into smaller groups and discuss Schwarz's three-color model. How do participants see this as applicable in their life and ministry?

- Have participants complete a gifts inventory test (Schwarz, page 65) and share their finding with one another. Have mentoree share if the results were what they expected or not.

- Have mentorees share with one another practical ways they can begin to express their gifts.

- Spend some time in the group reflecting on the various definitions of each gift.

Mentoring Matters

■ Mentoree

- Discuss the results with your mentor of the "3-Color" test (Schwarz pages 38-40). Do they agree with his premise or what is their perspective of the varied emphasis of the gifts in the Body.

- Do you see yourself in one of these three areas? What steps can you take to become more balanced?

- Consider how your gift mix and your personality type combine to give you a particular sphere of ministry.

■ Mentor

- Go through the results of the gift test with your mentoree. In those areas where you can, confirm and affirm the gifts you see in them.

- Consider the mentorees latent gifts and help provide opportunities for them in ministry that will enable them to express them. Give your mentoree ideas as to how they can better express the gifts that they have.

Your Calling: What You Do

Main Theme and Objectives

■ The participant will be encouraged to:

- appreciate the call that is upon every believer's life, as *ministers of reconciliation*.

- begin to reflect upon their own life (through the use of a *Timeline*) to determine the sphere of influence, or ministry role, that God specifically has for them.

- understand the complexities of their calling, career, vocation etc. and learn to apply steps to evaluate where they are at in their life and how they can reconcile these life roles for themselves.

Preparation and Resources

■ Supplementary Books

- *God's Call* is a helpful workbook by Neil Knierim and Yvonne Burrage, which focusses primarily on those called to vocational ministry.

- Two additional books, which take a more general view of "call," are *The Power of the Call* and *Called & Accountable* by Henry Blackaby.

■ Additional Bible References to Study

- A study of the reality of the priesthood of all believers (1 Peter 2:5, 9-10) and how this relates to the ministry of every believer as ministers of reconciliation (2 Cor. 5:18) is foundational to this approach to our specific call or role.

- A study of the lives of Jeremiah, Isaiah, Ezekiel (as well as others), to apply the lessons to be learned from their "excuses" to not fulfill their call.

- A study of being "set apart" and the application of this truth to those who are called.

- Reviewing the "gifts" in terms of their application in light of our call (Rom. 12; 1 Cor.12; Eph. 4)

- A study of "brokenness" and its prerequisite to fulfill one's call.

Key Questions

■ Insight

- If you are in ministry, consider your motivations for entering ministry. Allow God to deal with your heart on this issue.

- Retrace God's calling in your life to ministry. What confirmations did you have? How did God reveal his will to you?

- Have you gone through this process of brokenness in your life and ministry? What have you learned through these times?

- Notes -

■ Discussion

• Discuss the statement, "Every believer is called."

• Discuss the biblical concept of the *priesthood of all believers*. How does this truth apply to you in your ministry (vocational and otherwise)?

■ Application

• If you have not seen your job or career as a means by which to fulfill God's purposes for you in this life, what steps can you take to realign your perspective?

• Consider your current sphere of influence. Who do you influence? What kind of influence do you have?

• Consider your personality style, gifts and calling. With this in mind, what role or sphere of influence do you seem best suited for?

• Honestly assess what stage of life you are at. How does this affect your effectiveness in your particular ministry? What steps can you take to improve your effectiveness?

Group Learning Options

• Provide opportunity for participants to write out their own personal testimony and then share with others in the group.

• Review key highlights from the chapters, *Personality* and *Giftings* and help participants see how this relates to their call. Then provide opportunity for mentorees to begin to formulate a personal mission statement based on what they have learned of themselves and God's direction in their life.

• Provide opportunity for each mentoree to complete a *Timeline* (at back of manual). Divide into small groups and have them share with each other what they discovered through this process.

Mentoring Matters

■ Mentoree

• Discuss with your mentor how you can fulfill your call within your particular job or vocation.

• Be accountable to your mentor to take opportunities within your own church/community to serve others.

• Discuss with your mentor the affect of your calling on your marriage relationship. If married, meet as couples together to discuss this.

• Discuss with your mentor your time line. What have you seen of God's hand in your life? What stage of life are you in and how does this currently affect you?

■ Mentor

• Share as openly as possible with your mentoree how you arrived at your particular vocation. How much did a "call" have to do with your current position in life? What coincidences seemed like mere "chance," until years later when God's hand became apparent.

• Share with your mentoree how your specific "call" or "role" has affected your life. Are there any regrets or things you would do differently?

• Help your mentoree evaluate their "call" and give appropriate feedback (sensitively and carefully).

Your Foundation: The Personal Disciplines

Main Theme and Objectives

■ The participant will be encouraged to:

- learn and experience the difference between a legalistic approach to the spiritual disciplines and their practice as an expression of a personal relationship.

- establish habits of Bible meditation, prayer, fasting, as well as ongoing study and learning.

Preparation and Resources

■ Supplementary Books

- Fosters book, *Celebration of Discipline*, has become a classic and is one of the best books on the subject. Another important classic to read would be Dietrich Bonhoeffer's, *The Cost of Discipleship*.

- An excellent book on how to read and interpret the Bible is *How to Read the Bible for all its Worth,* (Fee & Stuart). This is a very readable resource that helps the reader understand the issues of interpreting Scripture. Others are also indicated in the Reference list.

- For additional information regarding fasting, Arthur Wallis', *God's Chosen Fast* is seen by many to still be one of the best books on the subject.

■ Additional Bible References to Study

- A study of external righteousness versus true righteousness as expressed in the disciplines: Matt. 5:20; Phil. 3; Eph. 6.

- A study in Psalms concerning meditation: Psa. 1:2, 63:6, 77:12, 143:5 and others.

- Jesus' prayer, Matthew 6; David's prayer, Psalm 51; as well as see other prayers, Matt. 26, James 5.

Key Questions

■ Insight

- How can the spiritual disciplines not become legalistic or mere obligation?

- How is it possible to be in a constant state of prayer? How does this differ from having a specific prayer time?

- Why is it important to keep your meditations biblically focussed on the meaning of the text? How is biblical meditation different than Bible study or reading?

- **Discussion**
  - What has been some of your experiences in Bible meditation?
  - Share with whole group (or smaller groups) your experiences in fasting.
- **Application**

  - Read a book (or two) on Bible study and interpretation (hermeneutics) in order to more effectively read and study God's Word (recommendation: Fee & Stuart's book).
  - Be accountable with your mentor, or accountability partner, in these areas of the spiritual disciplines.

Group Learning Options

- Discuss and ensure that participants understand the difference between practicing the disciplines out of legalism or obligation and out of relationship.
- Provide opportunity for mentorees to begin a prayer journal. Have someone from the group who has kept a journal share their experiences with the others.
- In small groups discuss the *A-C-T-S* method of praying. Which of these four aspects of prayer (ie. Adoration, Confession, Thanksgiving, Supplication) do mentorees most commonly pray?
- For those who are interested and able, commit as a group to fast for a specific time and purpose. At the next meeting discuss participant's results and experiences.

Mentoring Matters

- **Mentoree**
  - Commit with your mentor to daily spend time in prayer, as well as take time to regularly pray with your mentor.
  - Develop a daily Bible meditation plan and be accountable to your mentor for its implementation.
  - Ask your mentor regarding their experiences in fasting.
- **Mentor**
  - Share with your mentoree both your successes and failures in the area of Bible meditation, prayer, and fasting.
  - Discuss with your mentoree study habits you have acquired over the years that you have found helpful for ongoing lifelong learning.
  - Recommend any other books for your mentoree that you think would be helpful. Periodically lend books from your personal library for your mentoree to read and discuss together.

Your Challenges: The Big Three

Main Theme and Objectives

■ The participant will be encouraged to:

- be able to honestly evaluate their vulnerability in the areas of money, sexuality, and power; recognizing both their strengths and weaknesses.

- establish disciplines and habits in order to gain mastery over weaknesses in these areas, as well as eliminate possible areas of temptation.

- be able to live a godly life, redeeming each of these areas for the Kingdom and expressing them the way God intended.

Preparation and Resources

■ Supplementary Books

- Foster's book, *The Challenge of the Disciplined Life,* handles these issues in a very direct, yet balanced way and is a great resource on this topic.

- Two books which deal with male and female issues, particularly related to Christian marriage and ministry are *Beyond Sex Roles*, by Bilezikian and *Why Not Women,* by Loren Cunningham. Particularly interesting is Bilezikian's handling of the Ephesians 5 passage and the meaning of "headship."

■ Additional Bible References to Study

- Study Jesus teaching regarding money in the Gospels (Matt. 25:18, 27, 28:12, 15; Luke 9:3, 19:15, 23, 22:5, etc.)

- Meditate on 1 Tim. 6:10 to understand its meaning (" ...the love of money is the root of all evil..")

- From Genesis chapter two (as well as Song of Solomon) gain an understanding of God's view of the goodness of sex. See Pauline thought in 1 Cor. 7 regarding the value of both the single and married life.

- Review some of the Scriptures (listed in text) referring to sexual relations before marriage.

- The issue of "Power" will be dealt with in greater detail in Chapter 3.1, in relation to servant-leadership and so consequently is only introduced in this chapter.

Key Questions

■ Insight

- Is money merely a neutral form of exchange or does it hold a power all its own?

- Is God or Money the deciding factor in your economic decisions? What is the difference between *faith* and *presumption* with regards to trusting God for our finances?

- Have the men reflect on their view of women and their attitude towards them. If there are feelings of domination or control (often masked as "authority") allow God's Truth to replace these (see above mentioned books).

■ <u>Discussion</u>

• Discuss the idea that as believers our sexuality cannot be separated from our spirituality.

• Encourage participants to spend some time to discuss with their spouse the reason they married each other and, if necessary, establish new expectations of how their marriage can be a positive influence for the Kingdom.

• Also encourage the married participants to evaluate (with their spouse) their marriage as to their communication level, ability to deal with conflicts, common goals and expectations, as well as level of intimacy. If possible, mentorees can get together as couples with their mentor to discuss these matters (if they have this level of honesty in the relationship).

■ <u>Application</u>

• Have mentorees evaluate their giving principles before the Lord. Are finances being used for Kingdom purposes or selfish ones?

• Have participants evaluate their own particular weaknesses in the area of sexuality. Have them submit to the Lord anew those areas which they find a particular struggle and then find an accountability partner to help them in this area (their mentor or someone else).

• Have mentorees share with each other what their guidelines and standards are for their relationships with those of the opposite gender? Do they need to make changes in order to avoid even the appearance of evil?

• Does *Power* or *Service* motivate you in ministry? Ask the Lord to show you your heart.

Group Learning Options

• Due to the subject matter it may be helpful to divide the group into same-gender groups or married/ single. This will have to be evaluated in light of the participants of the small group, maturity level etc.

• Divide into smaller groups again to discuss the Insight or Discussion questions that you may want to emphasize.

• Have participants evaluate their accountability relationships. Are they open in these areas with this (these) individual (s)? If mentorees do not have such a person encourage them to find someone they can trust in these areas.

Mentoring Matters

■ <u>Mentoree</u>

• Reflect and evaluate which of these areas you are strong in and which are a greater temptation. Discuss this with your mentor or mentoring group.

• If you are single, discuss with your mentor, or accountability partner, your level of success in controlling your passions. What practical steps can you take to grow in this area?

• Is your ministry and life characterized by servanthood? Look for those around you who seem to have learned this and, if possible, spend time with them in order to learn this attitude.

■ <u>Mentor</u>

• Share with your mentoree your principles of giving as well as (if applicable), your principles of raising funds for the ministry.

• Share with your mentoree how you have dealt with the temptation to use power, as your ministry and influence have grown. What steps would you suggest a mentoree take to protect themselves from this temptation?

Your Direction:
Being Led of God

Lesson Plan 2.3

- Notes -

Main Theme and Objectives

- The participant will be encouraged to:

  - evaluate what their current emphasis is on being *led of God*.

  - begin to develop habit patterns which focus on a balanced approach to hearing God's voice in their lives and ministries.

  - become more stable in their Christian walk as they see how God intents to lead and guide them.

Preparation and Resources

- Supplementary Books

  - An excellent study in knowing and following God is *Experiencing God*, by Henry Blackaby (in both book and workbook format).

  - While many other books have certain chapters devoted to this topic, God *When God Speaks,* by Henry & Richard Blackaby deals exclusively with this topic (another good resource is Loren Cunningham's, *Is that Really You, God?*)

- Additional Bible References to Study

  - Study the promise of the coming of Holy Spirit in the Gospel of John (14:17, 16:13), the fulfilment in Acts (2:1-21) and the application for New Testament believers in being led by God's Spirit (1 Cor. 3:16, 12:3, 12-14; Eph. 1:13-14, 5:18).

  - Study the theme of being filled with the Spirit (Eph. 5:18) and the promise for every believer (Acts 2:1-21; 1 Cor. 12:3, 12-14; Eph. 1:13-14).

  - Study how Jesus was led by Scripture throughout his life and ministry (Matt. 1:22; Luke 2:21-24; Luke 3:4-6; Matt. 4:1-10; Luke 4:14-21; Matt. 5-7; Matt. 12:1-98; Matt 26: 24, 31, 54, 56 etc.)

Key Questions

- Insight

  - Have mentorees evaluate if they tend to over-spiritualize God's leading or undervaluing the experiential nature of God's leading in their life.

  - How can we learn to practice the presence of Christ more consistently in our daily life?

  - What is meant by the statement, "to some degree our circumstances will affect our understanding of God's leading in our lives." ? Is there an inherent danger in this?

■ Discussion

- In light of New Testament teaching, what is the primary role of prophecy in the believer's life? Have participants discuss how they should deal with prophecy and visions when it comes to seeking God's direction in their lives? Discuss if they agree or disagree with the cautions given in the text?

- What is the purpose of prophecy in the believer's life?

- Discuss the criteria given for testing our inner leadings, as well as some of the other cautions given. Do you agree with all of these? Why or why not?

■ Application

- Discuss the issue of "open" and "closed" doors in receiving guidance. Have participants list some of the dangers of relying on this. What part do circumstances play in being led by God.

- Have mentorees reflect on "wilderness" times that they have gone through and what they learned during this time.

- Have participants reflect on some of the "memorial stones" that they have in your life (perhaps by reflecting on their *Timeline*) and have them share how these have built their faith in God.

Group Learning Options

- Divide into smaller groups in order to discuss the "cautions" listed in the text (as well as other questions listed above). Reassemble as a larger group and have each group share their perspectives.

- Have several mentorees share with the others how they practically "hear" from God.

Mentoring Matters

■ Mentoree

- What have you learned about discerning between God's voice and your own desires? Discuss with your mentor your understanding of your desires and God's desires for you.

- Discuss with your mentor your current church situation and the degree of openness and accountability that you have to a local body of believers. What is your limit of accountability to a local body of believers. Explain.

- Discuss with your mentor your understanding of God's leading and what you have learned in this session. What changes in your thinking and understanding do you think you have to make? How will God's truth regarding how he wants to lead you affect your future decision making process?

- If you are currently in a wilderness or dry time, discuss this with your mentor and gain new perspective through your mentor's experiences.

■ Mentor

- Share with your mentoree some of the wilderness times you have gone through and how you have dealt with them.

- Share any other insights you may have learned in being led of God. Though this is a very personal matter, share with your mentoree how God leads you.

- Discuss your perspective regarding relying on externals, visions, dreams, prophecy etc. for leading. What part have these played in your life and ministry?

Your Foundation: Servant Leadership

Main Theme and Objectives

■ The participant will be encouraged to:

• recognize that the foundation of Christian leadership is servanthood; it is focussed on people not position.

• understand the structures, or models, of ministry which encourage servant leadership and those which do not.

• view their gifting, calling, and sphere of ministry expressed within the context of a servant leadership model.

Preparation and Resources

■ Supplementary Books

• Many of the leadership books listed have chapters dedicated to servant leadership, but Stacy Rinehart focuses exclusively on this in his book, *Upside Down - The Paradox of Servant Leadership,*. This one book will give the facilitator a good foundation on this topic.

• An excellent little book by Gene Edwards (his best, in my opinion), tells the story of David's dealings with Saul and Absalom. In *A Tale of Three Kings,* Edwards studies the theme of brokenness and provides a powerful tool for discussion regarding the topic of servant leadership.

■ Additional Bible References to Study

• Jesus' life is the greatest example of servanthood (Matt. 23:10-12; Mark 10:43-44; John 13:1-17, and others). A key passage being Philippians 2.

• A study of Paul's ministry (2 Cor. 1:24) would also be helpful background, as well as other passages such as 2 Cor. 1:24, 4:5; & 1 Peter 5:3.

Key Questions

■ Insight

• Have participants formulate (on paper or through discussion) what their current leadership philosophy is and how they developed it?

• Historically, how has the concept of a "professional" clergy limited the mission of the Church?

■ Discussion

• Have participants discuss with each other any new insights they have gleaned from a study of Jesus' ministry and particular his role as a servant.

• Do you think forms can remain flexible, or is it inevitable that they become inflexible? Discuss the ramifications for leadership.

■ Application

- Do you see areas in which you manipulate others with whom you have influence? How can you change these patterns of control?

- How does the concept of the *priesthood of all believers* reflect the Church as an organism, rather than an organization? What direct application is there for your leadership?

- How does the relational model of Church structure, as opposed to a hierarchical one, affect the style of leadership? What part of this concept do you struggle with?

- What are your particular challenges in living as a servant-leader? What steps can you take to align your leadership with the biblical pattern.

Group Learning Options

- Have mentorees divide into smaller groups to discuss their current approach to leadership and what they need to change to become true servant-leaders. Choose other questions from above that participants can discuss.

- Between group sessions, have mentorees do a study of Jesus' ministry in terms of his role as servant.

- If possible obtain copies of *A Tale of Three Kings* (Gene Edwards) and have participants read it (it is a very short book) and then come together to discuss their personal reflections.

- Have mentorees discuss together as a class and list the attributes of leaders who release and equip others rather than lead by position or "pyramid-structure." Also list ways that we can release and equip others in the Body. Be specific.

Mentoring Matters

■ Mentoree

- Reflect on your particular spiritual gifts and sphere of ministry. Are you frustrated or finding fulfilment at this time in your life?

- Do you have a plan to equip and develop others in your ministry? Can you think of others who are doing a good job of equipping and releasing God's people for ministry? What can you learn from them?

- Discuss with your mentor steps you want to take in order to become a better servant-leader. What misconceptions do you have to change in your own attitudes and thinking?

■ Mentor

- Discuss with your mentoree how you release others for ministry and help them apply these principles within their ministry and life.

- Discuss what being a servant-leader looks like in your ministry.

- Share with your mentoree your view regarding "structures" and their importance to facilitate servant leadership.

Your Development: Growing as a Leader

Main Theme and Objectives

■ The participant will be encouraged to:

• learn that leadership has to do with influence and that each person has a degree of influence.

• see what preparation is needed in order to be a leader and begin to develop these qualities in their own life.

• be aware of some of the perils of leadership and how to mitigate them in their life.

• obtain an accurate view of leadership and be able to count the cost of leadership.

Preparation and Resources

■ Supplementary Books

• An excellent book on the personal development of a leader is John Maxwell's, *Developing the Leader Within You*.

• Another good resource which covers many leadership topics is *Spiritual Leadership*, by Blackaby.

■ Additional Bible References to Study

• A study of the life of Daniel is a good background to the subject of leadership.

• Meditate on Paul's criteria for leadership in 1 Tim. 3:2-7. Which of these qualities are applicable for all leaders?

• The principles for determining the appropriateness of an activity: 1 Cor. 6:12; 8:12-13; 10:31.

• A study of giving up of our rights: 1 Cor. 4:9, 6:12, 8:12-13, 9:15-18.

Key Questions

■ Insight

• What is your view of the definition that leadership as the *ability to influence*?

• Are leaders *born* or *made*? Explain your opinion.

■ Discussion

• Discuss the Pareto Principle and its ramifications for your leadership.

• Discuss the difference between being a visionary and a person of vision. Are your visions based on God's vision?

• Interact with the statement, "leaders are required to pay a higher price than others." Have mentorees respond to what they think they will have to personally

give up in order to be an effective leader.

- **Application**

  - What steps are required to live a life of integrity? Have participants evaluate their level of integrity.

  - Have mentorees evaluate the practical steps they have taken (and may need to take) in order to protect themselves from sexual impurity.

  - How do you react to those who point out your weaknesses? What does this indicate about your heart condition?

  - If some participants have struggled (or are struggling) with depression, assist them get the help and understanding they need in this area. Have others share their own struggle with depression.

Group Learning Options

- Have mentorees evaluate their time over a week and compare this with the Pareto Principles. ie. Are they spending most of their productive time doing the right things? With the right people?

- In the next session together, divide into small groups and have participants share their discoveries with one another.

- Have mentorees share (and pray) with one another in smaller groups regarding some of the pitfalls of leadership and particularly those that they struggle with.

- Lead a discussion on the price of leadership and have mentorees interact with this topic.

Mentoring Matters

- **Mentoree**

  - Reflecting over the chapters covered thus far, in which areas have you grown and what steps can you take to continue to develop as a leader?

  - Reevaluate your current priorities and discuss these with your mentor.

  - What steps have you taken to become a life-long learner? Discuss with your mentor any areas of spiritual or mental laziness and take steps to change this.

  - Evaluate if you are truly willing to pay the price necessary to become a person of influence.

- **Mentor**

  - Discuss your perspective regarding *influence* versus *position*. Use your own personal experiences to highlight the difference.

  - Discuss with your mentoree the character qualities you consider most important for a leader.

  - Share your process of determining what is God's vision for your ministry, church, organization etc. and then how you implement that vision.

  - Share with your mentoree some of the perils of leadership that you have personally dealt with.

  - Discuss with your mentor your perspective regarding the concept that, the more we mature the less tangible guidance we receive from God.

Your Legacy: Developing Others

Main Theme and Objectives

- The participant will be encouraged to:

  - see the possible positive influence that they can have with others.

  - learn *who* to develop and then the principles necessary in order to help others reach their full potential.

  - gain an overview of the mentoring process and be encouraged to take steps to begin to mentor others in order to leave a legacy.

Preparation and Resources

- Supplementary Books

  - Two books by Maxwell are excellent on this topic: *Developing the Leaders Around You*, and *Becoming a Person of Influence.* Some of the other listed books on leadership and mentoring also deal with this to some degree.

  - If there are men in your group who are in the mid-season of life (though I know women who have also really enjoyed the book), Patrick Morley*'s, Second Half for the Man in the Mirror,* is a great book to realign ones' purposes and direction in life, which is essential before being able to develop others.

- Additional Bible References to Study

  - A study of biblical characters illustrates the biblical foundation for mentoring and developing others: Eli & Samuel, Elijah & Elisha, Moses & Joshua, Jesus with Peter, James and John, Paul & Timothy, to name a few.

  - The New Testament principles of equipping the saints (Corinthians, Ephesians et al.) are also applicable in this study of developing others.

Key Questions

- Insight

  - Who are some of the key people around you who you are committed to developing?

  - What have you learned that has helped you regarding motivating others.

- Discussion

  - Discuss how it is possible to be a meek (not weak) leader, not resorting to manipulation and self-strength, even when attacked or challenged

  - Discuss with your mentor lessons they have learned with regard to developing and working with a team.

■ Application

- Do you feel that you are able to mentor others? Why or why not? Identify those things that inhibit you from being involved in mentoring others.

- Do you feel threatened by developing others around you? What practical steps can you take to change this attitude and perspective.

- Have mentorees list someone that they are mentoring or have the potential to mentor. Have participants discuss practical steps that can be taken to develop others.

Group Learning Options

- During the course of this chapter, have mentorees list at least one person who they feel they have an influence with and could mentor. Have them discuss with their mentor practical steps that they can take in this regard.

- As a class, discuss some of the potential threats in developing others (ie. they take over your contacts and ministry). Is it still worth developing others? Why or why not? Is it possible to eliminate these threats or risks? What should be our response as servant-leaders?

- As a group list some of the benefits of developing others.

Mentoring Matters

■ Mentoree

- Evaluate what level of influence you have with the key people around you and how this affects your leadership role.

- Discuss your time-priorities with your mentor, what changes need to be made in order to develop others.

- Evaluate your attitude and actions as a mentoree. Are you maximizing this relationship? Ask your mentor for feedback.

- Do you see any weaknesses in your life which have the potential to keep you from finishing well? Be accountable with your mentor to take steps to strengthen these areas.

■ Mentor

- Provide feedback for your mentoree regarding your relationship and how effective you feel it has been. Also receive feedback from your mentoree regarding their evaluation to this point.

- Share with your mentoree benefits you have seen from developing others over the years.

- If appropriate, perhaps you could connect your mentoree to one of your contacts who needs to be mentored. In so doing you can expand your own effectiveness.

Your Motivation: Being God's Person

Main Theme and Objectives

■ The participant will be encouraged to:

• take the opportunity to reflect upon their heart motivation for service and ministry within the context of God's grace.

• discover what the proper motivation for ministry is and how to serve from "life message."

• learn how to guard their heart against that which can harden and poison it in the ministry.

Preparation and Resources

■ Supplementary Books

- Notes -

• A helpful workbook by Michael Miller, *Keeping Your Heart for Ministry*, is a great tool for self evaluation and *heart check-up*.

• Through the course of life and ministry the unexplainable happens which can threaten to harden our hearts and even invalidate us for ministry. In, *When God Doesn't Make Sense,* Dr. James Dobson addresses how to keep hope alive when all hell seems to have broken loose.

• From our own personal experiences we have also written a book titled, *This Pile of Stones* (Phil & Nancy Jeske). Through telling our story, which included several traumatic and dramatic events, we seek to give hope to the reader that God is still present even when we cannot see him or are even angry with his dealings in our lives. Our desire is that others will also discover that it is possible to live a purposeful life even in the midst of the unplanned and unexplainable. The Introduction is posted on the webpage where this resource can be ordered (www.thispileofstones.org).

■ Additional Bible References to Study

• Proverbs regarding the heart: Prov. 4:23, 7:9, 11:20, 12:20, 16:5, 18:12, 17:3, 17:20, 21:2, 21:4, 28:14.

• Why we serve: 1 Peter 5;1-4; 1Tim. 1:5.

• A study in brokenness and serving others with transparency: Psa. 51:16-17; 2 Cor 1:4, 2:4; 2 Cor. 6:11; 2 Cor 7:2-3; 1 Tim. 4:16.

Key Questions

■ Insight

• Take some time to consider your call and how this affects your motivation for what you do.

• Describe ways in which you currently guard your heart in reference to other relationships, your leadership responsibilities, and your personal activities.

■ <u>Discussion</u>

- What does ministering or leading from "life message" mean to you? What would you have to change in your ministry, leadership style, or attitudes, in order to serve in this way?

- Discuss what it means to live and minister "transparently" before others.

■ <u>Application</u>

- Prayerfully examine your heart and respond to the Lord's prompting regarding any steps you may need to take.

- Are there areas in your life in which you are more focussed on pleasing others rather than God?

- Have you become stagnant in any area of your life? What steps are you taking to continue to grow spiritually, intellectually, personally?

Group Learning Options

- This is a very personal topic and one that individuals must deal personally with God. As a facilitator, you need to give direction by asking the right questions and provide a setting conducive to sharing.

- Between group meetings, have participants commit to spending time with the Lord in order for him to reveal the motives of their heart to them. Also have each mentoree keep a record in their journal of these insights.

- Divide into smaller groups and have mentorees share with each other their attitudes towards those who do not personally know Christ. Compared to Jesus' attitude, how would they characterize their attitude? What adjustments would they need to make in order to have his heart attitude for the world?

Mentoring Matters

■ <u>Mentoree</u>

- Identify and discuss with your mentor some of the challenges in your life which have affected your heart condition. Together with your mentor commit together to see God bring clarity and healing in those areas where it is needed.

- Together with your mentor, evaluate your priorities in all main areas of your life and ministry. What steps do you need to take in order to realign your priorities?

- Be accountable with your mentor in those areas of necessary change that the Lord has showed you from this chapter. Keep these action steps in mind as you study the last two chapters regarding our mission in the world and your responsibility as a leader in that mission.

■ <u>Mentor</u>

- Share honestly with your mentoree how you keep your heart motivation pure and what you have learned regarding the need to do this in your life and ministry.

Your Mission: Having God's Heart

Lesson Plan 4.2

Main Theme and Objectives

- ■ The participant will be encouraged to:

  - gain a biblical perspective of God as the missionary God who has a heart for "all peoples" and desires to work in partnership with man to see this accomplished.

  - receive an overview of missionary activity after the New Testament period and will be introduced to the need for both *nurturing* and *sending* structures for the Church to fulfill its mandate.

  - be exposed to various missions principles in order to appreciate the task and challenge for world evangelization.

Preparation and Resources

- ■ Supplementary Books

  - *Perspectives on the World Christian Movement*, by Ralph Winter is recognized worldwide as the premier course on missions. It includes a reader, a study guide as well as can be done at various levels (college credit, audit etc). It is also possible to take this excellent missions course online through the ICM webpage: www.icm-international.org

  - A must for every world-Christian is Patrick Johnstone's book, *Operation World*. It itemizes the state of world missions, country by country, people group by people group. This is an invaluable resource for global intercession.

- ■ Additional Bible References to Study

  - A study in Isa. 52-54 in relation to the Suffering Servant and future harvest.

  - Genesis 12:1-3 and Gal. 3 on what it means to be a *blessing* and the Church's role in this.

  - Tracing the theme of Matt. 28:19-20 throughout Scripture.

Key Questions

- ■ Insight

  - What have you discovered from the Old Testament regarding God's purposes that you had not seen before?

  - Through a study of Isaiah 53 and 54, what insights have you gained concerning Jesus' redemptive work and the task of reaching the harvest?

  - What do you see as your personal role in fulfilling the Mandate?

- ■ Discussion

  - Respond to the statement, "There is a church because there is a mission, not vice versa."

- Notes -

- Discuss the concept that the Great Commission of Matthew 28 has more to do with making disciples than mere evangelism. What is the difference?

- Discuss the differences between *Modality* (nurture) and *Sodality* (sending) structures. Why are both important for the spread of the Gospel?

- Within your culture is there a reproducing church witness? Is your church/ministry involved in planting a church within a people group that does not have easy access to a church? If not now, does your ministry have this as one of its goals?

- ■ Application

  - If you are part of a church or group that was started by foreign missionaries, analyse your structures, do they have both nurturing and sending aspects? Are you also sending missionaries?

  - Every "mission field" is in a particular stage (Pioneer, Partnership, etc). Reflect upon the particular stage of where you are and some of the practical implications for your own ministry.

  - In relation to the different types of evangelism (the "E" scale) what is your current ministry emphasis and does this reflect your ministry gifts and calling?

Group Learning Options

- Divide into smaller groups and discuss the nurturing and sending aspects of the Church. Do you see this dual priority in your ministry? Share with each other how this relates to your personal ministry gifts.

- If you are in a non-western country, discuss how the influence of western culture has affected the values of those in your region or ministry. How has the transition from Western powers to local governance affected missions and the expansion of the Church in your region?

- Discuss, in smaller groups or as a whole group, in which *Modern Missions Era* your church or denomination was birthed. How does this affect your group's understanding of the mission of the church and your role in this mission?

- In smaller groups, have participants define the people groups within their sphere of ministry/influence and evaluate them according to the "E" and "P" scale. Then have participants analyse their particular ministry strategies and determine if they are applicable to the needs of their community.

- Arrange for interested mentorees to enroll in the Perspectives Course onLine (www.icm-international.org).

Mentoring Matters

- ■ Mentoree

  - Discuss with your mentor how this chapter has influenced you in seeing how the mission of the Church relates to your personal life mission.

  - Consider what you have covered thus far and reflect upon what you have learned about your personality, gifts and calling, and specifically how this affects your involvement in the Great Commission.

- ■ Mentor

  - In light of the subject matter in this chapter, discuss with your mentoree their potential role or sphere of ministry in relation to fulfilling the Great Commission. How can you help release them in this ministry?

Your Ministry: Following God's Strategy

Main Theme and Objectives

■ The participant will be encouraged to:

- learn of the need for a balance in the nurturing, training, and sending functions of the Church.

- gain an understanding as to how local churches grow and practical ways to apply these principles.

- see the need to become intentional and targeted in the mission of the Church and then be mobilized to use their gifts and calling in order to effectively participate in this task.

Preparation and Resources

■ Supplementary Books

- *The Church is Bigger than You Think*, by Patrick Johnstone, covers key themes and I am indebted to him for initially directing me to the structural issue of world missions that is discussed in the text of the manual. To have a fuller understanding of this, the second half of this book is particularly invaluable and cannot be more highly recommended.

- *The Purpose Driven Church*, by Rick Warren has influenced many in their rethinking of how we do church and how we reach into the community. In this section, I have included books from both missions and church growth fields, for they really need to be seen as part of the same continuum.

- For a more scholarly discussion on these topics, Hesselgrave have written two excellent works, *Communicating Christ Cross-Culturally*, and *Planting Churches Cross-Culturally*.

■ Additional Bible References to Study

- A study of the equipping gifts of Ephesians 4:11-12 and their application in the task of church planting. Also studying the other gifts (1 Cor. 12 and Rom. 12) in relation to functions in the local church.

- Selected biblical passages on the church: Matt. 5:13-16, 11:28-30, 18:19-20, 22:36-40, 28:18-20; Mark 10:43-45; Luke 4:18-19, 4:43-45; John 4:23, 12:34-35; Acts 1:8, 2:41-47, 6:1-7; Rom. 12:1-8, 15:1-7; 1 Cor. 12:12-31; 2 Cor. 5:17-6:1; Gal. 5:13-15; Eph. 1:22-23, 3:14-21, 4:11-16; Col. 1:24-28; Heb. 10: 224-25; 1 Pet. 2:9-10; 1 John 1:5-7; 4:7-21.

- An examination of the targeted approach seen in Scripture: Matt. 10:5-6; 15:24; Gal. 2:7, etc.

Key Questions

■ Insight

- What insights have you gained from looking at the nurturing and expansion models of the Church?

- What is your view of the interrelation between the early church and the early apostolic bands?

- Warren lists five purposes of the church. Why do you think that there must be a correct structure to ensure that each of these is in balance with the others?

■ Discussion

- Discuss how your ministry releases all members as ministers, regardless of their function.
- Discuss how the application of your gifts is affected by your sphere or role of ministry.
- Do you agree or disagree with the statement, "Only as the local church sees its purpose as missions can it really be a biblical church."
- Does adapting how we present the message mean that we are compromising that message? Why or why not?

■ Application

- Discuss why it is important that a local church is indigenous and, as a group, create a list of practical steps that can be taken to move a church in this direction.
- Have mentorees divide into smaller groups and evaluate the programs in their ministry according to the purposes of the ministry. Have them list changes that need to be made.
- Have participants evaluate their existing church attenders and leadership team in relation to the needs of the target group; those who they are attempting to reach. Are they gifted and called to meet these needs?

Group Learning Options

- Have mentorees evaluate (speaking to church members if possible) their church's first impressions on a visitor and then determine what steps can be taken in order to better assimilate new members.
- In small groups evaluate the cultural makeup and spiritual condition of your community or target group and begin to determine their values and worldview.
- Have participants ask members of their church (with permission of their leadership) if there are any barriers (cultural or otherwise) facing the church in reaching those within the community it finds itself. In the following group session have mentorees arranged in small groups to discuss their findings and practical steps that can be taken in order for them to be more targeted.

Mentoring Matters

■ Mentoree

- Together with your mentor, evaluate your gifts in relation to church planting (if you feel called to this ministry). Think through issues such as your calling, timing, gifts, motivation, abilities and interest.
- Discuss with your mentor what you have discovered about yourself, your calling and your ministry through this program. What practical steps have you already taken in order to reach your full potential? What steps do you still need to take?
- Are you reproducing others who are then able to do the same? Are there key leaders that you are beginning to mentor?

■ Mentor

- Discuss with your mentoree where you see growth in their life in the last year.
- Determine with your mentor the future level of your relationship together. If you will continue meeting together reevaluate the frequency and purpose. Discuss the ongoing needs and expectations that each of you have.

Mentoring Agreement

Mentor   _____

Mentoree: _____

1. Purpose/Expectation (personal growth? ministry growth? life/ministry skills? other specific goals?)

_____

_____

2. Meeting frequency/length of meetings

_____

3. Other Contact desired (phone? e-mail? etc). **Frequency desired.**

_____

4. Accountability Level (personal? ministry? all areas? any areas excluded?)

_____

5. Level of Confidentiality

_____

6. Reevaluation (3 months? 6 months? etc.)

_____

7. Duration of Commitment

_____

Date: _____

Signed: _____
                                            (Mentor)

              _____
                                          (Mentoree)

Personality Style Survey

The first step in successfully relating to others is understanding yourself: your strengths and weaknesses. This survey is designed to give you a quick pulse of your behaviour tendencies and should only be used in conjunction with additional training.

DIRECTIONS

1. Check to make sure you circled just one word on each of the 24 rows.

2. Begin your scoring by identifying the word you circled on question #1. Remaining within that column, go straight up and make a mental note of the letter at the top of the column: A, B, C, or D.

3. Now on scoring table circle the appropriate letter (A, B, C, or D) for question #1.

4. Proceed to question #2 and repeat the same process until you have circled 24 letters on the scoring sheet.

5. Count the circles on the first column of scoring sheet and write the number in the space provided at the bottom of the column. Do the same for the second, third, and last columns. All four columns should total 24.

6. At the top of the first column write the letter "D" in the space provided – then proceed to the next three columns: write the letter "I" at the top of the second column, the letter "S" for the third column, and the letter "C" for the last column.

7. Notice the two highest scores of your four columns. Put the appropriate letter (D, I, S, C) for your two highest scores. Space is provided on the bottom of page 3. Note: In case of a tie, write down both letters.

Used by permission of Walk thru the Bible, Inc. Atlanta, Georgia

(Directions: Circle ONE word in each row that you feel describes you best:)

	A	B	C	D
1	Restrained	Forceful	Careful	Expressive
2	Pioneering	Correct	Exciting	Satisfied
3	Willing	Animated	Bold	Precise
4	Argumentative	Doubting	Indecisive	Unpredictable
5	Respectful	Out-going	Patient	Daring
6	Persuasive	Self-reliant	Logical	Gentle
7	Cautious	Even-tempered	Decisive	Life-of-the-party
8	Popular	Assertive	Perfectionist	Generous
9	Colorful	Modest	Easy-going	Unyielding
10	Systematic	Optimistic	Persistent	Accommodating
11	Relentless	Humble	Neighbourly	Talkative
12	Friendly	Observant	Playful	Strong-willed
13	Charming	Adventurous	Disciplined	Deliberate
14	Restrained	Steady	Aggressive	Attractive
15	Enthusiastic	Analytical	Sympathetic	Determined
16	Commanding	Impulsive	Slow-paced	Critical
17	Consistent	Force-of-Character	Lively	Laid-back
18	Influential	Kind	Independent	Orderly
19	Idealistic	Popular	Pleasant	Out-spoken
20	Impatient	Serious	Procrastinator	Emotional
21	Competitive	Spontaneous	Loyal	Thoughtful
22	Self-sacrificing	Considerate	Convincing	Courageous
23	Dependent	Flighty	Stoic	Pushy
24	Tolerant	Conventional	Stimulating	Directing

1	B	D	A	C
2	A	C	D	B
3	C	B	A	D
4	A	D	C	B
5	D	B	C	A
6	B	A	D	C
7	C	D	B	A
8	B	A	D	C
9	D	C	A	B
10	C	A	D	B
11	A	D	C	B
12	D	C	A	B
13	B	A	D	C
14	C	D	B	A
15	D	A	C	B
16	A	B	C	D
17	B	C	D	A
18	C	A	B	D
19	D	B	C	A
20	A	D	C	B
21	A	B	C	D
22	D	C	B	A
23	B	C	A	A
24	D	C	A	B

My two highest scores: 1. _____ 2. _____

TIME LINE for: _____

Values/Lessons Learned	. . . .	. . . .	. . . .	. . . .
Major Roles	. . .	. . .	. . .	. . .
Sphere of Influence	. . .	. . .	. . .	. . .
Developmental Phase:				
KEY INCIDENTS:				
Family/Personal	. . . .	. . . .	. . . .	. . . .
Ministry/ Professional	. . . .	. . . .	. . . .	. . . .
Influential People/Mentors	.	.	.	.

Additional References

In the Introduction, one key book was listed for every chapter. This list is meant to enhance this, to help enrich the understanding and ministry of both the mentor and mentoree. These additional references have been arranged according to subject (not alphabetically according to author) in relation to the order of this manual for ease of reference. This is obviously not an exhaustive list on these subjects, merely a starting point. Along your journey you will undoubtedly discover many more.

Person

Positive Personality Profiles, Robert Rohm. Personality Insights Inc, Atlanta, GA, 1993.

Solving the People Puzzle. Walk thru the Bible, Atlanta, GA, 1999.

DISC Personality Profile. Carlson Learning Company, Minneapolis, MN, 1994. (there are various versions)

The 3 Colors of Ministry Schwarz, Christian Schwarz. Church Smart Resources, Germany, 2001 (NCD - Natural Church Development).

Your Spiritual Gifts, Peter Wagner. Regal Books, Ventura, CA, 1979.

Breakthru - A Spiritual Gifts Diagnostic Inventory. LEAD Consulting, Raleigh, NC, 1992.

God's Call, Knierim, Neil and Burrage, Yvonne. Convention Press, Nashville, TN, 1997.

The Power of the Call, Blackaby, H. and Brandt, H.

Called & Accountable, Henry Blackaby, and Kerry Skinner. New Hope Publishers, Birmingham, AL, 2002.

This Pile of Stones, Phil and Nancy Jeske. Zinzendorf Publishing, Canada. 2002.

Disciple

Celebration of Discipline, Richard Foster. HarperCollins Publishers, New York, NY, 1978.

Secrets of the Vine, Bruce Wilkinson. Multnomah Publishers, Sisters, OR, 2001.

Too Busy Not to Pray, Bill Hybels. InterVarsity Press, Downers Grove, IL, 1989.

How to Read the Bible for all its Worth, Gordon Fee & Douglas Stuart. Zondervan Publishing, Grand Rapids, MI, 1981.

Understanding & Applying the Bible, McQuilkin. Moody Press, Chicago, IL, 1983.

Living by the Book, Howard Hendricks. Moody Press, Chicago, IL, 1991.

Cost of Discipleship, Dietrich Bonhoeffer. The MacMillan Company, New York, 1963.

God's Chosen Fast, Arthur Wallis. Christian Literature Crusade, Fort Washington, Penn., 1971.

The Challenge of the Disciplined Life, Richard Foster. HarperCollins Publishers, New York, NY, 1985.

Beyond Sex Roles, Gilbert Bilezikian. Baker Book House, Grand Rapids, MI, 1985.

Why not Women, Loren Cunningham & David Hamilton. YWAM Publishing, Seattle, WA, 2000.

Experiencing God, Henry Blackaby & Claude King. Broadman & Holman Publishers, Nashville, TN, 1994.

When God Speaks, Henry & Richard Blackaby. LifeWay Press, Nashville, TN, 1995.

Leader

Upside Down, Stacy Rinehart. Navpress Publishing, Colorado Springs, CO, 1998.

The Purpose Driven Life, Rick Warren. Zondervan Publishing, Grand Rapids, MI, 2002.

Spiritual Leadership, J. Oswald Sanders. Moody Press, Chicago, IL, 1967.

Spiritual Leadership, Henry & Richard Blackaby. Broadman & Holman Publishers, Nashville, TN, 2001.

A Tale of Three Kings, Gene Edwards. Tyndale House Publishers, Wheaton, IL, 1980.

Be the Leader You Were Meant to Be, LeRoy Eims. Cook Communications, Colorado Springs, CO, 1975.

Developing the Leader Within You, John Maxwell. Thomas Nelson Publishers, Nashville, TN, 1993.

Developing the Leaders Around You, John Maxwell. Thomas Nelson Publishers, Nashville, TN, 1995.

Becoming a Person of Influence, John Maxwell. Thomas Nelson Publishers, Nashville, TN, 1997.

Mentoring, Bobb Biehl. Broadman & Holman Publishers, Nashville, TN, 1996.

Connecting, Paul Stanley & Robert Clinton. NavPress, Colorado Springs, CO, 1992.

Halftime, Bob Buford. Zondervan Publishing, Grand Rapids, MI, 1994.

Second Half for the Man in the Mirror, Patrick Morley. Zondervan Publishing, Grand Rapids, MI, 1999.

Minister

*Keeping Your Heart for Minist*ry, Michael Miller. LifeWay Press, Nashville, TN, 2001.

When God Doesn't Make Sense, Dr. James Dobson. Tyndale House Publishers, Wheaton, Ill., 1993.

Perspectives on the World Christian Movement, Ralph Winter & Steven Hawthorne, ed. Paternoster Press, UK, 1981, 1991.

Perspectives, Study Guide, Steven Hawthorne. Paternoster Press, UK, 1999 Edition.

Operation World, Patrick Johnstone. Paternoster Lifestyle, UK, 2001.

The Church is Bigger than You Think, Patrick Johnstone. Christian Focus Publications, UK, 1998.

Communicating Christ Cross-Culturally, David Hesselgrave. Zondervan Publishing, Grand Rapids, MI,

Planting Churches Cross-Culturally, David Hesselgrave. Baker Book House, Grand Rapids, MI, 1980.

The Purpose Driven Church, Rick Warren. Zondervan Publishing, Grand Rapids, MI, 1995.